She Builds

ALSO BY JADAH SELLNER

Simple Green Smoothies

She Builds

The Anti-Hustle Guide to Grow Your Business and Nourish Your Life

JADAH SELLNER

HARPER
BUSINESS

An Imprint of HarperCollins*Publishers*

HarperCollins books may be purchased for educational, business, or sales
promotional use. For information, please email the Special Markets Department at
SPsales@harpercollins.com.

FIRST EDITION

Designed by Bonni Leon-Berman
Interior artwork by Rachel Pesso

Library of Congress Cataloging-in-Publication Data has been applied for.

ISBN 978-0-06-313543-7

22 23 24 25 26   LSC   10 9 8 7 6 5 4 3 2 1

To my mom, Joy, who taught me to
build with my hands and my heart.

To my daughter, Zoe, a creative
soul building a better future.

#shebuilds

CONTENTS

She Builds

She (noun)
[shee] / ʃi /
   1. anything considered, as by personification, to be feminine.

Builds (verb)
[bilds] / bɪlds /
   1. to engage in the art, practice, or business of building.
   2. to establish, increase, or strengthen.

o o o

I recognize and welcome people of all genders and identities. If you feel drawn toward the holistic blend of feminine and masculine energy in business, this book is for you. You understand the importance of structure and action as well as trust and intuition. Representation of women of color is a topic close to my heart. I wrote *She Builds* from the perspective of being a multiracial cis-gendered woman. People who identify as women or were assigned females at birth receive implicit and explicit messages from society, social circles, and their families. I center women's stories and voices throughout this book, because this is what I wish I could have read when I became an entrepreneur. The beloved author Toni Morrison said, "If there's a book you want to read, but it hasn't been written yet, then you must write it." My wish is that you feel inspired to share your story, too.

There are no unique messages,
only unique messengers.

Introduction

FROM F.E.A.R. TO L.O.V.E.

I sat in the driveway at midnight, struggling to start my car. On the third try, the 1995 Toyota Corolla sputtered to life in the Kaua'i humidity. As I attempted to pull out unnoticed, my husband, George, ran outside frantically in nothing but his plaid boxers.

"Jadah, stop!" He spread himself across the windshield as I hit the brake.

"What are you doing?" I asked, rolling down the window, my voice reverberating in the darkness.

"Don't go," he begged.

"You're crazy!"

"You can stay mad here," he moved toward the door handle.

"GET. OFF. THE. CAR!"

o o o

George and I had opened a day care center, Little Sprouts Playhouse, together at the height of the economic downturn in 2009. Owning a day care center had not been in our original plan. When we got married, we were both creatives trying to make it in Hollywood: I was a spoken-word poet, and George was the lead singer in a band with dreams of becoming a famous rock star. But once I got pregnant with our daughter, we needed stability in our lives. We had made the decision to leave California for Hawai'i because my mom had moved there three years earlier and could help with child care. I had a secret fantasy that George would get a "real" job and provide for our growing family, while I stayed home with our daughter full-time. The big dream was that George would be able to make multiple six figures a year by selling time-shares, as did my bonus dad (many people might refer to him as my stepdad).

George did get his Hawai'i real estate license to financially support our family, but hiring freezes were happening all over the United States. We started Little Sprouts Playhouse out of necessity. Our decision to open a day care center stemmed from numerous factors. George wasn't able to find work. I wanted to work, but with our eighteen-month-old daughter, Zoe, close by. Though it felt stressful and chaotic at the time, looking back, I can see how it was the perfect lead-up to starting my first business—another secret dream I'd always kept close to my heart. The early seeds of my entrepreneurial spirit had been planted with the help of my father. I remember him telling me stories about his entrepreneurial ventures as a kid, like buying bubble gum at the local store and selling it to his classmates for twice the price. When I was nine, he taught me how to spell the word *entrepreneur*. I'd repeat the spelling, "E-N-T-R-E-P-R-E-N-E-U-R," over and over again to myself. I guess it stuck.

The initial months of launching Little Sprouts were exciting, but the honeymoon phase quickly faded. Despite my passion for entrepreneurship, I didn't have a college degree or any business knowledge or experience. I treated Google as my advisor, flying by the seat of my pants. During business hours, I greeted families at drop-off, taught the kids lessons, and made snacks. I hired and trained other day care workers, returned calls to potential clients, promoted the business online and via social media, and cleaned the toilet. After hours, I worried about making payroll, managing my staff, and keeping the customers happy. I focused more on the administrative and marketing side of the business, and George's superpower was making music and bringing joy to the kids. When he wasn't at the playhouse, he juggled odd jobs such as catering staff for weddings, evening server at an Italian restaurant, church choir director, and fulfilling random Craigslist postings. He did everything in his power to provide for our family during a recession. Money was tight, and we were both committed to doing what we could to keep our bills paid.

I felt a constant pull between my family and my business. Although I was with Zoe all day long, the realities of running Little Sprouts meant that I had less attention for her than ever. The stress of the business also put a lot of strain on our marriage. I was stretched too thin, and I had become a moody mom and partner who would snap without warning. I was exhausted and overwhelmed.

After pouring our savings into Little Sprouts, George and I discovered that we couldn't afford to pay both the rent for our home and our business. I proposed a solution: Instead of paying $1,600 per month for the house and $1,800 per month on our business lease, why not move into the playhouse? George laughed, but I was serious. A few months after opening, we moved our family into the day care center with its turquoise-painted walls, just a short walk from the beach. George and I slept on a futon in the main room that converted to a couch during the day, and we added a door to the large storage closet to make a room for Zoe. Our "kitchen" included a minifridge, a hot plate, and a George Foreman grill outside. The one bathroom in the playhouse, which housed a table for diaper changes and a sink to wash sticky toddler hands while singing "Itsy Bitsy Spider," also had a shower that George, Zoe, and I used only when we weren't open for business.

One afternoon during pickup, as a dad put on his child's shoes, he said to us, "Julia keeps saying you live in the back of the playhouse." George replied, "Yeah, we do." The dad's face turned red, and his eyes widened. I don't know if he was embarrassed that he'd asked or shocked that we lived in the playhouse (and that his two-year-old daughter had been telling the truth). Either way, the moment struck a nerve, sending me into a shame spiral: *We are not okay. What was I thinking, moving my family into our place of business? I have no idea what I am doing. Who am I to run my own company?*

○ ○ ○

A week later, my shame erupted like hot lava as George and I confronted each other in the driveway. I needed time and space to think. I felt as though I wanted to burn down everything that we'd built. My heart was pounding and my thoughts ran wild as I sat there behind the wheel, thinking:

1. This had better not wake up Zoe.
2. I don't know if our marriage will survive this.
3. Fuck this business for getting me to this place of exasperated rage.

"What do you want me to do?" George asked in frustration as he hopped off the car's hood. "I'm working all the time, too, and the money just disappears. I never get a break."

"Something has to change," I replied, not even sure what I meant. "I can't figure all of this out on my own."

I shifted into reverse, leaving my husband standing there on the gravel as I peeled out and sped off down the Kuhio Highway. As I drove, listening to the waves crashing on the beach through my open window, I thought, *Marriage, raising a young daughter, and running a new business? It's all too much. I can't do it anymore.* After a few miles, I pulled over, parking on Wailua Beach. I got out and pressed my feet into the cool sand, then sat down on a large piece of driftwood and looked toward the sky.

My eruption wasn't about George or our marriage. We'd be fine. We fought fairly and truly cared for each other, and after over fifteen years of marriage we still do. Our Little Sprouts experience even paved the way for him to create his own business blending his love of children and love of music years later. Some of our greatest joys come from our greatest losses. That breakdown-to-breakthrough moment was really about me stepping fully into my role as a leader.

I was struggling to reconcile the demands of holding it all together as a woman, a partner, a mother, and a business owner. We had a mountain of debt. We had no medical insurance. I felt lethargic in my body, and my mental energy was zapped. I ate more comfort food to self-soothe, which then triggered more shame because women in Western society are *supposed* to be a certain size to be considered healthy. I felt as though I had no control over the direction of my life. And I was the only one who could change that. Though I knew I wanted to build a business and be there for my daughter, I wasn't willing to sacrifice my health or relationship. As I sat on the beach, I thought, *There has got to be another way. Burnout is not an option.*

Burnout is not an option.

o o o

As women entrepreneurs, we are not only the CEOs of our companies. We don't just go to work, run our businesses, and come home at night to put our feet up. Once the workday ends, we are still partners, mothers, school volunteers, home cooks, cleaners, and the ones who stay home when our kids are sick. Even if we are not parents or in a partnership, as women we most likely take on the caretaking role for the people we love. Our hearts are that big. But when we add hustling, overwork, and people pleasing—tendencies that often accompany entrepreneurship—to the equation, we burn out.

There are many reasons why we are susceptible to burnout, a syndrome defined by the World Health Organization as "resulting from chronic workplace stress that has not been successfully managed."[1] One of the primary reasons that women face burnout is that we are often doing double duty at home and at work. In some cases, we are the primary breadwinners in our families, yet we still do more child care and domestic labor than our partners, who may be underemployed or out of work completely. In other cases, both partners have full-time jobs, but caregiving and household chores fall primarily on the woman. Still others have no partner at home, further increasing the burden.

Another reason for burnout among us is so-called hustle culture, which has become synonymous with entrepreneurship. Many self-employed women feel an unspoken pressure to participate in hustle culture because of the messaging we hear from the male-dominated start-up world about what it means to be a "real" entrepreneur. Elon Musk, the founder of SpaceX and CEO of Tesla, summed it up with this Twitter post: "There are way easier places to work, but nobody ever changed the world on 40 hours a week." Mark Cuban, an investor, *Shark Tank* personality, and owner of the Dallas Mavericks, didn't take a vacation for seven years when he started his first business. And entrepreneur and internet personality Gary Vaynerchuk preaches, "Not only am I working eighteen hours a day, but I'm working fast as hell in those eighteen hours."

Hustle culture was created by and for men, who are typically not juggling caregiving responsibilities with their careers. Women like us who want to be involved caregivers, while also doing meaningful work and providing for our families, are simply not willing to make these types of sacrifices if it means less time with our loved ones. And when we *do* try to do business this way—forced to choose between professional ambitions and missing important moments in our personal lives—it depletes our joy. We find ourselves losing sleep, wracked with guilt about where we should be spending our time. The stress takes its toll in the form of physical symptoms such as adrenal fatigue, abrupt weight changes, hair loss, and mental health issues such as anxiety and depression.

Many of us question whether it is even possible to build a successful business while living a fulfilling life outside work. We wonder whether we should scale up or shut down; franchise or file for bankruptcy; go back to a stable nine-to-five or give up and become backpacking world travelers. We have the constant pressure to be doing, creating, and caregiving—often at the cost of our health, well-being, and relationships. The 24/7 rise-and-grind approach does not work for us, and it is not the only way to build a successful company.

The COVID-19 pandemic in 2020 magnified the economic realities that working women have long been struggling with, including low wages, the high cost of housing, and the expense of child care. For some women, starting a business is the only viable option because it allows them the flexibility to care for their loved ones while also earning income. There are millions of other women in the United States who are running businesses started out of necessity, even though society doesn't support or even acknowledge them.

That was my situation when I started Little Sprouts Playhouse. In 2011, as a first-time entrepreneur who was burning the candle at both ends, my worst-case scenario came true: Little Sprouts was failing, and we had to shut down. The business wasn't making enough to support itself or our family, and George and I were unable to keep up with the constant demands of trying to keep it afloat.

With few options, we decided to leave Hawai'i and move in with my in-laws in California. I felt that my world was falling apart. George got temporary work at an educational theater company, and I juggled two part-time jobs making $15 an hour while also taking care of Zoe. One morning I got into my car and realized I didn't have enough gas to get to work. I checked my bank account, twice. My stomach turned as I read the message on my phone screen: INSUFFICIENT FUNDS. I had to call my boss and say, "I can't come in to work today. I have no money for gas. I'm so sorry."

I had reached a breaking point. Worn down by living paycheck to paycheck and barely scraping by, I knew something had to change. But deep down I was also driven by a desire to pursue my passions and do work that was fulfilling. I wanted to start a business that would give me scheduling flexibility along with more financial freedom so that I didn't have to sacrifice time with my family. I needed to find a new way of making money and building a business I loved while still enjoying my life.

Build with L.O.V.E.

I read tons of business books searching for answers, but as a multiracial woman, wife, and mother (I'm African American, Chinese, and White), I didn't see myself or my experiences represented in anything that I found. I was looking for evidence that someone like me could build a successful company. But at the time it seemed every book on entrepreneurship out there was written by a man, usually White, single, without kids, and with an ability to pour eighty hours into his workweek. The bookshelf wasn't reflecting my reality, so I had to piece things together on my own.

Clearly Little Sprouts was not a sustainable business for us. We built it out of necessity and survival mode. Over the years, I went on to create three more businesses, each with a little more intention and a lot less hustle. The second was Family Sponge, a parenting blog cocreated with my friend Jen Hansard. Business number three was Simple Green Smoothies, a product and information-based blog also cocreated with Jen. When I decided to sell Simple Green Smoothies to Jen in 2016, we had built a community of over 1 million followers in a very short amount of time. We also made more than $1 million in revenue in our first two years and published a top-selling recipe book.

The company I run today at jadahsellner.com guides women to build at a pace that works for us, growing our businesses out of love for ourselves, our families, and our communities. We need a business plan that is aligned with a greater mission for our lives, beyond just the metrics. We need to focus on the meaning behind the numbers, too.

Through my professional coaching practice, speaking, and *Lead with Love* podcast, I am on a mission to help women entrepreneurs build sustainable businesses and recover from burnout. I help my clients take their businesses to the next level while remaining fulfilled in the rest of their lives. As a woman of color without a typical business background, it is also my mission to redefine who gets to write business books and give advice on entrepreneurship. I want to challenge the belief that creatives can't make money while doing world-changing work that they love.

While each business taught me very different lessons (which I'll share with you in future chapters), collectively all four businesses helped me develop my signature "Build with L.O.V.E." approach, the core framework of this book. Building with L.O.V.E. is about building a business sustainably, with love at the center of every decision. It's the antidote to building with hustle, something female entrepreneurs around the world have been craving (whether we consciously realize it or not). Here are the four pillars:

BUILD WITH L.O.V.E.

- **LEAD.** Building our businesses sustainably means learning to *lead* from the inside out. This begins by leading ourselves with clarity and purpose, followed by leading our families, our teams, our communities, and the customers we serve. To become better leaders while avoiding burnout, we need to establish a compelling vision for what we want from our lives and our businesses. Then we gather allies who will help us make this vision a reality.

- **OPTIMIZE.** We need to set up internal support systems to *optimize* the way we run our businesses and our personal lives, systems that will enable us to thrive and allow us to achieve sustainability and scale. This includes redesigning how we use our time, building our team, and streamlining our businesses. In this section, we'll stop overcomplicating things and make time for what matters most.

- VISUALIZE. We must step away from daily distractions and *visualize* what we want, the big picture. This is about moving from being reactionary managers to being visionary CEOs. We'll learn how to celebrate our past accomplishments and how to map out where we want to go by creating a clear action plan. In this section, we'll also learn the three simple questions to ask to realign the direction of our businesses, so that we can double down on what's working and eliminate what's not.

- EXPAND. In the final section, we will *expand* our most valuable asset: *ourselves*—as leaders, founders, partners, parents, and friends. This pillar is about learning to communicate our needs and establish boundaries, so that we can prioritize taking care of ourselves and our businesses. We'll cultivate a mindset that enables us to build sustainably, at a pace that works for our lives, while feeling confident in the choices we make.

Building with L.O.V.E. helped me balance my personal growth with my business goals, while still having time to enjoy my life. In the pages to come, I will show you how to tailor this process to meet your needs.

She Builds is a road map for you to build and scale your business in a new way. It is an anti-hustle handbook to help you move from overwhelmed founder leading with fear to empowered CEO leading with love. From burnout to balance, from exhausted to energized, from frustration to freedom, this book will get you off the hamster wheel of busyness, stress, and self-doubt and onto a clear path toward leading with more heart.

You will learn to think like the visionary CEO your business needs. You will also learn how to shut off your work brain at home (even if you work from home) and be fully present to the people who matter the most to you. I'll show you how to engineer systems of support, view self-care as a business strategy, and extract yourself from the daily grind to move into intentional planning so that you can grow your business to the next level without burning out.

This book is an interactive guide. Think of me as a personal coach on your nightstand (or in your earbuds), cheering you on as you complete the exercises along the way. Grab a journal and a pen, and get ready to write! You can also download and print out all of the interactive exercises in the book at shebuilds.com/resources.

She Builds is an invitation to redefine the way you work, lead, and love. It is time to become the architect of your business without sacrificing your life—and avoid the stress of the hustle. Let's get started.

she builds with

Intention.

1

Detox from Hustle Culture

The secret of change is to focus
all your energy not on fighting
the old but on building the new.[1]

—*Dan Millman,* Way of the Peaceful Warrior

It was 7:55 a.m. I had been up for over twenty-four hours. I sat on the floor surrounded by manuscript pages, still dressed in yesterday's yoga pants. My book, *Simple Green Smoothies,* was due to my editor in an hour, and the recovering perfectionist in me knew that it was my last chance to make changes. I was the cofounder of a health and wellness brand. I was also a walking contradiction, routinely pushing myself to exhaustion and eating poorly as I did sprints like this in my business. I knew this wasn't sustainable, and I didn't want to model this way of working for my daughter. Yet here I was again.

I somehow managed to get the manuscript to my editor before pushing ahead with the rest of my massive to-do list that day. Over the next nine months, I would rinse and repeat the same unhealthy work patterns, culminating in the November 2015 launch of the book.

Each year I vowed to unplug during the holidays, but as a co-founder of a healthy lifestyle company, that seemed impossible. I felt pressure to prepare for the "New Year, New You" season in January, which was the time of year when we'd make the most money. And that particular year, the book launch meant that things were busier than ever leading into December. Unsurprisingly, my body was the first part of me to say "No." I got very sick, and on Christmas morning, instead of being fully present with my daughter, sipping eggnog and watching Christmas movies, I was under the covers with a high fever. "This is it," I told my husband. "I can't do this anymore." In that moment, something clicked. I needed to make a change. But another eleven months would pass before I could summon up the courage to sell my half of the company to my business partner, Jen, and make my exit.

The Hustle Is a Lie

Like many female entrepreneurs who have absorbed messages from the male-dominated business world on what it means to be a *real* entrepreneur, I had bought into the hustle culture: working long hours, feeling guilty if I spent time on anything non-work-related, and sacrificing my personal well-being to build my business. No one was forcing me to hustle. Instead, the sneaky subliminal messaging of the patriarchy was telling me: You're not smart enough. You're not fast enough. You're not doing enough.

As one example of how this harmful messaging plays out for women, in a 2017 study conducted by the Institute for Gender and the Economy (GATE), researchers interviewed high-earning men and women at an oil and gas company to assess their perceptions of their ability to juggle work and parental responsibilities.[2] According to the responses, women experienced an intense work-life conflict. They didn't see a way to balance motherhood with career ambition. Feeling trapped between the two, many ultimately opted to leave their positions. Men, however, felt that work-life balance was attainable, with "balance" meaning working longer hours to climb the corporate ladder. They were almost universally supported by a stay-at-home partner who shouldered the primary responsibility of caretaking at home.

Hustle culture is built around norms that favor the way most men like to work. Underlying these norms is the unspoken assumption that every working adult has the equivalent of a 1950s housewife providing free, all-day support services: housework, running errands, child care, and so on. There's only one problem: most women don't have this kind of support, even if their partner helps out on the domestic front. (Many men don't have support, either, by the way.) And often, because women tend to be paid less than men for doing the same work, it is hard for us to pay for a team of helpers to get everything done, especially in the early days of running a business. As a result, we resort to squeezing more and more out of ourselves and cutting into our personal time, to the detriment of our physical and mental health. I call this pattern of behavior *toxic productivity*, and we'll explore it in more depth later in this chapter.

Many business owners also succumb to the hustle culture because of the social pressure to belong and be accepted by other entrepreneurs. We hustle as a badge of honor, especially if we work in industries where we're the only women in the room. We become addicted to the chase, determined to prove that we can do the work and that we deserve success. We overcommit and overschedule ourselves for fear of missing out on an opportunity to get ahead. Yet the finish line always moves farther away, and our best is never enough.

Patriarchal standards also drive us to compare ourselves to others whose lives and priorities may be different than ours. We beat ourselves up when our homes are not perfectly organized, when the meals we cook (or replace with takeout) are not gourmet, when we can't volunteer for a school event that conflicts with work. When the way we work looks different from that of our male counterparts, or when our lives and careers don't seem Instagram-worthy, we compare and despair, and we are more likely to buy into self-perpetuating lies such as:

- "My business is a hot mess."
- "I stumbled into this work and don't know what I'm doing."
- "I'm not qualified enough to do this."
- "I'm not working hard enough to be successful."

If we keep proving, pushing, and people pleasing our way through business and life, we are destined to burn out and sabotage what we've built. So repeat after me: "My business is not a hot mess. I am enough."

We need to recognize that many popular models of success that work for men (and that the media celebrates) aren't good models for us. Books that are about hustling and scaling up by any means necessary—even if it means no sleep, no time for family, and no time for ourselves—don't consider the things we value. Even business books that embrace a slower-paced lifestyle don't acknowledge the realities of our lives as women. I got excited by the promise of working less, traveling more, and automating everything in Tim Ferriss's *The 4-Hour Workweek*. But as I read the book, I came to doubt that his life of freedom and flexibility was possible for me. Ferriss presents himself in the book as a young Ivy League–educated man who travels the globe while running a financially successful business and relying on time-saving hacks such as delegating the purchase of flowers for his girlfriend to an assistant in India.[3] As the parent of a young daughter who was drowning in debt and living with her in-laws to make ends meet, it was tough to relate.

Remember: Your business is not a hot mess. You are not a hot mess. Your business is growing. And you are growing it while leading a busy adult life. Your business looks different because you are

Building with L.O.V.E., and it is unfolding at a different pace and in a different way than that of a start-up founder who starts a project, scales it up, sells it, and moves on to the next one. Let me also remind you: you *can* live the life you want while creating a mission-driven business that represents who you are and what you stand for. But you can only do this if you stop competing in the race of hustle culture and commit to running at your own pace.

The Passion Paradox

It's not only hustle culture that sucks us into burnout. Sometimes it's an even sneakier culprit: passion. "Pursue your passion" is a common rallying cry that draws many women to the entrepreneurial path. It certainly influenced me. My father, a man with many side hustles, often said, "Do work you love and marry someone who loves what they do, too." I took that advice, letting passion be the guiding light that pointed me toward each job I took and each business I started. However, the downside of relentlessly pursuing my passion was that I ignored my health and my important relationships more often than I'd like to admit. One time I took my laptop to a playdate, and Zoe bit the screen, cracking it, to get my attention. I was angry with her but even angrier at myself. I didn't like who I was becoming, yet I was so obsessed with my work that I couldn't stop. I was also spending so much time on my computer that I became sedentary, ignoring my body's signs that I needed to take breaks and be more active. My work was too important, and there wasn't enough time in a day. There was always *one more thing* to do.

Don't get me wrong; there is a lot to be said for doing what you are passionate about as an entrepreneur. But there is a dark side to passion. It can be hard to find the "off" button when you're running your own business, with no external forces telling you to stop. Many women entrepreneurs feel that there's always more to do. We're never done with our workday, and although we try to create some security and stability in our lives, we lack the support many people get from a traditional job. This puts us into a constant state of stress that can break us down.

THE HIGH COST OF PASSION

Did you know that the way you manage your passion can determine your odds of working sustainably throughout your career versus flaming out? A study in *Harvard Business Review* looked at the causes of burnout among entrepreneurs by examining the two distinct types of passion:[4]

- HARMONIOUS PASSION. Believing your work is an important part of who you are and feeling easily motivated by your work because it brings you joy and fulfillment.
- OBSESSIVE PASSION. Defining your internal value by your work because of the status, money, or recognition it brings.

The research found that business owners who reported high levels of obsessive passion were more likely to experience burnout. Those entrepreneurs worked very long hours, which led them to experience frustration, exhaustion, and constant stress and anxiety. They reported feeling distracted, ignoring self-care, and neglecting relationships with family and friends. They had to battle the urge to be productive 24/7 and felt emotionally dependent on their work.

In contrast, the entrepreneurs who characterized themselves as having harmonious passion, although excited by their businesses, were more flexible and more willing to take breaks. This left them better able to focus while working. They designed lives that allowed them to spend time on other things without guilt when they weren't working.

Which group sounds happier? Most entrepreneurs I know would rather approach their businesses with harmonious passion. However, for many working women, obsessive passion is hard to avoid because you almost have to be obsessed with your career to be able to juggle the double shifts of paid work and household work. Fortunately, if you're trapped in obsessive passion, it's possible to break your addiction to overwork. It's a matter of actively choosing harmonious passion and setting yourself up to embrace it every day of your life.

Warning Signs That the Hustle Is Crushing You

In my coaching practice, I've found that there are two major signs that people need to make a serious change in how they run their businesses: high-functioning anxiety and toxic productivity. Let's explore what these warning signs look like, and whether they may be affecting you.

High-Functioning Anxiety

Anxiety is our body's natural response to stress. In certain situations, such as public speaking or taking a test, a certain amount of anxiety is typical, even healthy. It becomes problematic, however, when it's so intense that we can't live our lives or get our work done. High-functioning anxiety is a type of anxiety that's common to women entrepreneurs. Though not an official mental health diagnosis (and I highly recommend seeking professional support if you think you may need it), it's a term used to describe individuals who struggle with anxiety while appearing to function optimally to others.[5]

As business owners, we tend to stretch ourselves thin and push ourselves to the limit. Often, we are also experts at hiding our stress from others, wanting to appear successful, calm, and confident on the outside. This may even drive us to overachieve, rather than holding us back as we strive for perfection. This is high-functioning anxiety in action.

We pay a price for our achievement in the form of disrupted sleep due to racing thoughts, an inability to relax, a struggle to enforce boundaries, and having feelings of overwhelm and personal pressure. Some of the world's most successful women, including Oprah Winfrey, Adele, Kristen Bell, and Lady Gaga, have spoken publicly about their struggles with high-functioning anxiety. Those of us with this type of anxiety may look as though we have it all figured out, but our private reality is different. Although every person experiences the condition differently, here are some signs of high-functioning anxiety.

- Identifying as a "people pleaser" and having difficulty saying no
- Struggling to let go of perfectionism
- Constantly making to-do lists to stay on task
- Being afraid to disappoint others
- Tending to procrastinate
- Having an intense fear of failure
- Overpreparing for work and projects
- Imagining catastrophic outcomes of events before they happen
- Dwelling on small mistakes
- Becoming irritated easily and snapping at people out of nowhere

If you identify with any of the qualities on this list, you are not alone. Myself and many strong women all over the world have struggled with high-functioning anxiety behind closed doors. The following strategies may help you manage your stress more effectively.

- **MEET YOURSELF WITH COMPASSION FIRST.** Don't beat yourself up for feeling anxious. Instead, talk to yourself as you would talk to your child or best friend. Something like, "I see that you're worried about not having enough time to do it all. I completely understand. That must feel really overwhelming." If self-compassion is a real challenge for you right now, connect with others facing similar struggles and share what you are going through. Deep breathing can also help you feel a sense of control. I listen to guided meditations in the Insight Timer app by Vanessa Michele and Sarah Blondin. Some great ones to start with are "Finding Calm: SOS Anxiety Relief" and "Healing Through Letting Go."

- FEEL THE FEELINGS. If you experience anxious thoughts, don't dismiss or try to minimize the emotion. Instead, give yourself permission to name the emotion and to really feel it. Set a timer for twenty minutes, and sit with your full range of emotions. Once the timer is done, share what you are going through with a partner, friend, or therapist, or write it in a journal. This exercise allows your fight-or-flight response to calm down, so that more rational thinking can enter the room. If you'd like to connect to your feelings in a self-guided way, Amber Rae has written *The Wonder Journal: A Guide to Explore Your Emotions*. It's a choose-your-own adventure playbook to discover your feelings and yourself.

- NAME YOUR FEAR. Find a way to separate your worries from who you are beneath the fear. You can name what you're afraid of, draw a picture of it, or purchase an item that symbolizes your inner critic. I named my self-critical voice Patronizing Polly. She's the voice that says, "You don't know what you're doing. You're lazy. You can't do anything right." Once you have named your fear or worry voice, tell her she's safe, and engage in positive self-talk to counteract the negative messaging. My friend Amy Ahlers teaches a compassionate approach to connecting with your self-critic and developing inner wisdom in her book *Reform Your Inner Mean Girl*.[6]

- GET CURIOUS. Observe the root of your anxious thoughts. What triggered your feelings? Put your consultant hat on and challenge your assumptions. Consider whether your fears are founded, if you may be overreacting, or if there's another way to look at the situation. Reaching out to a skilled coach or therapist can guide you through questions to help alleviate anxious thoughts and reframe your perceptions to more empowering truths.

- BORROW FROM YOUR PAST. Think back and consider whether you have been in a similar situation before. How did you cope? What worked, and what didn't? You can reuse strategies that helped you through similar experiences in the past. Create a menu of activities that have worked. I refer to my self-care menu (you'll create one in chapter 11). For example, if I start to worry about money, I schedule a call with my therapist, talk to a friend who would understand, or read "The Abundance Prayer" in Tosha Silver's book *It's Not Your Money.*[7] This doesn't solve my money problems, but these actions help my racing mind relax a little, so I can come up with more creative solutions.

Toxic Productivity

Another sign you're hustling too much is that you are trying to do everything on your own. Wearing too many hats is exhausting. The first step toward building the business you want and living your life with more joy is letting go of toxic productivity, which is the belief that getting more done is the only way to achieve success. Answer the following questions to determine whether toxic productivity may be present in your life.

- Do you find yourself distracted while at work, thinking about the many responsibilities you might be neglecting at home?

- Are you constantly thinking about your business when you're with your friends or family?
- Do you feel guilty if you're not doing something that you think is constructive, such as learning, making, creating, or moving a project forward?
- Do you feel a lack of self-worth when you are resting and taking care of yourself instead of tending to the needs of others or your business?
- Do you find yourself working at night or on the weekends out of habit, regardless of whether you are managing a time-sensitive deadline or not?

If you answered yes to any of these questions, toxic productivity is probably sabotaging your efforts both at work and at home. Hustle culture has made you believe that you are only valuable, lovable, and worthy enough when you are being productive. It's no surprise that you're burnt out. The antidote: Stop playing the game. Stop hustling. Stop trying to do too much. Get comfortable with the discomfort of not getting everything done, so you can be present for what matters most to you. This may be easier said than done, especially if nonstop working has become your autopilot mode. To actively break these patterns of behavior, you must choose to slow down, trust yourself, and start making conscious business decisions from a place of love. In other words, embrace Intentional Living.

Overcoming Burnout with Intentional Living

The good news is that if you're caught on the hustle treadmill, there is an off button. The solution is to choose Intentional Living over the hustle lifestyle. Intentional Living is about living your life by design and not by default. It's about envisioning where you want to go next, setting a goal, and prioritizing what you need to do to get there. It's about making time for what *really* matters to you, as opposed to hustling to keep up with societal expectations of how you *should* be living. Intentional Living will enable you to achieve better focus, more fulfillment, and even fun when you work. It involves giving yourself permission to embrace your pace, reflect on how far you've come, and celebrate the smaller milestones of progress along the way.

Part of Intentional Living is making room for serendipity and surrender. Even if you are moving toward a desired destination, there are going to be bumps in the road. This approach to living will help you hold your intentions lightly, loosen your grip on your goals, recalibrate after disappointing detours, take rest stops, and enjoy the journey. You'll learn to trust the process and love yourself each step of the way.

THE HUSTLE LIFESTYLE VERSUS INTENTIONAL LIVING

To stop proving your worth through productivity, it helps to identify the differences between these two choices. Here are some examples of what people in each category do.

THE HUSTLE LIFESTYLE	INTENTIONAL LIVING
Is obsessively passionate	Is harmoniously passionate
Focuses on outcomes and productivity	Focuses on processes and fulfillment
Networks for social acceptance	Builds authentic friendships
Pursues accomplishments for status	Pursues projects for growth and learning
Is driven by the desire for more money	Is driven by the desire for more meaning
Neglects relationships and health	Makes time for relationships and health
Has the urge to work 24/7	Takes guilt-free breaks and downtime

Anti-Hustle Strategies

When we are caught up in the hustle, how do we get off that tread-mill and onto the path toward Intentional Living? I have discovered that there are three primary ways, which I call my Anti-Hustle Strategies:

1. Break the Cycle of F.E.A.R.
2. Give yourself permission to be a slow cooker.
3. Do a Business Detox.

Here I will give you an overview of each strategy, and in the coming chapters, I will guide you through how to implement them as daily practices in your work and in your life.

Break the Cycle of F.E.A.R.

As I've mentioned, the balance that many of us are trying to maintain—working nonstop, overcommitting our schedules, and putting everyone else's needs before our own—isn't sustainable. Running a business while hustling to live according to unattainable expectations leads us to what I call the Cycle of F.E.A.R., which we need to break free from.

I've identified four mental loops that keep us stuck in this endless cycle and racing toward burnout: *forcing, exhaustion, avoidance,* and *rigidity.* Here's how these four factors play off one another.

1. FORCING. When we attempt to force desired outcomes or force our bodies and minds to perform past a healthy threshold to keep up with the daily demands of our lives, we're operating from a place of time scarcity. We exist in a state of panic, feeling that there are never enough hours in the day to get everything done. Forcing also applies to holding impossible standards of who

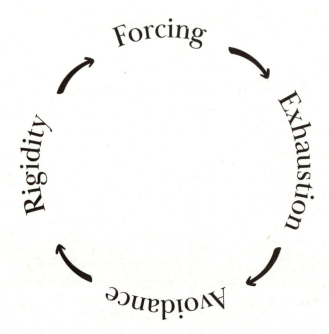

we should be as entrepreneurs, partners, friends, parents, and neighbors—and the ways we judge ourselves when we don't measure up. We force instead of trust. We give ourselves no physical or mental rest, which then leads to the next stage . . .

2. **EXHAUSTION.** As women, we often overcommit and overschedule ourselves in an effort to keep others happy while also pursuing our own dreams and ambitions. This people pleasing leads to exhaustion—and when we're exhausted, we're moody, frustrated, and irritable, which affects our relationships. We feel apathetic and phone it in, and having depleted our energy and resources, it's no surprise that we soon find ourselves in the next part of the cycle . . .

3. **AVOIDANCE.** When we're tired, we avoid important projects that require mental energy and creativity. In denial about how much is on our plates, we lose sight of the big picture and hide in busy-

work, which leaves no time for the projects and people that matter most. We focus on putting out the urgent fires, instead of on what will make the biggest impact. We can no longer see the forest for the trees. Our to-do list is so long that we can't prioritize. So we freeze, second-guess every decision, and procrastinate, leaving no room for creative flexibility, which leads to . . .

4. RIGIDITY. As entrepreneurs we make plans. We commit and act. Then we stick to the plan, regardless of whether it's working, because we've invested so heavily in it (this is known in economics as the "sunk cost fallacy"). Or we simply do the same thing over and over out of habit because it's what we've always done. When anxiety overwhelms us, we default to old, familiar patterns of behavior. We have tunnel vision, unable to take a step back to assess and reimagine whether there's a better way to accomplish the results we desire. This inflexible thinking causes more fatigue and overwhelm and leads us right back to forcing.

The first step of breaking the Cycle of F.E.A.R. is acknowledging that we're caught up in it. We're sacrificing sleep, skipping meals, and working late-night hours to make sure our clients, partners, and kids (or "fur babies") are happy. No one is forcing us to live this way, yet our perfectionism is causing us to push ourselves to burnout. How can we stop repeating the pattern of forcing, exhaustion, avoidance, and rigidity? We decide who and what gets our attention and when.

Give Yourself Permission to Be a Slow Cooker

Intentional Living requires some shifts in how we think. There are two work modes: fast and slow. Working fast gets the accolades for accomplishing a great deal in a short amount of time. Working slow is perceived as lazy and inefficient. It reminds me of two popular kitchen appliances: the pressure cooker, which cooks meals in less than an hour, and the slow cooker, which makes a meal over the course of a full day. The difference is the amount of time it takes to have a delicious meal on the table. Neither is wrong or better than the other. Both get the same results, but they work in different ways.

To get everything done, many of us have been operating in our businesses and lives as though we're cooking with a pressure cooker. We multitask and work through our to-do list as quickly as possible. In my experience, doing everything in the fastest way distorts our perspective, making it impossible to keep sight of the bigger picture and live mindfully.

What would happen if you gave yourself permission to be like a slow cooker? A slow cooker allows you to let a dish simmer for hours, while you go about the other activities of your day. You have the space to leave and do other things, while also knowing you can check on the progress of the food whenever you want or need to.

Rather than attempting to do the impossible single-handedly, honor your work style and let your business simmer. When we let things simmer, we're able to slow down and trust that the most important things will get done with perfect timing.

Do a Business Detox

When I ran Simple Green Smoothies, I hosted 21-day plant-based cleanses in which participants eliminated certain foods to help eat healthier and release toxins from their bodies. The first few days were the most intense, with everyone irritable and "hangry" while detoxing. A Business Detox may cause a similar effect. You may feel worse before you feel better when you release the toxic behaviors that got you caught in the Cycle of F.E.A.R. in the first place. But you will ultimately find that by letting go of the things that are no longer working for you (or never did), you will free up mental space and energy to be more creative and to grow your business in new ways.

My first Business Detox at Simple Green Smoothies involved finding ways to work less instead of more as the company grew. I didn't want to fall out of love with my business or customers, so I hired a part-time assistant for five hours per week to respond to social media comments and emails. I worked four days a week instead of five to give myself more time to rest and recover. I turned down projects and opportunities that didn't align directly with my focus for the next three months to one year. I scheduled family dates and added them to my work calendar on Fridays, Saturdays, and Sundays so that I wouldn't let work overflow into my weekends.

Even if you're in the earlier stages of business and aren't quite bringing in enough money to buy yourself more time, there are creative ways in which you can lighten your load. When I first started my business, I did child care swaps, created more boundaries around my time (like stepping down from the board at my daughter's preschool), and invited a friend to be my accountability partner when I couldn't afford a coach. By prioritizing what mattered most to me, I was able to increase both my business profits and my personal income in a very short amount of time. I chose "love over metrics," focusing on people instead of just the bottom line (which I'll describe in more detail in chapter 7).

Breaking away from hustle culture won't happen overnight. It happens gradually, and it begins with imagining a different life for yourself and shifting your mindset so that you can start to heal. I'll lead you through the process of doing this in the coming chapters, and I'll share stories of female entrepreneurs who successfully detoxed their businesses, too.

Make a Mental Declutter List

Let's start your Business Detox now. Pull out a notebook or journal and a pen. Set a timer for ten minutes. Find a blank page, make two columns, then write down every possible thing you can think of that you have to do in your business (column one) and your personal life (column two). Keep writing until ten minutes is up. Some people call this exercise a "brain dump," but I prefer not to describe the thoughts and tasks running through our minds as trash. Instead, let's call it a "brain sneeze," a term coined by my friend Nikki Elledge Brown. Need some inspiration to get your gears turning? Here's the beginning of my list.

BUSINESS	PERSONAL LIFE
Write newsletter	Make a grocery list
Research flights to New York	Do back-to-school shopping
Record podcast interview	Drop off donations
Design website home page	Buy baby shower gift
Send proposal to potential client	Pay credit card bill
Research retreat locations	Reschedule dentist appointment

Anything and everything goes onto the list, whether it will take you two seconds or two weeks to complete. Though this may seem like the kind of exercise that you could easily skip over, here's why I don't want you to do that: it is like clearing out the junk drawer in your kitchen, only in this case, the junk drawer is your mind.

Once your mental clutter is on the page and you've freed up space in your mind, rip out a second piece of paper and fold it in half twice. Then unfold it. You now have eight squares, four on the front and four on the back of your page. Next, I want you to label the squares with the following eight action categories, which we will use to organize the brain sneeze activities you listed. Creating these categories enables your brain to organize and focus. Then, when it's time to execute, you'll be able to batch similar tasks and get them completed more quickly rather than bouncing back and forth among different kinds of tasks. Feel free to adjust the following eight categories based on your needs.

- CREATE. These are things that you need more time and creative bandwidth to accomplish, including writing something new, or editing or reviewing something you've already created.
- DELEGATE. These are things you can ask someone on your team or in your family to do. I usually add them to my next team meeting with my assistant or to my next couples meeting with my husband.
- ELIMINATE. These are items that you've decided don't need to be done in the next thirty to ninety days. If you think you may want to revisit them, you can add them to your Dream Bank (which I'll discuss in chapter 8).
- COLLABORATE. This includes bigger projects that you know you can't complete on your own, for which you will have to hire an outside paid consultant, such as a designer, or brainstorm with a thought partner, such as someone on your team.
- EMAIL. This category is for important emails that you don't want to risk losing in your inbox.
- CALL. You can list all calls that are on your mental declutter list, whether for making an appointment or for catching up with a friend or family member.
- PAY. These are any purchases for which you need to pull out a credit card and make a payment online or write a check.
- PERSONAL. These are more personal tasks that need to be done at home or errands that need to be done outside in your neighborhood.

Once you have your categories, write each item from your brain sneeze under the corresponding heading. When all your tasks have a home, go through them and estimate how long it will take you to complete each one. This can range from five minutes to three hours, and I suggest overestimating the length of time necessary. Write that amount next to each item.

Next, total the time it will take you to finish all the items listed in each category. Write that number next to the category title. This will give you a clearer sense of how long it will take you to complete the items and how much you can expect to get done in a day.

Here's my example using my brain sneeze list.

Front Side

Create (2 hours, 30 minutes) Write newsletter (1 hour) Record podcast interview (1 hour, 30 minutes)	Delegate (1 hour) Research flights to New York (30 minutes) Drop off donations (30 minutes)
Eliminate ~~Research retreat locations~~	Collaborate (3 hours) Design website home page (3 hours)

Back Side

Email (30 minutes) Send proposal to potential client (30 minutes)	Call (5 minutes) Reschedule dentist appointment (5 minutes)
Pay (35 minutes) Buy baby shower gift (30 minutes) Pay credit card bill (5 minutes)	Personal (2 hours, 30 minutes) Make a grocery list (30 minutes) Do back-to-school shopping (2 hours)

You can now start to add these items to your calendar as scheduled time blocks. For example, I could see where I have a little more than one hour of time available and could complete all of my calls, emails, and purchases. I could also schedule a "Create" day, where I block off three hours in my calendar to record a podcast interview and write my newsletter. Once I transfer all the tasks under "Delegate" to someone such as my husband or assistant, I see that I will save myself more than an hour by getting them off my plate.

Looking at the commitments you already have in place and making an honest assessment of what you can get done and when, helps you start to reclaim control of your time. (We'll identify how much time you have for work in chapter 5.) But for now, doing this exercise will help you lighten your mental load.

This mental declutter exercise is a great way to jump-start your Business Detox, and you will use it again and again. I like to do it once a month or whenever I feel overwhelmed by all that I have on my plate.

o o o

When I think about stepping away from the hustle and what it means to me, I get an image of nine-year-old Zoe in my mind. She is grinning from ear to ear with a matcha green tea ice cream cone in her hand on a trip that we took as a family to Japan—a *real* two-week vacation when I wasn't working. I had just finalized the sale of Simple Green Smoothies to my cofounder a few weeks earlier. That decision was one of the hardest I've ever had to make. I loved the community and team we had built together, but I was exhausted and my soul was calling me in a new direction. I wasn't sure exactly where I was headed, but as soon as I signed the papers to release me from the company, I felt a weight lifted off me that I hadn't even known I was carrying.

I realized that the trip to Japan was the first time I had left my laptop at home while on a vacation. I didn't send my family off to a separate activity so I could get some work done, as I usually did, saying "Just one more email" or "I have to take this call" or "I need to write this sales page right now." I'd been an entrepreneur for more than eight years, and I finally gave myself permission to let work rest and be fully present with my family. I didn't let my work bleed into my life. I created boundaries and let go of the "do whatever it takes" mentality so that I could prioritize what matters the most in my life.

Ultimately, being a woman in business is your superpower, not your weakness. Stepping into the next level of leadership requires a new way of thinking and being. How can you build a life that works for you? How can you trust that it's okay to build your way? We will answer these questions together. It won't be easy, but it will be worth it. In the next chapter, I want to help you build a strong foundation by showing you how to become really clear on what matters most in your life.

It's okay to build YOUR way.

2

Simplify Your Life

My mission in life is not merely to
survive, but to thrive; and to do so with
some passion, some compassion, some
humor, and some style.

—*Maya Angelou*

Have you read the parable by Paulo Coelho about the fisherman
and the businessman?[1] This is my spin on it, which I call "The Yoga
Teacher and the Businesswoman: A Tale of Simplicity."

*A wealthy businesswoman visited her friend, a yoga teacher, on the idyl-
lic northern California coast. They had brunch together and then walked
along the beach, sharing updates about their families, their work, and
their health. They sat down on a blanket where the sand met the ocean,
and the yoga teacher moved her body up and down in a cat-cow position,
which helped her to digest her meal fully. The businesswoman compli-
mented her friend: "Your classes are so calming and easy to follow. How
long have you been teaching now?"*

"Twenty years," the yoga teacher said.

The businesswoman asked, "How often do you teach?"

"I host a ten-week class four times per year. I also lead retreats in Maui and California."

Then the businesswoman asked, "How many students are in your classes?"

"Fifteen."

"Do you ever think about expanding your teaching practice to serve even more students and make more money? You are such a gifted teacher, and you could be doing so much more with your talents."

The yoga teacher replied, "My two retreats and four sessions make enough money to pay for my home close to the beach and provide for my family. I really love where I live. It's a small town with no traffic. Lots of space and nature. Life has a slow pace here."

The businesswoman stared out into the ocean, "So if you only work a few months out of the year, what do you do with the rest of your time?"

The yoga teacher sat up straight, "That's the best part! I make my kids lunches in the morning, walk them to school, do my own yoga practice in my sunroom, have lunch at home with my husband, rest in the afternoon, snuggle with my dog, write a few pages for the book I'm working on, take my kids to their after-school activities, and then walk into town to meet with friends, where we laugh and share our dreams over kombucha and wine."

The businesswoman pulled out her phone and punched numbers into her calculator. She said, "That all sounds great, but you could reach so many more people by systemizing your business. I can show you how to do it. First you increase your prices; then you increase your class sizes; then you add more classes to your schedule. Then, with the extra profit from the classes, you'll move to a more populated city so you can maximize your reach. You can lease a bigger building to teach your classes and hire a studio manager. And with the money from the bigger studio, you can train and certify teachers, open even more studios, license your IP, and franchise your business. You'll travel the world to train other teachers in your model. If you want to add even more profit to your bottom line, you can create an online yoga course, hire a social media manager to build your following, and do brand partnerships. You'll be making money in your sleep!"

The yoga teacher ran her fingers through the sand, then said, "I could reach a lot more people and change a lot more lives. How long will this take to expand my business in this way?"

"Scaling your business would take about twenty years, working about eighty hours per week," the businesswoman replied.

"And what happens next?" asked the yoga teacher.

The businesswoman smiled. "That's the best part! You'll come up with a strategic plan to exit your company, sell it for a lot of money. And never have to teach again. You'll have so much money you won't even know what to do with it."

"And then what happens?"

The businesswoman replied, "And then you can retire and move to a small town near the coast, visit your kids in college, do your own yoga practice in your sunroom, have lunch at home with your husband, rest in the afternoon, snuggle with your rescue dog, write a few pages for your book, and then walk into town to meet with friends, where you laugh and share your dreams over kombucha and wine."

o o o

The story of the yoga teacher and the businesswoman reminds me of why I built my business in the first place: to provide for my family, have time to enjoy my relationships, and do meaningful work that doesn't take up my entire life. And it's based on a true story. My dear friend Michelle Long, the founder of The Practice, had a boutique yoga studio with a teacher certification program and was advised by several business consultants to franchise her curriculum and studio model. She followed their advice, excited by the prospect of expanding her reach to impact more lives, but there was a cost. Instead of doing what she loved—teaching yoga—she became CEO, brand strategist, project manager, accountant, substitute teacher, and HR manager. She had little time or energy for her kids or husband. She had to manage teachers, deal with workplace conflicts, and consult with lawyers.

Eventually she burned out, closed the doors of her studio, and moved to a smaller town with a slower pace of living. She wanted to heal, restore, and find a way to serve her students that was simpler but still felt expansive. She calculated what I call her "enough number," the yearly income she needed to earn to live at a pace that worked for her, have time to travel, and be present for her family. (We'll talk more about getting to your enough number later in this chapter.) Today, Michelle leads two retreats a year and four ten-week immersion classes, serving sixty clients a year. Her ambition is still there, her creativity is still alive, but her vision for her business also includes her vision for her life.

Many of us yearn to simplify our lives and our businesses, so that we are not constantly juggling competing demands. Regardless of where you currently are in building your business, it can be helpful to plan out that simplified vision *now*, as opposed to waiting until you've scaled up or hit some other milestone. You can adopt what I call an "integrated life" right away.

The Integrated Life

Living an integrated life is about creating harmony among your health, wealth, and relationships—bringing your whole self to each part no matter how much of your attention it's getting. It's not about trying to compartmentalize "career" and "life" into separate pockets of time. Your attention will be divided, and that's okay. An integrated life means that you can upshift and downshift according to your priorities at any given moment and depending on the situation.

THE INTEGRATED LIFE

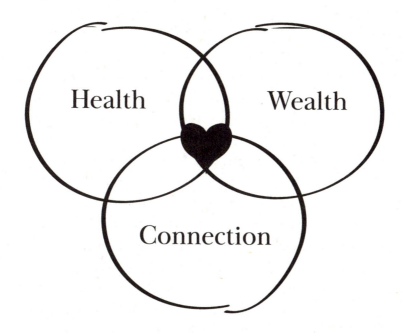

I call the end of my workweek "Free-Flow Fridays" and often meet up with friends for a brunch-and-brainstorm session, where we talk about our businesses and our lives. This model works when I'm traveling, too. For example, when I spoke at ProBlogger, a training event in Brisbane, Australia, I took my husband and daughter with me. While I practiced and delivered my keynote speech, they did fun activities on their own, such as going to the gorgeous Surfer's Paradise Beach and riding the giant Ferris wheel on the iconic South Bank. Then, after I was done with my work, we flew to Fiji, where I was able to fully unplug and be on vacation with them.

What I like most about the integrated life approach is that it works just as well when things don't go according to plan. Not long ago, I had accepted an invitation to speak at an event, but when the event rolled around, Zoe was extremely sick. I decided to cancel to be there for my daughter, but there was a part of me that worried, *What will this do to future speaking opportunities?* Then I remembered my commitment to working in a way that allows me to make choices that honor my whole life. An integrated life is one where you build a business that fits into your life rather than cramming your life into your business. And once you do, it'll set you free in ways you may never have imagined.

What Season of Life Are You In?

Before you can simplify and integrate your life, you first have to become clear on what you want, big picture. To do this, I've found it is important to understand what season of life you're in. Maybe you have young children, you're caretaking aging parents, or you are managing a chronic or mental illness that affects your energy and focus. Maybe you are swamped in debt and have taken on additional work to pay the bills or you're in a season of expansion and need to reinvest personal profits back into your business. Whatever circumstances or constraints exist, it's helpful to know and accept that some timelines for reaching your desired destination may take longer because of the other demands on your time or energy.

My client Meggan Hill, the founder of the food blog Culinary Hill, has grown from running a one-woman business to having four full-time employees and three contractors since we started working together. She is also raising three children under the age of ten. When publishers approached Meggan to produce a cookbook, she was excited about the possibility of having her recipes on bookshelves around the world. Then she considered the season of life she was in. She assessed the time commitment it would take to produce a cookbook: developing and testing recipes, styling the food, taking and editing photos, writing the copy for the book, and a whole lot more. She was also navigating a divorce. With all she was juggling in her professional and personal life, she knew she had only so much time in a day for new projects. Pardon the pun, but adding a cookbook to her plate would have likely put her over the edge and created a recipe for burnout. Being present for her family was a priority, so she decided to wait.

Meggan made what I call an Intentional Trade-Off, saying no to one opportunity to free up mental bandwidth and energy for something else. To make an Intentional Trade-Off, you need to know what you want for your life at the moment. She dug deep and became specific about what was most important to her during that season of her life, while also considering what she wanted and what she had the capacity to do. She decided that instead of focusing on writing a cookbook, she would hire a team to help her develop recipes for her blog, which was her main source of income. Having a team has freed up her time for other priorities, such as volunteering in her children's classrooms and taking the kids for bike rides on the weekend. Her trade-off was postponing her cookbook to a few years in the future. She had no regrets about the decision once she became clear about what she truly wanted. It's time to become clear on what *you* really want by asking:

- WHAT SEASON OF LIFE AM I IN? What are your constraints when it comes to time, energy, and commitments?

- WHAT INTENTIONAL TRADE-OFFS AM I WILLING TO MAKE? What do you want to pursue now? What can you pause for now and revisit in the future?

No one has the ability to do everything at once. You'll be much happier when you don't try to wear all the hats and give your full focus to what matters most. That's why it's important to figure out what you really need to do to thrive.

Determine Your Enough Number

At the start of this chapter, we discussed how my yoga teacher friend Michelle calculated her enough number, the yearly income that she needed to earn to thrive. In this section, we'll discuss how to calculate *your* enough number, which will be key to simplifying your business and living an integrated life. Your enough number is the amount your business needs to earn each year to support the life you want to be living. To determine what that number is, consider these questions:

- How much do you *want* to make?
- What do you truly *need* to thrive?

A business that compromises your health & relationships is not sustainable.

In our society, there's a constant pursuit of more—more money, more square footage, more awards, more stuff. And what's it all for? When does our happiness quotient get filled? We can become addicted to achievement. And as women with ambition, we can still feel as though we're not doing enough, being enough, earning enough.

But remember: the number in your bank account does not determine your self-worth. You need to earn an income to afford the necessities of life, but constantly chasing more money can lead to an empty feeling alongside the accomplishment. Why chase more when your loved ones never get to see you? Why chase more when it's destroying your health? A business that compromises your health and relationships is not sustainable.

Instead, you can simultaneously meet your needs and be rich in abundant time and energy. And with the right optimization strategies, which we'll discuss in chapter 5, you can leverage your resources to make more money without stripping away your other newfound wealth.

So let's calculate your enough number. Look at all of your living expenses per year. Look at your fixed and variable expenses, including your mortgage or rent payment, utilities, transportation, insurance, food, subscriptions, travel, and entertainment. Don't forget to include expenses such as contributing to savings and retirement accounts, making stock and real estate investments, and paying your personal taxes. Write all these expenses down and total them. This number is the minimum yearly income you need to make to sustain your life while supporting your ideal lifestyle.

ENOUGH NUMBER =

Fixed personal expenses + Variable personal expenses +
Investments + Taxes

Keep in mind that as you navigate the different seasons of life, your enough number may change. You will want to revisit and calculate your enough number at least once a year. Now think about how much you need to earn in your business each month and over the course of a year to be able to thrive. We'll use what I call a Revenue Map to discover this amount.

Create a Revenue Map

Once you define your enough number, you can calculate how much money your business needs to make each year to support your desired lifestyle. Just as you calculated your personal expenses for your happiness and life, you will do the same for your business. Your business expenses will include cost of goods, payroll, contractors' fees, office rent, marketing, software, education, travel, and meals, as well as building up your business savings. Then add your enough number to your business expenses, and you have a total of how much you'd like your business to bring in. That's your base business revenue goal. Once you have your business revenue goal, you can create a visual story of how much revenue you'd like your business to generate in a year to grow and thrive, and to support your enough number. This visual story is what I call a Revenue Map.

BUSINESS REVENUE GOAL =

Business expenses + Enough number

Let's use Michelle as our example of how to create a Revenue Map. Michelle and I determined that her enough number for her personal life was $150,000 and her business expenses were $100,000 per year, making her base business revenue goal $250,000. She knew that to achieve her desired lifestyle and professional goals, she wanted to lead two yoga retreats and four ten-week immersion classes per year. To get to her business revenue goal, she could have twenty-five people at each retreat for $3,200 per person and fifteen people in each of her immersion classes for $1,500 per person. She could adjust the pricing or the number of people she wants to have attend her programs, but this would be a starting point to help her reach her enough number. If she wanted to increase her revenue, she could raise her prices, increase class sizes, or increase the frequency of her programs.

It's helpful to see all the numbers on one page in the form of a Revenue Map, because when you see your financial goals laid out, you won't feel as though you're throwing out an arbitrary number as your target. When you write the numbers down and do the calculations, your money goal also feels more attainable. I walked Michelle through this exercise, and we noted the following.

MICHELLE'S ENOUGH NUMBER: $150,000 +

MICHELLE'S BUSINESS EXPENSES: $100,000

= Michelle's business revenue goal: $250,000 in the next 12 months

To meet this business revenue goal, she would need to sell:

15 students × 4 immersion classes per year

= 60 immersion students per year @ $1,500 each

= $90,000 (total)

AND

25 students × 2 yoga retreats per year

= 50 retreat students per year @ $3,200 each

= $160,000 (total)

Taking the time to figure out your enough number before you work on your Revenue Map will give you a sense of peace and clarity. I often see new business owners create a revenue goal that feels impossible because they haven't thought through what's enough to survive and be personally happy. Or someone who has a fast-growing business keeps chasing a bigger revenue number for the business but is exhausting herself trying to reach that goal. If she knew her enough number, she would see that she doesn't have to push so hard.

REVENUE MAP

$250,000

THIS YEAR'S REVENUE GOAL

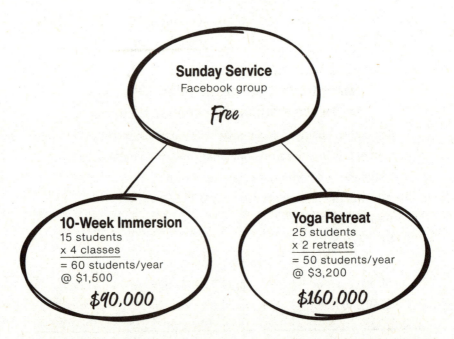

Sunday Service
Facebook group

Free

10-Week Immersion
15 students
x 4 classes
= 60 students/year
@ $1,500

$90,000

Yoga Retreat
25 students
x 2 retreats
= 50 students/year
@ $3,200

$160,000

YOUR REVENUE MAP

Now it's time to create your own Revenue Map. Start by writing down how much you want to earn (your enough number, plus your business expenses), followed by the services or products you'll provide to your customers to reach that revenue goal:

I want to earn $_____ in the next 12 months. To do this I will need to sell:

_____ (insert number of units or customers)

of _____ (insert good or service)

at $_____ (insert dollar amount)

= $_____ (total)

In the appendix, you'll find a blank Revenue Map you can personalize according to your goals. You can also download a worksheet to print out at shebuilds.com/resources.

When Your Enough Number Isn't Enough

As you will recall, when I started Little Sprouts, we were in survival mode and my goal was to make enough money to feed my family, pay our essential bills, and keep the lights on. When we made the difficult decision to close the business and move in with my in-laws, I felt like a failure. But deep down, I'd also known that the business model wasn't quite right. I loved serving people, coming up with marketing ideas, and having something I could call mine. Yet watching other people's kids was not my dream.

I knew I had to build a new kind of business, one that would inspire me without exhausting and depleting me. I also had to get to my enough number. After I closed Little Sprouts, Jen Hansard and I cocreated a parenting blog, Family Sponge, in the hope of building a profitable business where we could work from home with our kids close by. I set a goal of making a yearly income of $180,000, my enough number, through the blog. That broke down to $15,000 a month to cover my family's expenses while also allowing my husband to leave his job to start his own business, which would give him more flexibility with his schedule. I also took into account that I would need to put aside 30 percent of my income for taxes, 10 percent for giving to charities I believed in, and a certain amount to cover the costs of medical insurance (since we would no longer have medical benefits through George's full-time job).

As it would turn out, my second business attempt with Family Sponge did not create the income and the lifestyle I desired. Jen and I tried to make money through sponsored blog posts and affiliate links, where we got a commission for recommending products, but even with all the hard work and long hours, the blog was not able to make a profit. Still, I was not ready to throw in the towel of getting to my enough number. I remember telling my husband one day, "I got this. I don't know how we're going to make money or when it's going to happen, I just need a little more time." I kept going, and my third business, Simple Green Smoothies, which I cocreated with Jen, would finally get me there. By 2014, I was making more than $200,000 in income from that business.

In my previous companies, I had been all over the place trying to offer too many products and services to too many people. What was different about my approach to my third business was that I focused on building a community around one person with one problem and delivering one promise and one solution. The person we helped: a busy mom with kids. The problem: making healthy eating quick, simple, and delicious. The promise: more energy and confidence in the kitchen. The solution: sharing beginner-friendly, plant-based recipes without complicated ingredients.

We became the go-to resource for tasty smoothies because we built a brand, not just a business. We appealed to people who valued beautiful photos and design. We shared tips on how to make a healthy eating lifestyle easier for people who had limited time. Our company was fun and playful. We used expressions such as "rawkstar," "kale yeah," and "peace, love and leafy greens." We responded to every comment and question that we received through social media, our website, and emails.

I was passionate about helping people fall in love with kale and spinach. And by helping others achieve their goals, I achieved my personal income goals, too. I thought of it this way: if you want to make more money, find a way to help more people. And we did it. We grew an online community of over a million followers. I loved changing people's lives through the business, but I was burning myself out because I was disconnected from my personal vision.

What Is Your Next-Level Vision?

After five long years of trial and error, I had surpassed my enough number of $180,000 in income per year. Now what? While running Simple Green Smoothies, I spent hours sitting at our dining room table (aka office headquarters), focused intently on my laptop. My daughter would say, "Mama, you're making that face again." "What face?" I'd ask her. Zoe would squint her eyes and hunch her body over as if typing. I'd say, "Oh, that's my moneymaking face."

Adding more guilt to the equation was the way that work stress was affecting my connection with George. Since I worked from home, there wasn't a lot of physical separation between my work and home life. One day, I was sitting at our dining room table, typing frantically on my laptop. I was in the zone.

"How's your day going?" my husband asked.

Without turning away from my screen, I snapped, "Baby, I'm launching right now! I need to focus." Couldn't he see I was busy? I continued tapping on my computer keys.

"You're always launching," he said, raising his voice in desperation. Those words gutted me. I was ashamed that I had built a "healthy lifestyle" business for my family, yet they were getting the shortest stick in the equation.

I had thought that getting to my enough number would solve all our problems. But I realized that achieving my income goal wasn't all that I wanted. I was yearning for more space and ease, and I would not be truly happy until I set things up that way.

Now when I'm coaching clients who want to feel more aligned with their businesses, I ask them this important question: What is your next level? "Next level" doesn't have to mean more money. It can also mean more meaning, more experiences, more personal growth, more contribution. Reaching a new level is not just about what you have and do; it's about how you spend your time and who you become. Our money goals have an end goal. Connect with what you want your money to do separate from the expectations of others. To help my clients connect with their Next-Level Vision, I ask them to consider the following four questions, thinking about their emotional, physical, intellectual, and spiritual goals.

- EMOTIONAL. How do you want to feel?
- PHYSICAL. What experiences would you enjoy?
- INTELLECTUAL. What do you want to learn?
- SPIRITUAL. How do you want to serve?

IMAGINE YOUR NEXT-LEVEL VISION

As you move through the following questions, jot down your responses while considering the examples I share. You can use the Next-Level Vision template in the appendix or download at shebuilds.com/resources. Spend no more than three minutes on each of these questions, and don't overthink your answers!

Emotional: How Do You Want to Feel?

We are emotional beings, so let's start with your desired emotional state. Think of all the ways you want to feel throughout the day in your business and your life. If you do this on a regular basis, you'll start to notice patterns. I always want to feel inspired, confident, and energized. I pay attention to the situations that make me feel that way, such as taking my women-only Hipline dance class, where we shake our booties to Beyoncé under disco lights.

Here are a few examples from my clients of desired emotional states:

- Martha, who owns a PR firm, responded that she wants to feel connected and present with her two school-aged children.
- Meggan, who runs an online food blog, said that she wants to feel engaged with her audience and subscribers.
- Meri, who runs a process art studio, shared that she wants to feel as playful as she feels on the tennis court.

Physical: What Experiences Would You Enjoy?

We are also physical bodies living in a physical world. Imagine the things you may want to own, fun activities you'd like to try, or places you'd like to visit throughout your life. What would spark the most joy for you? Your experiences can even include an identity you'd like to try on, as in "I'd like to experience being a *New York Times* bestselling author or a founder of a million-dollar business." Here's what comes up for me when I do this exercise: I want to own a home with tree views, a hot tub, a fireplace, and a creation studio; I want to lead writing retreats in inspiring locations; I want to live in Paris for six months; I want to host board game nights.

Here are a few more examples:

- Enrika, who runs a video marketing agency, responded that she wants to live in a place with warm water and travel with her family.
- Brandilyn, who is a personal brand photographer, said she wants to build her dream house and invite everybody over.
- Lisane, who creates journals, shared that she wants to experience no more working on the weekends.

Intellectual: What Do You Want to Learn?

As entrepreneurs, we have a strong desire to solve problems and to learn. How can we fulfill the part of ourselves that constantly yearns to grow intellectually and creatively? First, think of areas in your life in which you'd like to deepen your knowledge and experience of something you're already good at. For example, I open my public speaking keynotes with spoken-word poetry, so one summer, I signed up for a few poetry workshops to help improve my craft.

You can also brainstorm some things you'd like to learn for the first time. How do you want to grow in your personal and professional relationships? How do you want to evolve as a business leader? As a parent? As a creative person? In my own case, this is where I'll usually include healthy habits I'd like to try, such as meditating daily or learning how to cook vegetarian recipes that my daughter would enjoy. Once you finish this list, head to the library or bookstore and pick up some books on your area of interest or sign up for a workshop or course to learn more. Things I've added to my personal "learn" list: deepen my connection to my emotional self; study podcast storytelling; establish a consistent morning routine.

Spiritual: How Do You Want to Serve?

Think of your spiritual self. You want to be a part of something bigger. How do you want to shake up the world and make a difference? What's your deeper purpose?

This doesn't have to be some huge contribution. Oprah shared in an interview that Maya Angelou told her, "You have no idea what your legacy will be. Your legacy is what you do every day. Your legacy is every life you've touched . . ."[2]

Think of how you want to contribute with the resources you have: time, energy, money, and relationships. This can be as simple as volunteering in your local community for two hours with your family. When I do this exercise, these are my answers: mentor young entrepreneurs in underserved communities; fund schools in Ghana and Mozambique to honor my Sub-Saharan African heritage; host a volunteer day with my team.

Here are a few additional examples.

- Jen, who runs multiple companies including a family-owned vine-yard, wants to become an Angel investor in women-led companies.
- Nicole, who leads self-care retreats, shared that she wants to spend time volunteering at the animal shelter and tip 100% with ease.
- La'Kita, who is a company culture strategist, wants to coach 10 people for free each year.

NEXT-LEVEL VISION

FEEL	ENJOY
Connected	Travel with family
Engaged	Build dream house
Playful	No working on the weekends
LEARN	**SERVE**
Take a poetry class	Become an Angel Investor
Cook vegetarian recipes	Volunteer at an animal shelter
Study podcast storytelling	Coach 10 people for free

The answers you wrote down in response to each of these four questions will help you build the foundation of writing your Future Vision, which I'll guide you through in the next chapter. Your answers will serve to unlock the meaning behind the metrics of your business.

Life is not a dress rehearsal. It moves fast. And if you continue to move at an unsustainable pace, you could miss the most precious parts of your life. Slow down, simplify, and remember what matters. Your ambition to do big things in the world may be at odds with your desire to live a simple life, one that allows you to be present for the day-to-day moments.

I like to think of my approach to business and life as more like floating down a lazy river than riding the rapids. I'd rather not exert so much effort to get everything done. I have ambition, but I don't let it override my peace. I accomplish big projects that take a lot of effort, but I don't allow them to take over my whole life, to the point where I don't have time for my family, for sleeping, or for eating well. I want my life to be a journey that follows a natural flow between my ambition and my life. And I want the same for you.

It's time to create a compelling vision for the way you are going to work that will prevent burnout while pulling you forward. In the next chapter, I'll walk you through how to develop a Future Vision that will create space for your ambition, your dreams, and your life.

3

This life is mine alone. So I have stopped asking people for directions to places they've never been.

—*Glennon Doyle,* Untamed

On January 1, 2012, George and I sat on the floor of our living room as I begged him to make a vision board with me.

"Baby, pleeeeease," I implored. George half nodded, strumming the strings of the guitar in his lap.

"You have to focus," I insisted.

George finally put down the guitar as I grabbed a large hair tie and whirled my waist-length dreads into a pineapple bun. I turned my laptop volume up, tapping the plus sign five times more than necessary, so that we both could hear the audiobook *Awaken the Giant Within*, with its promise to "take immediate control of your mental, emotional, physical, and financial destiny!" Here was another attempt to feel inspired after closing Little Sprouts; I wanted a personal shift in my finances, but I was running out of ideas for how to make that a reality. Tony Robbins's voice boomed from the speakers: "If you could have anything in the world, what would it be?"

We were surrounded by glossy magazine cutouts of inspiring

words, beautiful homes, fancy cars, and dream vacations in Tahiti. As I flipped through the pages, my inner mean girl voice got loud. Infinity swimming pool overlooking the Pacific Ocean. *I'm a total failure.* Remodeled kitchen with a white porcelain farmhouse sink. *I can't even support my family.* First-class airline seats that recline into a bed. *How will this ever be possible?* The headlines taunted me with their bright colors and fancy fonts: *Choose happy! Imagine your next adventure! Change the world!* My husband and I looked at our vision board materials, then looked at each other, and we started *craughing.* You know, laughing and crying at the same time because it was so sad that it was funny.

We were living in a cramped apartment in a quiet suburb twenty-five miles east of San Francisco. Beyond the walls of our modest apartment complex, our neighborhood was filled with lawyers and engineers making six-figure salaries, living in big houses, and driving around in luxurious SUVs. George popped me out of my Tony Robbins trance and said, "We have $42,000 in credit card debt. Neither of us has a college degree. We're living paycheck to paycheck. When will we get a break?"

Three months earlier, we had managed to move with our four-year-old daughter out of my in-laws' house, where we'd been staying for half a year. We'd had to borrow money from a friend for the rental deposit on our new place, and my mom had agreed to cosign our apartment lease due to our low credit score. This was a privilege and a blessing even though at the time it didn't feel like one. In addition to the mountain of credit card debt, we had no medical insurance. All of the odds were stacked against us. I was twenty-eight years old, and my confidence in the future was already shaken.

George and I were both willing to do whatever it took to turn things around, including creating a vision board. We were skeptical that a craft project to "manifest our dreams" would really do any good, but we knew we needed to try something new. We would not abandon hope and the possibility of creating a brighter future for ourselves and our daughter. It seemed as though every other door had closed for us and the economy had fallen apart; the only thing we *could* do was dream.

I licked my thumb to turn to the next magazine page. I saw a slick midnight-black Range Rover. As I dreamed of heated leather seats, I thought about the car we had driven in Kaua'i, a sand-colored Toyota Corolla we'd named Joe Boo, barely functional with dingy hubcaps trimmed in rust. If we'd had to repair it, it would have cost more than it was worth. With my back leaning against our squishy $200 Craigslist couch, I said, "All I want is a car that isn't a hooptie* and won't break down on us." But Tony had told us to dream big, so I cut the Range Rover out for my vision board. I also added a Tiffany Legacy diamond ring to celebrate our marriage, a deep soaking tub with expansive city views, and the phrase "Prepare to be amazed" as a promise to myself for a better future.

My husband cut out images of a music studio and of Bob Marley, which expressed his love for making meaningful music; pictures of beaches and the Taj Mahal to represent his desire for world travel; a truck and a motorcycle as symbols of more reliable transportation for our family (well, at least the truck was); Mother Teresa and Mister Rogers to remind him to be of service, be kind, and see children as they are.

I wrote on a card with a bold black Sharpie pen with the hope that I would make $15,000/month. I had done the math and knew that that amount would give us enough to pay our bills; travel; order a bottle of wine, appetizers, *and* dessert in a restaurant at least once a week; and give 10 percent to causes we believed in.

Although I posted that amount on my board, my doubt and skepticism lingered. I stood up, pressed the vision board against my chest,

---

*   A worn-out car, especially an old or dilapidated one.

closed my eyes, and took a deep breath, secretly hoping that every wish would come true. I opened my eyes and hung the collage of our magazine dreams above my tiny desk.

The Power of Envisioning

When I decided to embark on that first vision board exercise, I didn't really believe it would help me build a successful business and make more money. Yet, given all I had been through in the past few years, I was willing to give it a try. Once I finished my vision board, however, I began to see the power of creating a visual representation of my ideal future.

According to neuroscience research, mental imagery impacts your brain's cognitive process so extensively that when you visualize something, you're training your brain for actual performance.[1] Visualizing sets your brain up for success. When you visualize what you want to achieve, you engage all of your senses, imagining what you want to accomplish before it happens.[2]

Successful athletes, entertainers, and celebrities use visualizations to build confidence, motivation, and momentum toward achieving their goals. In the 2015 Women's World Cup, US soccer player Carli Lloyd credited visualizations as the reason she had played so well, leading her team's win over Japan. She had envisioned herself scoring four goals and had actually scored three in the final game, the most in Women's World Cup history.[3]

In a biological process that neuropsychologists call *encoding*, we mentally store our goals and dreams, which facilitates decision making that will lead us toward them. Simply put, vision boarding provides us with visual cues that will increase our likelihood of accomplishing our goals.

As I stared at the images on that board—vacation destinations on beaches, a smiling couple sitting on a couch with guitars on the walls, a greeting card that read "Be bold in the dreams you dream for your life"—I immediately became clear about what I wanted and why: I wanted to explore the world with my family, I wanted a happy marriage with a home full of music and creativity, and I wanted to be confident enough to dream big and take action. I didn't know how or when those things would happen, but that was okay.

Maybe you're where I was when I started working on my first vision board, facing financial hardship. Maybe you have done envisioning exercises before, but you feel a desire for reinvention. Either way, if you're wondering what your next move should be or feel conflicted about the direction you need to take, make time to reimagine your future. You have changed, so your vision will change, too. Start the next chapter of your life with an anti-hustle mindset. Spend sixty minutes redefining your goals and dreams in a more intentional and creative way. When you take the time to connect to your vision, whether at work or in your personal life, you can approach your opportunities with an immediate "Yes," because you are in touch with what you really want.

A vision board helps you zoom out and see the bigger picture. You get clear about what you want and why you want it. For now, release yourself from worrying about how you're going to get it and when it's going to happen (you'll learn strategies for how to do this in chapters 8 and 9). As I often say to my clients, "Don't put a timeline on your dreams; put a timeline on your actions." Visualizing your future will only bear fruit if you show up and do the work. It starts with trusting the process, trusting the timing, and trusting yourself as to how your future will unfold.

Vision boarding is like setting up a slingshot: you hold the slingshot handle in one hand and pull the rubber band holding the shot back with your other hand, then scan the horizon to point it in the right direction. Once you focus on where you want to go, all you have to do is release the band. Just as with a slingshot, the momentum of the release will propel you forward in the direction of your dreams. Ask yourself: Does this bring me closer or farther away from my dreams? (If you aren't any closer to where you want to be in a year, it's possible that you need to do more work to get clear about your ideal direction or honor your capacity for this season of your life. But at least you'll have gotten started.)

Keep in mind that a vision is a compass, not a step-by-step road map. It also doesn't include specific dates, so it will not have any S.M.A.R.T. (specific, measurable, attainable, relevant, time-bound) goals with deadlines, either. It's *not* about execution, it's all about opening your mind to possibility, to create a mental story of what your future can look and feel like. That's something many of us don't give ourselves permission to do.

If this seems like a big undertaking, consider that you've most likely already created some type of vision to get to where you are right now. It may have been in the form of writing down your goals in a journal, typing notes on your phone, creating an actual vision board collage, or even writing a letter to yourself/the universe/a higher power about where you want to go in life. But as the saying goes, what got you here won't get you there. So you have to dream again to move to the next level in your personal and professional lives. For example, after I left my company Simple Green Smoothies, I created a new vision board to help me step into a new vision for my life.

Create Your Vision Board

It's time to put your vision board together. Gather materials such as magazines, poster paper, scissors, and glue sticks, and use them to create a collage of the things you want to have in your life. Hang your vision board someplace where you will see it regularly for inspiration. It also helps to have a "TPP" for your vision board: a designated *time* when you will work on your board, a *place* to work on your vision, and a *person* who will hold you accountable for taking the steps to make your vision a reality.

Time: Make a Date with Your Future Self

To begin, I want you to carve out time in your schedule to make sure that your vision boarding really happens. Otherwise, your more urgent tasks and responsibilities will get in the way. Many of my clients say they want to think about the big picture, but they never get around to doing it because they're bogged down in the day-to-day tasks of their businesses. So while I'm on the phone coaching my clients, I have them look at their calendar, pick a day when they have at least one uninterrupted hour to work on their vision board, and then schedule a "date" with their future self. You can do the same thing for yourself now. Treat it like a doctor's appointment.

Place: Choose a Vision Retreat Location

Did you know that Lin-Manuel Miranda came up with the idea for the Broadway musical *Hamilton* while on vacation with his family? It was the first vacation he'd taken in years. He had been working nonstop and wasn't able to envision his masterpiece until he allowed himself the time and space to think and dream.[4]

Most of us are pulled in many different directions on a daily basis, but in order to dream bigger, we need to slow down and give ourselves time and the optimal environment for letting ourselves imagine a new reality. I initially struggled to believe that I could make my vision board a reality because there was such a gap between our environment—with its borrowed and secondhand furniture—and my vision. It may also be difficult for a corporate employee to envision the start-up they want to launch because they are interrupted by constant emails. Or for a stay-at-home mom to envision the future business she wants to create because she is overwhelmed by the kids' schedules, laundry, and caretaking.

Create a separate setting for your vision boarding, one that will allow you to think more clearly and creatively, without the distractions of daily life. This will enable you to make better decisions about your future. You don't have to go on vacation or take a sabbatical to do this; you can simply sit on a bench at a local park or in the sun at an outdoor coffee shop. Research from the National Academy of Sciences shows that spending time in nature acts as a reset button for your brain.[5] After a few hours in nature, you'll feel more optimistic. You'll come up with out-of-the-box ideas. You'll see things you couldn't see before.

Now that I've grown my business far past the point where I have to worry about filling the gas tank of my car, I find it's best to create my Future Vision by mentally and physically stepping away from my day-to-day responsibilities. I schedule a "vision retreat" for myself whenever I need a reboot, in the form of a cabin getaway with my husband or a meetup with some friends in a beautiful location, where we set aside time to think, dream, and plan. I also host vision retreats for my clients, and it's my absolute favorite part of my business. There's something magical about being surrounded by inspiring women who are making time to stretch themselves and imagine their next level. I encourage you to schedule your own mini vision retreat. Book a hotel or vacation home for a night or two and split the costs with a friend, or invite your partner to join you in some dreaming. I find I get the best results doing this with other business-minded people.

Maybe you're thinking: What if everything falls apart while I'm gone? My business can't function without me. My kids need me. I have a lot of responsibilities, and it's hard to step away from them. You may feel uneasy about traveling away from home, but if you do step away, you're likely to get more high-level work done in a single weekend than you might in three weeks or even three months at home. It's hard to come up with million-dollar ideas in between loads of laundry.

Trying something new can be scary, and you may have to push yourself a little to overcome any reservations you're having. One spring, I hosted a vision retreat for women business owners. A few weeks before the retreat, Deanna Mason, a past client in my group coaching program who hosts the *Refreshed Moms* podcast and is a coach for busy moms, had paid to join the retreat, but she started to get cold feet. She worried about stepping away from her commitments at home. She sent the following email to my team.

Hi, Team,

I've spent the morning searching for flights into San Jose and San Francisco. The time of the flights (7 to 8 hours minimum) plus the cost of the flights, plus the cost of my transportation to and from the retreat, are pretty extensive for me. It's gonna cost me nearly $1,000 to travel there and get back home.

Plus, the time of the month for me to be away from home is not good. It's both of my children's last week of school (My daughter needs me home that week to wrap up the school year), and I'm traveling at the end of the week to Chicago for my nephew's high school graduation.

This just doesn't feel aligned for me—and I feel like I'm forcing it because I really want to be there. I'm going to have to cancel my reservation for the retreat. I'm completely and totally disappointed that I will not be attending. I've gotta go with my gut and SURRENDER my plans to what is the most needful thing.

Deanna

Here's how my team responded: "We honor you for surrendering and going with your gut." We did not push Deanna. We encouraged her to trust her inner knowing to prioritize what mattered most. I was drawn to a line near the end of her email: "I really want to be there." She felt that way, but she was listing every reason she could think of for why she shouldn't: time, money, family. She was facing her own resistance to leaving her kids behind and flying across the country. Within a few days, however, she continued to trust her gut and became resourceful. She researched more affordable flight possibilities, talked with the women in the group, and came up with a solution that worked for her and her family so she could get away.

Stepping away from your usual routine can feel challenging, but the rewards are huge. In giving yourself time to think about your future, you're not "stealing" time away from your business or your family; you're making a positive investment in yourself, one that will benefit everyone back home.

Person: Find Your Accountability Partner

Reach out to the person who will hold you accountable for sticking to your vision. The easiest way to do this is to invite someone else to work on their vision board, too. This could be a close friend or a business or life coach. I usually convince my husband to do it with me, which makes it easier for us to cocreate a beautiful life together and support each other's dreams. You can even invite a small group and make it a vision board party where everyone brings three to five magazines and some wine (or kombucha!). Schedule a time to meet with your partner(s) when you can share and explain your collage.

You can lean on this accountability partner even beyond creating your vision board. Imagine having a person who knows your biggest dreams and motivates you to keep going, someone who keeps track of your most important projects and reminds you of the next steps you need to take to move your ideas forward. Find someone you feel safe brainstorming with, and address your most pressing roadblocks. Creating in community makes growing a business fun and less lonely. I'll share more strategies on how to do this in the next chapter.

Once you have your TPP—time, place, and person—it will be easier to overcome resistance and guilt about taking time for yourself. I also find it helps to publicly share your "away" dates via email and put them on your calendar so that your team, clients, and others will know that you're unavailable to respond to nonurgent matters and can plan accordingly. You can share why you're going with those closest to you (friends and family), so that they understand your needs and boundaries. There are sample emails on how to do this on pages 115 and 116.

Write Your Future Vision

After you have created your vision board, it's time to write out your Future Vision. Through this writing exercise, you will describe what your life and business will look and feel like three years in the future. I recommend three years because this amount of time will give you room to include goals that require longer-term planning. It's been said by many business leaders that people overestimate what they can do in one year and underestimate what they can do in three, five, or even ten years.

Picture yourself exactly three years into the future, on today's date. Everything you've dreamed of creating is a reality. Your environment, relationships, brand visibility, impact, products, and services have hit or exceeded your wildest hopes and dreams. As you move through the prompts on the following pages, return to your responses from the "Imagine Your Next-Level Vision" exercise in chapter 2. Reflect on those responses as you write out your Future Vision, thinking about how you want your life to fulfill you in each of the four categories: emotionally, physically, intellectually, and spiritually.

Don't worry about turning any of your dreams into actions just yet. It's essential to spend more time on thinking about what you really want before you create a strategic business plan. This is a mistake that many entrepreneurs make—me included. We get on the hamster wheel of hustle but can't get off because we haven't clearly defined what our vision is. So please don't skip this step. I'll guide you through a process to build your Quarterly Plan in chapter 8, but for now, it's time to simply figure out what you want to create first.

YOUR FUTURE VISION

Grab your journal, and write out your Future Vision by answering the prompts below. Record your responses in the present tense, as if these things have already happened. Schedule at least an hour for the exercise, but if you have time, leave your home and your office and give yourself a few hours or even a few days to do it. Once you've written down your vision, share it with someone you trust, such as your accountability partner. **SAY YOUR DREAMS OUT LOUD.**

Your Home Life
- Describe your home. What do you see, hear, smell? Where in the world are you living?
- What are your thoughts when you first wake up? What do you look forward to the most in the morning?
- How do you move through your day? How are you spending your time?
- What do you look forward to every night? How do you wind down for the evening?
- What are your thoughts before bed?

Your Wellness
- How is your health? How are you moving and fueling your body?
- How are you growing intellectually? What are you learning?
- What are some ways you reconnect and take care of yourself? What

habits and rituals are you practicing? How is your spiritual practice?

- How is your heart? What do you feel throughout your day?
- How do you express yourself fully? Describe your creative outlets, interests, activities that nurture and inspire your soul.

Your Relationships

- Who are the people you are most grateful for?
- How do you nurture and spend time with the most important people in your life?
- What does your relationship with your partner or spouse (if applicable) look like?
- What does your relationship with your child or children (if applicable) look like?
- What does your relationship with your family members and friends look like?

Your Company

- What do you see and hear when you walk into your place of work? Where is your office located?
- What inspires you to get out of bed and show up fully for work? Why do you do what you do?
- What do you do every day in the company? What are the tasks, strategies, meetings, and activities you spend your time on? How many hours do you work each week?
- Describe your business and its mission. What do you want to create in the world as a result of the work that you do at your company?
- What are your company's values? How do you show up as a leader? How do you take care of your team?
- Describe your Dream Team and how its members support the company vision. How many team members do you have? How is the company running day to day?

- Who are your dream customers? How many customers' lives do you want to impact? How do you communicate and connect with them? What are they saying about your company?
- Based on what you see that may be missing in your industry, what's the gap that you want to fill? What makes your business unique and stand out in the marketplace?
- What programs, products, services, events, and books do you offer? What does your company's financial picture look like? What's your annual revenue and profit? What's your personal take-home income?
- What does your visual brand look and feel like? What's your reputation in your industry? What does the public think about you, as shown in the media and online?

Your Contribution

- What are you celebrating personally? What are you most proud of in your life?
- What is your company celebrating? What are you and your team most proud of?
- How do you celebrate, unplug, think, dream, rest, reset, and realign throughout the year?
- Your cup is full, and you serve from the overflow. How are you giving back with time, money, and resources?
- Finally, describe the person you are who lives a life and leads a business like this. Complete this sentence: "I am . . ."

Don't worry if your first draft feels messy. It's important to allow the various elements of your vision time to gradually integrate before it all clicks into place. You can see a copy of my Future Vision and have a digital copy of prompts to complete yours at shebuilds.com/resources.

Ximena Silva,* an executive coach and consultant for women leaders, was surprised by the power of committing her vision to paper. She attended one of my retreats in Sausalito, California, where I led all the attendees through the Future Vision exercise. Everyone in the workshop created a detailed handwritten vision for her life three years into the future.

Following our hour of silent writing time, Ximena read her vision aloud to the group, which included "I own a house in Ojai where I raise my family. We hike, walk to the farmers' market, and spend lots of time in nature." After she expressed that to the group, she told us that she felt the dream was too far away, as her partner had a full-time job in Los Angeles, California, where they lived. To make that dream house a reality, she realized, she would have to reach a certain level of revenue in her business.

A visioning exercise is the perfect opportunity to challenge assumptions like this one, so I asked her, "How much would it cost to buy a home in Ojai? What would your monthly expenses be?" When Ximena did the math, she realized that her cost of living in Ojai would be a lot less than it was in Los Angeles. Soon she and her partner came up with a creative solution where he could telecommute some days. Within three months of writing down her vision, they bought a house in Ojai. And within three years of writing about her vision of a family, she had her first child. With a clear picture of what she wanted from her life in her mind, she made the decisions that would support it.

---

* This name and identifying details have been changed to protect the privacy of this past client. She is fully embracing the anti-hustle mindset and unplugged from social media.

Say your dreams out loud.

Invisible Roadblocks

Like Ximena, many women stop themselves from pursuing what they want because they believe there's a certain order in which things have to happen: "If X happens, then I can do/have/be Y." "If I make $120,000, then I can buy my dream house." "If I grow my email list to one million subscribers, then I can write a book." "If I get a coaching certification, then I can host a retreat." These are invisible and unnecessary roadblocks we place in front of ourselves. Becoming clear about what you want for your life and business can help you challenge the idea that things have to happen in a specific order. Make sure that your business supports your life, rather than becoming a roadblock to the life you want to live and are free to live right now.

The flip side of this is that many people skip the visualizing phase of a project and dive right in, only to realize that they didn't think it through. They push a project forward without having a clear vision and are later derailed by self-doubt. Your three-year vision will help prevent that. Once you've completed the Future Vision exercise and know what you want to feel, enjoy, and learn and how you want to serve, it'll be easier for you to create an inspiring blueprint for your life and business the same way an architect creates a blueprint for building a house.

Maybe you're thinking that this is a waste of time. Or that allowing yourself to dream in this way, given the day-to-day reality of your life, just isn't you or isn't realistic. It may be challenging for you to acknowledge what you *do* want. This could be due to the way you were raised, a lack of support at home, trade-offs you are making for your kids, or the result of a personal or family illness. Don't beat yourself up if any of these is the case. You are not alone. Struggling to balance other people's needs with your own is much more common than people realize. You can expand your vision over time as you build your confidence in what's possible for you to do. Give yourself the grace and space for whatever season you're in.

o o o

Eighteen months after creating my vision board with George, I had started Simple Green Smoothies and was achieving my $15,000/month salary goal. I had also paid for a black SUV in full, and years later George had surprised me with a trip to Maui to renew our wedding vows in front of our close friends and family. We were living proof of the images on the vision board I had created. That's how powerful this exercise can be.

The actions inspired by this vision board exercise led me to co-create Simple Green Smoothies, the business that enabled me to work from home in my pajamas, take time off when I wanted to, and travel around the world.

I remember our first big launch vividly because it happened while my family and I were on our first real vacation in Cabo San Lucas, Mexico—similar to the magazine image of the dream vacation on the beach I had pinned on my vision board a year earlier. It was our first time selling our *Fresh Start 21* meal plan to our community, and we made $86,000 in ten days. (I'll share more details on how we did that in chapter 7.) When I made my vision board, I couldn't have imagined that eighteen months later I'd be on the beach with a Dos Equis in one hand and a book in the other while money was being deposited into our PayPal account. It's worth noting that this didn't all happen just because I made a vision board, but allowing myself to visualize the future I wanted definitely set me on the path to making that dream a reality.

o o o

As you create your Future Vision and move toward your goals, resistance will undoubtedly pop up along the way. You'll feel like an imposter and question if you have enough qualifications and certifications. You'll question if you have enough time to make it all happen. You'll doubt that you're worthy of success. You'll fear failing in public. Even if you've achieved a certain level of success, these sneaky thoughts will creep in as you grow to the next level. That is why it's important to find a safe space in which to say your dreams out loud. Find an accountability partner, coach, mentor, and group of like-hearted people to keep you on track. Once you have a compelling vision to pull you forward, it's time to identify who's going to help you get there. In the next chapter, we'll explore the different ways you can gather support throughout your entrepreneurial journey so that you don't feel you have to do this alone.

4

Behind every great woman is another
great woman replying to her frantic
texts in the middle of the night.

—*Nora McInerny*

Being a leader is hard. It brings up a lot of emotions. Scrappiness, resilience, and self-reliance get us only so far. To build our businesses sustainably and live intentionally, we need a Support Squad. This is a group of people we can count on to keep us motivated, focused, and accountable, who will provide support on both an emotional level and a soul level as we build our businesses and our lives. We need a safe circle of people to lean on. The members of our Support Squad are there to cheer us on and celebrate our wins, but they also know us well enough to let us know when we are drifting off course. A Support Squad is not the same as the team of people that we hire to support us at work and at home. Those employees, freelancers, and specialists are our Dream Team, and I will address how to build this team in chapter 6.

The Support Squad can be divided into three general categories: (1) peers and colleagues, (2) mentors and advisors, and (3) coaches and therapists. My Support Squad has members from all three categories, and I rely on them in various ways to keep me calm and focused, especially when life throws me unexpected curveballs.

In this chapter, I'll talk about how to build your Support Squad by building relationships in each of three categories: with like-minded business owners (aka the mastermind alliance); with mentors and advisors to propel you to your next level of growth; and with a life coach or therapist who can help you work through emotional and psychological blocks that are preventing you from achieving your goals.

If you tend to be a lone wolf in your entrepreneurial pursuits, I hope this chapter will convince you to broaden your circle and try a different approach, keeping the following in mind.

ACHIEVING SUCCESS IS NOT A SOLO SPORT. I am borrowing here from Minda Harts, the author of *The Memo: What Women of Color Need to Know to Secure a Seat at the Table*.[1] Being a founder can feel lonely and isolating, and the idea that a business can be built by one person alone is a myth. Yet women tend to be unconscious martyrs, trying to do everything by themselves. The truth is, you need other people to help you achieve your goals in a sustainable way. You do not need to go it alone.

HAVING CONSISTENT SUPPORT RAISES YOUR GAME. Create an environment that nurtures your growth personally and professionally. When you have consistent support, it enhances your performance in all areas of your life. When you don't, it takes much more effort and energy to get other people up to speed. There is a special momentum that is created when someone tracks what you're doing and observes how you're progressing.

YOU CAN'T READ A LABEL FROM INSIDE THE JAR. It's important to have thought partners you can brainstorm with to develop big-picture strategy—people who can reflect your strengths, see your potential, and call you out when they see you self-sabotaging by playing it small. When you're moving at a fast pace, it can be easy to have tunnel vision and miss an opportunity for growth.

YOUR COMMUNITY IS YOUR SUPERGLUE. I believe our lives are shaped by the people we surround ourselves with, so it's important to be intentional and find those who support, encourage, and uplift us on this wild journey called life. It's essential to gather with other women who are building companies, raising families, and facing challenges that are similar to your own. Community puts us back together when we fall apart. Find a safe and structured group of people where everyone is rooting for everyone else to win.

Evaluating Your Current Support Squad

Let's begin by taking stock of your current Support Squad. Consider the people you spend the most time with, personally and profession-ally. Are they helping you to grow and to take your business and life to the next level? Or are there areas where you need more support and need to focus on forging new relationships? Ask yourself the following questions, and list the names that come to mind for each of these three categories.

- PEERS AND COLLEAGUES. Do I have peers in similar stages of business and life to lean on for support? Who are they?

- MENTORS AND ADVISORS. Do I have a mentor and coach to guide and advise me on business strategy? Who are they?

- LIFE COACHES AND THERAPISTS. Do I have a life coach and therapist who is supporting my emotional and mental well-being? Who are they?

If you answered no to any of these questions, think of how you can build relationships and cultivate more support as you read this chapter. If you currently have Support Squad members in all three categories, think about how to strengthen those relationships in ways that will benefit your life and business goals. At the end of the chapter, we will return to your list of answers to create an action plan. For now, let's dive deeper into the three core areas of support.

Peers and Colleagues:
Harnessing the Strength of a Mastermind Alliance

After I closed my first business in Kauaʻi, Hawaiʻi, I wanted to figure out how to make a living as an entrepreneur. One of the books I read during that period was *Think and Grow Rich* by Napoleon Hill, in which I discovered the term *mastermind alliance*. Hill studied the habits of successful businessmen in the nineteenth and twentieth centuries, and the common thread he saw was that they had all formed partnerships to solve problems, overcome obstacles, and identify opportunities for growth. He wrote, "No two minds ever come together without, thereby, creating a third, invisible, intangible force which may be likened to a third mind."[2]

The idea of an alliance resonated with me deeply. When I was living with my in-laws, trying to figure out my next career step, I reached out to a friend who would become my very first mastermind partner, Tamika Lewis. Tamika and I had once been roommates and had known each other for years. I was considering going back to college for my degree, and I wanted to talk to her about her career path as a counselor with a master's degree in social work.

On a catch-up call one evening, I told her that I had closed Little Sprouts Playhouse and was living with my in-laws. I also told her that running a preschool watching other people's children was not my dream and I was burned out. I still wanted to be an entrepreneur so I could have more control over how I spent my time. But while I figured out how to do that in a sustainable way, I was working part-time as a virtual assistant for a family member as well as a front-desk receptionist at a yoga studio. Both jobs paid me $15 per hour. Tamika confided that her husband had cheated on her and that she had recently been laid off from her job as a high school counselor. As ambitious women and busy moms, we both craved more freedom and flexibility in our careers, and we believed that building our own businesses was the best way to achieve that.

During our call, we discovered that we'd both read *Think and Grow Rich* and felt inspired by the idea of a mastermind. We decided that we would create our own alliance to keep each other accountable as we worked toward our goals. Tamika's goals included writing books and having a private counseling practice. My goals were to start a business I was passionate about that I could run from anywhere in the world, make enough money to travel, and spend quality time with my family. Neither of us had things figured out. We were exhausted moms trying to crack the entrepreneurial code. But we understood the need for an accountability partner to help us propel our visions forward.

We scheduled a phone meeting for an hour every Tuesday evening after our kids were asleep. We'd spend five minutes catching up, then each of us would share what we were working on, brainstorm ideas, and identify the next steps we'd take before our next call. During those calls, we'd share resources, such as books we were reading and time-saving tools, and we'd encourage each other to keep going. Those calls were instrumental in our lives.

During our years of supporting each other, Tamika wrote and self-published her first book, *Next Generation Graduate: College Readiness for Low-Income Students*, and I completed my first digital ebook for Simple Green Smoothies. We not only gave each other advice to overcome resistance, we also deepened our friendship and felt less alone. Today, Tamika is a licensed psychotherapist practicing in Los Angeles, California, and the founder of WOC Therapy Inc., a mental health and wellness community that helps women of color heal from personal and intergenerational trauma. She is running a million-dollar business, writing her second book, leading a team of five therapists, and collaborating with diversity, equity, and inclusion (DEI) and nonprofit organizations to support teen girls.

There is a rich history of creatives and entrepreneurs banding together, meeting regularly, and leaning on their communities to learn and grow. Virginia Woolf had the Bloomsbury group; C. S. Lewis and J. R. R. Tolkien were in a literary group called the Inklings; Benjamin Franklin created the Junto, a "club for mutual improvement," in Philadelphia.[3] The members of those groups would meet to exchange ideas, critique one another's work, and creatively problem solve together.

As business owners, we tend to think that the key to success is hiring the right people and building the right team. But I've learned that as an entrepreneur, having a great team alone is not enough. What keeps you in the game for the long haul is having a group of peers who are on the same journey and understand what you're going through. Mastermind groups can be small or large, paid or free. The aim is to help each other grow.

There are mastermind groups for established business owners ranging from $10,000 to $100,000 and up per year. This can be cost prohibitive for many in the early start-up years. If you can't find a peer group easily on your own, join your local SBA (Small Business Association) where they offer free business counseling.

To find your people, you can also join an entrepreneurial membership community, which typically starts at $50 per month. I have met most of my best friends through online training programs like this. I made financial risks by reinvesting business profits back into the business, which is not always possible if you have limited access to funds. Check out programs like Hello Alice, an organization that offers small business grants and funding opportunities, including a Black-Owned Business Resource Center.

A successful mastermind group provides space to share knowledge, brainstorm ideas, and strengthen your business and personal skills. The key is commitment to accountability—making sure that all members follow through on their plans and their purpose.

Something I initially noticed when I joined my first mastermind group was that I was getting something different out of the women-centered groups I was a part of as opposed to those that were made up of mostly men. In the male-dominated groups, I often received feedback that didn't fully align with my personal vision, goals, and dreams. At first, I couldn't quite put my finger on what the issue was. Eventually I came to recognize that in women-centered groups, we tended to place more emphasis on building emotional trust, safety, and mutual respect. We weren't just solving business problems. We were also talking about our relationships, our children, and our health—the stuff that affects how we show up (or don't show up) in our businesses. Beyond discussing how to develop a business strategy and how to make more money, we were navigating life's big transitions, such as miscarriage, divorce, illness, and grief.

Being part of mastermind groups became my gateway to developing deeper friendships. I learned how to let women into my inner world and became more vulnerable by sharing the more tender parts of my personal life. Building a support system is about so much more than having someone to help you complete your tasks; it's about having trusted friends who will listen and offer advice when things are hard and you're in the trenches. Over the years, through my mastermind groups, I've also gained access to invaluable resources, including referrals and recommendations that would lead me to hiring my director of happiness and communications, Michele Morales, who's been with me for more than seven years, as well as bookkeepers, personal chefs, babysitters, lawyers, payroll companies, therapists, and podcast editors.

Create Your Mastermind Group

There is really nothing more valuable than having a community of like-minded entrepreneurs to strategize with and share common experiences. Let's get into how you are going to build your mastermind group with some general strategies.

Step 1: Decide who will be in the group.

Brainstorm a list of people you'd like to be your accountability and thought partner(s). Find women who run their own businesses, are in a similar season of life as you, and are willing to bring their whole lives to the conversation. This community will act as your personal board of directors in business and life. How many people do you want in the group? Four to eight has been an ideal group size for me to be able to track and support everyone.

Step 2: Invite your people.

Next, send out personal invitations to the group via email or text. Share your intention for the mastermind, what you are looking to build, and why you think the person you are inviting would be an asset to the group. This is how I form my peer-led Support Squads— through informal conversations and an email invitation. One afternoon in Lafayette, California, I had lunch with my friend Amy Ahlers, who, as I previously mentioned, helps with your inner mean girl. We covered a range of topics such as business ideas and challenges, our kids and our marriages, and being published authors. We also shared how much we were craving to be in a community with women who were building businesses *and* raising families. After hours of talking, we both agreed that we'd want to meet up consistently with a small group to talk about not only business but our whole lives. Here's the email Amy sent a few weeks after our lunch.

Subject: Gathering as Visionaries for some Masterminding & Support?

Hello Beautiful Souls!

I had the joy of doing lunch with Jadah a couple weeks ago and we were talking about how important it is for us entrepreneurs to stay in community and support each other. I know each of us is balancing so very much, including babies, partners, huge visions and callings. Jadah and I were thinking that perhaps the four of us could gather in circle to support, mastermind, vision and more? Let's start by getting together for an initial meeting and seeing what we are all up for and if it feels right? Thoughts? Feelings? Ideas?

With love,
Amy

Everyone in the group replied "Yes," and we called our Support Squad "The Soulful Sistermind." We started with four women business owners who were all moms, and we met in person once a month. This group has been meeting for more than five years.

Step 3: Decide where you'll connect.

If your group members are all in the same city, I highly recommend gathering in person and making it a special day when you can combine business and life brainstorming with a shared meal. If the group members are in different cities or countries, you can connect via a video call or select a central travel destination. You can set up online meetings with a free software like Google Hangouts or use a paid Zoom account.

Step 4: Decide when you'll meet.

Think about the frequency of connection. This could be weekly, monthly, quarterly, or annually. Choose a day of the week and time that works for everyone in the group. You will also want to decide on a length for your meetings. I would recommend allowing at least twenty-five minutes for each person in the group to speak (we call this a "hot seat"), and if you're meeting in person and enjoying a meal together, add two hours. For example, if there are three people in your group and you're meeting on a video call, you could meet weekly on Tuesdays from 10:00 to 11:30 a.m. If there are four people in your local group and your meeting includes lunch, meet monthly on Fridays from 10:00 a.m. to 2:00 p.m. With this setup, each participant can occupy the hot seat for twenty-five minutes. Schedule the meetings in your calendar, and don't flake. Essential to making a mastermind group successful, you need commitment, consistency, and reciprocity of giving and receiving.

Step 5: Decide how you'll structure the meeting.

Whether you meet in person or over the phone, creating a structure for your mastermind meetings can help you stay focused and get the most out of your time together. Assign a timekeeper for each meeting (this role should rotate), and make sure everyone gets equal time in the hot seat. In my group, we also like to set a timer for when there are five minutes left for each person, as a signal to wrap it up. Here's a sample framework that you can use.

- The first ten minutes are for celebrating personal and professional wins of the group.
- There is a twenty-five-minute hot seat for each person (set a timer with a five-minute warning).
- The person in the hot seat will describe a business challenge or an opportunity or ask the group a question for discussion. The

group can then ask questions to clarify, and the person in the hot seat will receive feedback, ideas, and possible solutions.

- To end, the person in the hot seat will share her insights and what she's committed to doing by the next meeting.

Each time your group meets, reconnect on the intention of the mastermind and your expectations for it. On a personal level, make sure you feel both fed and supported by the conversations that are happening among group members. You do not want to feel as though your opinions are not being heard or that you are being treated like the expert in the room, with everyone else turning to you for answers.

At a certain point, you may accelerate in your business and find that you need a more seasoned group of peers and fellow entrepreneurs for support. Or there may be a natural completion to the group's discussions and then you part ways, which is okay. If the dynamics of a group feel draining, creating more effort than ease to maintain consistency and connection, it may be time to leave. There are also times when a community is simply not the right fit. It may take a few tries before you find a group that works for you.

Here are a few ways that I've integrated mastermind groups and accountability into my business and life.

- Once a week, I schedule a call to check in with my dedicated accountability partner (as I did with Tamika). We meet on the phone and give updates, share tools, and ask for help on a specific problem.
- Once a month, I meet with the Soulful Sistermind. We meet on Fridays from 10:00 a.m. to 3:00 p.m. in the San Francisco Bay Area. Everyone gets a thirty-minute hot seat, and halfway through we have lunch together.
- Once a quarter, I meet with a small group of female CEOs and we stay at a vacation home or hotel for three nights. Since there are four of us and we live in different states (California, Georgia,

Hawaiʻi, and Texas), we call ourselves the sQuad, and we choose a different location each time. We talk about our businesses, our marriages, and our children and always have a dedicated spa day to restore.

- Once a year, I hold a meeting with a group of eight women where we're less formal about the structure. We all have businesses, kids, and primary partners. We know we'll talk about it all. We make an annual trip to a luxury villa in Tulum, Mexico.

Mentors and Advisors:
Seeking Out Strategic Guidance and Support

As entrepreneurs, we often need to close the gap in our knowledge quickly. Our cash flow depends on it. A mentor is an experienced and trusted person who believes in you and your vision (especially when self-doubt creeps in). They can share valuable resources with you and make suggestions for strategies you might not come up with on your own. Having a mentor who is steps and years ahead of you speeds up the process and helps you avoid costly mistakes such as holding on to a team member too long or overlooking opportunities to grow.

Mentors are also proof of what's possible. That's why I have become an advisor as a professional business coach. Representation matters, and I know that my life circumstances, my experiences, and the setbacks I've faced will resonate with certain people who may not have previously seen themselves represented in the entrepreneurial space. There are no unique messages, only unique messengers. If you're not gaining traction in your business, it could mean you haven't yet found a teacher who resonates with you. You want to find a mentor whose body of work aligns with your personal and professional values.

Mentorship was the one essential piece of the entrepreneurial puzzle I was missing when I started Little Sprouts Playhouse. I threw spaghetti at the wall without any feedback or guidance and tried to figure out everything on my own. When I invested time, energy, and money in interning with mentors, signing up for their courses and events, and hiring them as coaches, that's when my subsequent businesses started to accelerate with less doubt and more focus.

You can look for mentors in a variety of places: while you're doing an internship or a paid job in the industry you want to be a part of or by hiring a business coach who's been down the path that you want to take (more on hiring a professional coach later in this chapter). There are also rare opportunities when you could ask someone to advise you for free. Some successful business leaders allot a certain amount of their time to pay it forward and help others who are earlier in their journey. Another option is cultivating a mentor from afar—someone you don't have a direct, personal relationship with but whose experience you're still able to learn from and apply to your own business and life through reading books, listening to podcasts, and watching videos. This is an affordable and accessible way to learn from people who may be hard to reach.

My first business mentor was my husband's aunt Maria Veloso. We call her "Auntie Tutti." The best way to describe Auntie Tutti is that she wants everyone in her family to win. On family vacations, she has been known to give entire presentations on how she built her multiple-seven-figure online health and wellness business, which includes educational newsletters, books, and e-commerce products. She initially started her business because she wanted to pay for repairs to her mother's roof in the Philippines. Auntie Tutti does work that she loves to support the people she loves.

When George and I had moved back to California and were living with my in-laws, I asked Auntie Tutti if I could intern with her to learn how she ran her business. I told her I'd do whatever she needed, including picking up coffee and her dry cleaning. She agreed.

I went to stay at Auntie Tutti's house in Beverly Hills for two weeks. She was generous about sharing her hard-earned wisdom with me, and she also taught me how to make my first green smoothie (at the time, I had no idea that I would turn a spinach shake into a business). I also learned how to pull content together to create digital products and write newsletters that provided added value to subscribers, which would turn out to be the foundation of Simple Green Smoothies.

Auntie Tutti eventually hired me as her virtual assistant for ten hours per week so that I could continue working with her and learning about the business once I went back home. The $600 a month she paid me meant a lot. I was excited that I could get paid to learn. I still had so much I wanted to understand about running a business, and I was willing to work for free to gain experience. I also want to acknowledge what a gift it is to have a family member who could share business knowledge with me so freely. This privilege served me well and has been a factor to my success. This doesn't mean that I didn't work hard, but I know not every business owner has close access to a resource like this.

Working with Auntie Tutti was the bridge that I needed as I shifted from running a brick-and-mortar business to running an online business. Auntie Tutti not only mentored me and believed in my dreams, she showed me leading with L.O.V.E. in action, planting the seed in my mind for what would ultimately become my signature business approach and coaching method. Not only was Auntie Tutti generous with her wisdom and expertise, she gave me the greatest expression of love: her time.

TRANSFORMATIONAL OVER TRANSACTIONAL RELATIONSHIPS

When building your Support Squad, especially when seeking out mentors and advisors, it's essential to seek out people whose values align with yours. Look for people you feel genuinely drawn to and who inspire you with the way they show up in the world. Follow your impulse for connection. If someone's work inspires you or teaches you something, reach out and tell that person why. Ask them if they'd be willing to meet for a coffee at their convenience to connect (do **NOT** say that you want to "pick their brain"). Putting yourself out there may feel awkward at first, but it is so important and will lead you to some surprising opportunities. This sort of outreach is what I call "10 Seconds of Bravery," and I'll show you how to implement this simple strategy at the end of this chapter.

There's a heartwarming scene in the **TED LASSO** season two finale where Keeley is afraid to tell her good friend she's leaving her job. "I don't want to appear like I'm not grateful for the amazing opportunity she's given me here," she says.

"A good mentor hopes you will move on," Higgins tells her. "A great mentor knows you will."[4]

As my second business grew, I began to look around for mentors who had achieved entrepreneurial success while also raising young children. I wanted proof that it was possible to grow a meaningful business while being present for my family. Ultimately, I discovered dad and entrepreneur Jonathan Fields, the founder of the Good Life Project. I listened regularly to his podcast, where he passionately shared stories about his wife and daughter and running his business. He was someone I could see myself being friends with beyond a business transaction, and I initially made him my mentor from afar.

One day, I learned about a two-day mastermind event that he was hosting in New York City with twelve entrepreneurs, and I decided to sign up. That was a leap for me; I worried about the $2,500 investment required to attend and about flying across the country, but the opportunity to meet one of my mentors in person was life-changing. After the event, I told Jonathan, "If you ever need someone to speak at one of your events about how to build an engaged community online, I'm happy to share my experience for free if that would be helpful." I let him know that I wanted to help, without expecting anything from him in return. I genuinely believed in his mission. This is how I lead with all my business connections; I'm looking to build resonant relationships.

A few months later, Jonathan took me up on my offer and invited me to speak at one of his events. He was inspired by the story I shared, and in turn he introduced me to Chris Guillebeau, the author of **THE $100 STARTUP**. Chris trusted the speaker recommendations that Jonathan made, so after a personal email introduction, he invited me to deliver my first keynote speech. I spoke in front of three thousand people at the World Domination Summit, his annual event in Portland, Oregon. As my mentor, Jonathan opened up opportunities for me that I would never have had access to on my own. Today, we talk regularly about our businesses and our kids, and I have even shared a few meals and cozy conversations with his family in his home.

When building relationships in your industry, don't think only in terms of what you can get. Instead, focus just as much on what you can give.

Life Coaches and Therapists:
Finding a Safe Space to Be Seen

As business owners, we experience a full range of emotions on any given day, from excitement, pride, hope, and confidence to disappointment, fear, anxiety, and frustration. It's important to recognize that if we don't tend to these emotions, especially when we're feeling low, we can't operate at our best. We are forced on a regular basis to examine our triggers and cultivate greater self-awareness because running a business is the ultimate personal growth gym.

This is why, in addition to getting support from mastermind groups and mentors, we may want to seek out the help of a life coach or therapist to help us deal with the highs and lows of entrepreneurship. These professionals can support us by creating a safe space in which to explore what is going on for us emotionally, psychologically, and even spiritually. They help us identify how these issues may be affecting our professional success. I recommend adding a therapist or life coach to your Support Squad, depending on your goals and the resources at your disposal. If you have the means, you may even want to hire both (and some professionals are both licensed therapists and life coaches). Which is the right option for you? Here are the key differences between them.

- THERAPISTS. These individuals are licensed and regulated by their state and can diagnose and treat mental health conditions. They can also help you process trauma, grief, and loss and may be covered by health insurance. A therapist may be the appropriate choice for you if, in addition to career goals, you are struggling with emotional, psychological, and mental health issues such as anxiety, depression, and childhood trauma. An accessible option is to receive therapy from graduate students who have to complete so many hours to graduate but who are still supervised by experienced professionals.

- LIFE COACHES. These individuals are not mental health professionals. Instead, they are specialists who support you by facilitating skilled questioning and strategic planning, including reframing your beliefs, helping you get "unstuck," and holding you accountable. A life coach is most effective if you are looking for practical business and career-building strategies that will help you make progress toward your goals.

All the business strategies in the world will not work if there are emotional blocks in your path. These blocks need to be addressed before you can move forward. I have worked with the same coach, Rebecca McLoughlin, for more than five years. She is a life coach with a master's in counseling psychology, so her therapeutic background blends well with her action-oriented approach. When I work with my coach, I'm able to honor my productivity style, in which I have huge bursts of creative output (which leads me to run out of steam) followed by a need to recalibrate and recharge. Rebecca calls both of us "big-energy women." If you have intense productive workflows, followed by stagnant slumps where you want to plop on your bed, hide under the covers, and shut the rest of the world off, you might be a big-energy woman, too.

Rebecca has taught me to sustain my energy when I feel overwhelmed or stuck. She has witnessed and supported me in the messy middle of business breakups, major financial dips, self-doubt, and identity crises. She's also been there for big celebratory moments: getting book deals, speaking on big stages, buying a home. And she's helped me process life's biggest transitions, such as the loss of close family members, including my father, my youngest brother, my grandfather, and my rescue dog—all within two years. I like to say, "Everyone needs a Rebecca in their corner." In addition to supporting me, I invite Rebecca to join my coaching programs and retreats. During my retreats, she supports my clients and helps them work through their roadblocks around overwhelm.

As entrepreneurs, we're in the arena, putting ourselves out there every day, facing criticism, and dealing with rejection. Our struggles with feelings of worthiness come up as well when we make decisions about money and pricing. Entrepreneurship brings up some emotional stuff, and we need support, tools, and strategies to move through times of uncertainty and stress. We must face our fears, acknowledge our resistance, and address what is holding us back with honesty to stay accountable to our dreams. And there is no better way to do this than in partnership with a skilled therapist or life coach.

Build Your Support Squad

A big part of receiving support is learning to ask for what you want and need. Asking for help is critical, but it can also be an incredibly vulnerable and uncomfortable act, because it means admitting that we cannot go it alone. To assist you in the outreach necessary to help you find your new support people, I'd like to issue an invitation called "10 Seconds of Bravery."

At the start of this chapter, I invited you to take stock of your current Support Squad and make a list of the key people in each of your three support categories (peers, mentors, and therapists/coaches). As you moved through this chapter, you were thinking about how to cultivate new relationships in areas where you may be lacking and how to fortify your existing relationships to create even more support. Consider the areas where you have determined that you need more support, and think about whether there are acquaintances, colleagues, or friends in your current network that you could reach out to right now.

Next, decide who you'll reach out to and follow these steps.

1. Identify how you'll connect with each person (this could be by sending an email, writing a social media message, or attending an event they are hosting).

2. Make a personal connection. This is your ten seconds of bravery in action. Express why you are inspired by each person and their work. Do not make a request of them. The goal is to lead with generosity and not take or pick their brain.

3. If one of the people you contact responds, find a way to continue the conversation by connecting in person over coffee, scheduling a call, or finding a way to add value to that person's life. When you connect with someone new, ask, "What do you need the most help with right now?" If they have an answer, do everything in your power to share any knowledge that you have. You could share a resource or introduce them to a personal contact, to help accelerate their dreams and desires first. Do this before asking for anything in return.

Many people will not respond. This has nothing to do with you and everything to do with their own personal commitments and priorities. Take rejection as redirection. Trust that the right connections at the right time will grow into something deeper. For now, plant seeds and patiently wait to see what blossoms. This applies when looking to build friendships with peers and find mentors. If you're looking to hire a coach or therapist, the value exchange happens through investing money. So you need to focus only on asking your personal network to find a list of recommendations. Contact the top three, and schedule a call with each one to see which is the right fit for you.

True wealth is your relationships. To weather life's storms of business dips, broken dreams, and broken hearts, we need to surround ourselves with safe people during difficult periods. Whether it's your partner, spouse, best friend, family member, or a business peer, gather your Support Squad.

Developing your Support Squad and building your network of people to lean on takes time and dedication. It's not easy to find your people, but the effort is a worthy investment in yourself. There will be people who fizzle out and are not as committed as you are. At times, you will feel frustrated and rejected. Don't give up. Your people are waiting for you. I promise it will be worth the wait.

You are now ready to build a Support Squad of people who will not only keep you accountable to your dreams but be a source of love and encouragement. In Part II, "Optimize," you will develop a healthy relationship with time so you have the energy to bring your next-level vision to life. Once you identify how you're spending your hours in a week, you'll be able to identify the logistical support you'll need at home and on your team. This will help free up your time so you can streamline your business and grow in a sustainable way.

she builds with

Ease.

5

I wish I had not been in such a hurry to
get on to the next thing: dinner, bath,
book, bed. I wish I had treasured the
doing a little more and the getting it
done a little less.

—*Anna Quindlen,* Loud and Clear

On the night my child was born, nothing went quite as we had
planned. "First-time pregnancy?" the front-desk attendant shouted
as we rushed into the hospital and toward the nurse's station. I nodded between intense contractions as we were guided to a room with
blinding fluorescent lighting. I got onto a bed, placed my feet in the
metal stirrups, and the contractions became unbearable. I was ready
to tear up my seven-page birth plan that we'd spent months prepar-
ing and order a giant epidural.

"Ten centimeters!" the nurse said. "You're fully dilated. It's time
to have your baby!"

As it turned out, there would be no time to carry through my
thoughtfully conceived birth plan or an epidural or anything other
than getting the baby out of me pronto. As we entered the labor and
delivery room at 3:00 a.m., George and I exchanged a glance, as if

to say: What about the special robe, bouncing on the blue medicine ball, and the iPod with a playlist of Sade, Jill Scott, and Enya curated for this special moment?

"Okay, Jadah. We need you to push," said the midwife. I gathered my strength, took a deep breath, and pushed three times.

"You're doing great. You can rest for a moment." I looked up and saw a mirror in the top corner of the delivery room reflecting the scene—George holding up my right leg, my mom holding up my left, and my OB and midwife in front, ready to catch the baby.

"Jadah, we need you to push again." My whole world reflected back at me. "You're doing great, honey. Push a little harder this time." I gathered another deep breath and all my strength, and pushed again.

"The baby's crowning!" the doctor exclaimed excitedly. "One more time!"

I pushed again with all the might I could muster. Three rounds of pushing and fifteen minutes later, my baby was born. A slow-motion silence filled the room. The doctor unraveled the umbilical cord from around our baby's neck and patted its backside several times. "She's not crying," she said.

She? I had forgotten that we didn't know if our baby was a boy or a girl.

Then we knew.

But she didn't cry. My thoughts cycled from thrilled, triumphant, and exhausted to concerned. I skipped over how many fingers and toes she had to: Is anything wrong? Is she deaf? Is she mute? Is she breathing?

George cut the cord, and they placed our daughter, with her head full of jet-black hair and candy-apple cheeks, against my chest. I melted into my first day of motherhood. It turned out that Zoe was absolutely fine and that she wouldn't have her first cry until the next morning.

o o o

Before I was an entrepreneur, I had a full-time job. And the day I became a mother, everything changed. In the early days after Zoe's birth, I could go from feeling as though I was on cloud nine to feeling completely overwhelmed in an instant. I had no sense of what it would take to juggle motherhood and work when I went back to my office after my maternity leave. I was determined to balance my job responsibilities with being there for Zoe in the weeks to come, and, as all new moms know, that was *a lot*. I had to adjust my work schedule to accommodate child care drop-offs, pickups, and nursing breaks. That meant shifting my role at the educational theater program where I worked. Instead of touring at different schools each day as a performance educator, I worked from our office, answering the phone and booking the shows I had once performed in. I lost a bit of my soul working in a cubicle, and I left that job after four months. We couldn't survive on my husband's salary alone, however, so I found babysitting work that allowed me to take my daughter with me. I purchased a bright green convertible double stroller and wore my Mei Tai baby carrier to accommodate two babies under the age of one. I didn't have to pay for child care, but I still wasn't making enough money.

Motherhood inspired me to become an entrepreneur because it showed me a path toward freedom and flexibility that would also allow me to support my family financially. I knew I wanted a schedule where I could be a present mother, one who could be there for my daughter during the big and small moments. I also knew I wanted to enjoy my life, taking vacations and traveling the world. On top of that, as a spoken-word poet with a performing arts background, I knew I needed to do work that was mission-driven and creatively fulfilling.

In search of having more control of my schedule, I made the leap to being my own boss and starting Little Sprouts Playhouse when Zoe was eighteen months old. Little Sprouts did not fulfill all of the categories I mention, however; I enjoy teaching children, but it's not the best use of my creativity and talents. And financially, things did not work out. But the experience with my first business did teach me some important lessons about how I wanted to use my energy and my time in my next ventures. I discovered that instead of fighting my new identity as a mother, I needed to allow the new time constraints of parenthood to bring a new level of focus and commitment to my life and how I used my time.

Becoming a parent is one identity shift that a person can go through. Other identity shifts include moving to another town, losing a loved one, or starting a new partnership that impacts not just who you are but how you spend your time. Whether you are starting a business or have been running one for years, it can take awhile to find a way of working that allows you to be there for your family, not to mention make time for yourself, while generating an income and getting fulfillment from your work. In this chapter, we'll examine how you are currently using your time and evaluate whether that approach supports your priorities. Then we'll create an anti-hustle work schedule that makes time for what matters most to you in your business and your life.

What Really Matters?

Sometimes a big life change, such as becoming a parent, selling a company, or changing careers, calls for a major overhaul and reinvention of your identity. Or maybe you are navigating a challenging period, such as caring for elders, adjusting to life after divorce, or managing your energy due to a health diagnosis. At other times, there are short-term changes that call for smaller adjustments, such as having a sick child who must stay home from school, your partner traveling for business, or experiencing a temporary loss of revenue. In any of these cases, you will need to rethink what matters most to you in this moment or season of your life and plan your days accordingly.

What stage of life are you in right now? What really matters to you? Have your identity or your responsibilities shifted in a way that affects the way you spend your time? You may have heard the expression "How we spend our days is how we spend our lives." Whatever season of life you are in, one of the most important questions to consider is: How do you want to spend your days? If you're not sure, remind yourself why you started your business in the first place. Does that reason still resonate with you now, or is it time to change your focus to reflect your new priorities?

Rethink what matters most.

Time Abundance versus Time Scarcity

In the early start-up days of my first few businesses, I had way more time than money. Instead of paying for advertising to get new customers, I leveraged the time I had to build a community to generate awareness about my business. Instead of paying for child care, a friend and I took turns watching each other's kids.

Once I started to generate a healthy income from my companies, and as Zoe grew older, I expected that managing my time would get easier. I figured that I would finally have more time for the things that were most important to me, including picking my daughter up from school, making time to work out, and going on date nights with my husband. I was at a place in my business where I could pay to outsource the tasks I didn't want to spend my time on, such as cleaning the house, writing newsletters, and responding to social media posts. However, I came to realize that that wasn't exactly true because as my companies grew, new responsibilities were always being added to my plate, and no matter what I tried, it felt as though there weren't enough hours in a day to get them all done.

The problem was that I was operating from a place of "time scarcity," constantly feeling as though my time was limited to the point that it caused me incredible stress. I'd find myself saying "Five more minutes" to my daughter repeatedly as she waited for me to wrap up work and spend time with her, but it was never just five more minutes. I'd be so tired at the end of each day that I couldn't even respond to my husband when he asked how my day was. My heart wanted to be with my family. But my actions showed that the most important thing in my world was a thirteen-inch laptop screen. That led me to realize that time is our most valuable resource—and a limited one—which means we must spend it wisely. I became a more conscious spender of time, embracing a mindset that I call *time abundance*, which means that we believe there's enough time available to do what matters most.

I've been caught in a time scarcity mindset more times than I'd like to admit. One day, I was frustrated and frazzled because Zoe was sick and I had to stay home to care for her, missing a day that would otherwise have been devoted to running my business. Then I asked myself, "Instead of thinking 'I *have* to stay home,' what if I thought 'I *get* to do this'? Isn't this why I stopped working for some- one else? I started a business so I could have the flexibility to be there for my daughter when she needs me."

Where in your life can you say to yourself, "I *get* to do this"?

This is the anti-hustle way we need to think about our time as entrepreneurs. We *get* to design our schedules to make space for our competing responsibilities. We *get* to make space for life's circum- stances and the unexpected. It's a privilege to have that type of con- trol over our time. Yet we often become the world's worst bosses of ourselves. We recreate the unhealthy work environments that we stepped away from. We drive ourselves to constantly produce by any means necessary, even though we're bone tired.

When we adopt a time abundance mindset, our constraints can become the greatest asset of our businesses. When we know what matters and schedule our days to reflect it, we can become more focused, more efficient, and more selective about what we say yes and no to.

Rethinking Your Relationship to Time and Productivity

How can you reclaim your time and energy and shift from a mindset of time scarcity to one of time abundance? It starts with a three-step process that we will use to reconfigure your schedule so that it better supports your goals and your desired lifestyle.

1. TRACK YOUR TIME. So that you know exactly how you are spend- ing your hours each day.

2. AUDIT YOUR ENERGY. So that you can identify what fuels and drains you throughout the week.

3. CLARIFY YOUR CAPACITY. So that you become clear about how much time you really have to do the things that matter to you.

Let's take a closer look at each of these steps.

Track Your Time

Let's see how you are spending your time right now. You are going to create a Weekly Time Log and track exactly how you use your hours for a full week. Think of this exercise as keeping a schedule diary, documenting the activities you do throughout the day. The more detailed your log, the better. This weekly log will give you an idea of where your time is going. If you forget to track hour by hour, do your best at the end of the day to remember what the core things were that you did. And don't try to wait for a "typical" week. Your life is constantly shifting, and waiting for the perfect moment to track your time is a way to avoid doing this important exercise. In addition to the scheduled events that take place throughout your day, don't forget to log:

- When you sleep, eat, and play
- When you move your body
- When you connect with others
- Unplanned phone calls or in-person conversations
- Time spent on email or social media (note if it was for business or leisure)

On the next page is an example of how to record your time over the course of one week. You can also review the Weekly Time Log in the appendix or download your own worksheet for free at shebuilds. com/resources.

WEEKLY TIME LOG

🕐	SUN	MON	TUE	WED	THU	FRI	SAT
6AM	sleep	Check Email	Check Email	Check Email	Check Email	Check Email	sleep
7AM	sleep	Morning Ritual	Morning Ritual	Morning Ritual	Morning Ritual	Morning Ritual	Breakfast
8AM	Phone Scroll	Meditate	Meditate	Meditate	Family Hike	Meditate	Zoom Workshop
9AM	Meditate	Prep	Team Meeting	Check Email	Meditate	Squad Zoom	Zoom Workshop
10AM	Zoom Event	Quarterly Planning zoom	Client Call	Co-Working	Client Call	Master mind	Zoom Workshop
11AM	Zoom Event	Quarterly Planning zoom	Check Email	Co-Working	Check Email	Master mind	Zoom Workshop
12PM	Couple's Meeting	Quarterly Planning zoom	Lunch	Co-Working	Client Call	Master mind	Zoom Workshop
1PM	Phone scroll	Lunch	Creative Course	Lunch	Lunch	Lunch	Lunch
2PM	Lunch	Check Email	Exploration Call	Homeschool Meeting	Co-Working	Check Email	Phone scroll
3PM	Poetry Class	Grocery Delivery	Phone scroll	Phone scroll	Nap	Nap	Phone scroll
4PM	Poetry Class	Call Grandma	shopping	Friend Hike	Talk w/ George	Writting Class	Nap
5PM	Order Groceries	Hang w/ Zoe	Talk w/ George	Friend Hike	Phone scroll	Writting Class	Hang w/ Zoe
6PM	Family Dinner	Hipline Dance	Cook Enchiladas	Tidy	Family Dinner	Writting Class	Hang w/ Zoe
7PM	Watch SNL	Family Dinner	Cook	Family Dinner	Family Dinner	Takeout Dinner	Leftovers
8PM	Watch SNL	Laundry	Family dinner	Fold Clothes	Journal	Family Movie	Meditate
9PM	Phone scroll	Laundry	Zoe Grades	Talk w/ Zoe	sleep	Family Movie	Watch show
10PM	Phone scroll	sleep	sleep	sleep	sleep	Watch show	Watch show

Audit Your Energy

Energy is the life force that allows you to show up and do the work, play with your family, and hang out with friends. It's incredibly important to pay attention to the activities that drain your life force and those that energize you throughout the course of a day.

Being constantly plugged in—that includes literally—can fool us into thinking that we have lots of energy left in us. We see the charging battery icon on our computer desktops, and we keep going. But we are *not* computers. We are humans, and we do run out of steam. (Bonus hack: sometimes I don't plug my laptop into an outlet, so I can use my battery's running down as a sign that my brain and body need to recharge, too. Once my battery drains, it's a sign to pause work.) That's why it's important to audit your energy and plan your days to match your output.

To start, identify the times of the day, week, or month when you typically have more energy, as opposed to when you tend to feel run down. Are you alert in the morning, but dragging after lunch? Are you dragging by Friday, making it a bad day to schedule important meetings or focus on demanding projects? I use an app on my phone to track my energy based on my menstrual cycle. I know that when week four in my cycle comes around, tasks that once seemed easy become the biggest mountains to climb. Pay attention to your natural patterns of output and disengagement.

Next, look back at your Weekly Time Log from the previous exercise. Ask yourself these two questions:

- Which experiences in my log give me energy?
- Which experiences in my log drain my energy?

While in lockdown in 2020 during the COVID-19 pandemic, I felt my energy getting depleted a lot more quickly than usual, and I did an Energy Audit, based on my Weekly Time Log, to figure

ENERGY AUDIT

Activities	Energizing, Draining, or Neutral	Notes
Morning Ritual	Energizing	Feels good to start the day tending to my wellbeing and I feel less reactionary
Dance Class on Zoom	Draining	Love my teachers and having disco lights in the living room, but miss being in person. Sometimes I sit on the couch because no one can see me
Hike with friends and family	Energizing	Feels good to be outdoors talking with my friends and family while moving my body
Cooking	Neutral	I love mindful slow cooking for my family every now and then, but not as a daily obligation
Co-work with friend	Energizing	Very focused, productive, and a great way to keep me accountable to work I'd rather avoid
Quarterly planning call for clients on Zoom	Draining	I love gathering women to dream and plan, but miss being in person. And online tech glitches are frustrating.
Spoken Word Poetry Workshops	Draining	I feel so behind. I don't have any time to read all of the poems, post in the comments, and write a new poem every week
Exploration calls with potential clients	Neutral	Love connecting with new women, but don't like lots of calls on my calendar
Writing Class	Energizing	Like learning a specific topic on writing (versus broad topic like creativity) in an intimate group of 12 people or less

out what was going on. I separated my daily activities into several categories—personal, connection, learning, work, and home—and I rated each activity as "energizing," "draining," or "neutral," depending on how it made me feel.

Based on my notes for each activity, I had the following takeaways.

- Being on Zoom for client work, talking to friends, movement classes, and learning drains me. #zoomfatigue
- Moving my body with people I love spending time with energizes me.
- I sign up for online courses because I love to learn, but I overcommit and take on too much. I then get frustrated when I can't keep up with all of them.
- I like to cook special meals occasionally, but I don't enjoy making quick everyday meals.
- I love coworking with friends and having the opportunity to talk about what I'm working on with people who know me well.

Then I came up with action steps I could take to shift how I used my energy throughout the week:

- Decline invitations for learning and social group hangouts on Zoom.
- Catch up with friends via phone while walking or while taking an in-person hike together.
- Pick one learning class or workshop per quarter (don't overcommit).
- Create a meal plan where George cooks the easier, quicker meals throughout the week.
- Schedule a weekly coworking date, and create a calendar invite for my friends to join me.

By making a list and identifying which activities energized or sucked the life out of me, I was able to adjust how I spent my time. I removed activities from my schedule that drained me and increased those that boosted my energy. In cases where an activity drained my energy but still needed to happen, I found a way to delegate it— for example, having George cook quick, easy meals throughout the week. In chapter 6, I'll share how to use your Weekly Time Log to hand off tasks within your business.

I also gave myself permission to be more intentional about how I was spending my time each week so that I could make different choices. For example, I noted that I had signed up for many on-line courses and workshops, which meant that I wanted to prioritize learning in my weekly schedule. However, I had gone overboard by signing up for too many, I didn't have time to digest the content, and I was behind on the assignments. I also knew that I liked smaller, intimate groups. Based on this data gathering, I chose to continue the memoir-writing class I'd signed up for, but I took a pass on other learning courses and workshops, no matter how much I thought I wanted to do them; the workload of multiple classes was too much.

Take a moment to fill out your own Energy Audit in the appendix or download the template at shebuilds.com/resources. Notice if you have overcommitted to activities in your schedule. Is there anything you could take off your plate to create more space? Being aware of what's working and not working for you gives you a lot of clues on how to increase your engagement and energy and decrease the overwhelm.

Clarify Your Capacity

Your capacity is your ability to perform and get things done as a function of your time and energy. Determining your capacity isn't about pushing yourself to extremes; just because you *can* stay up un-til 2:00 a.m. working doesn't mean that you *should*. Your capacity is what you truly have time and energy for while maintaining balance and avoiding burnout. Ask yourself: How much time do I have available to work on my business? How much time would I like to spend on my personal needs, desires, and relationships outside work? When you're clear about your capacity, you can be honest about what you can take on and show up for.

One way that I honor my capacity is by deciding how many hours a week I want to dedicate to my business. I have ideal office hours where I work from 9:00 a.m. to 1:00 p.m., twenty hours per week. When I'm working on a bigger project, I'll work until 3:00 p.m. or later. Even though I have time in my calendar to work more hours, my energy starts to drain in the late afternoon, and I'm not as focused or efficient. My optimal work hours are in the morning before lunch. Think about your natural energy spurts. Are you an early riser who likes to get started on work as soon as you start your day? Or do you prefer to work in the evening?

After reviewing my Energy Audit, I had some ideas about how to shift my schedule to better honor my capacity. I began to experiment with changes, and there was some trial and error before I figured out what would truly work for me. For example, Fridays were blocked off for working on my book, but I had also committed to a weekly group call with friends on Fridays at 9:00 a.m. I had originally thought that those calls would make me feel inspired and fuel my writing, but they did the opposite, leaving me feeling drained and distracted. With the insight gained from my Energy Audit, I initially moved these group calls to Monday afternoons, but with the new day and time, I found myself canceling the calls at the last minute. The truth was, during that season of my life, when my priority was writing my book, I couldn't give that kind of time to group calls with my friends. I was at full capacity. So I let my friends know that, for a time, I would no longer be joining the calls, which helped to reduce my feeling of overwhelm.

Once you track how you're currently spending your time and gather insights into your energy, create a schedule that works for your whole life. You can't increase the number of hours in a day, but you can change your relationship with time.

Design Your Weekly Workflow Plan

Now that you have more clarity about your allotted weekly time and energizing activities, it's time to optimize your workflow.

WEEKLY WORKFLOW PLAN

Mondays // Momentum & Money
6:30am – 8:00am Morning ritual
8:00am – 8:30am Meditate
9:15am – 10:15am Team Meeting
10:15am – 11:00am Plan Week
11:00am – 1:00pm Priority Cash Projects
1:00pm – 2:00pm Lunch
2:00pm – 3:00pm Emails + social
5-6pm – Hipline Dance with Lisha

Tuesday // Talk Days
6:30am – 8:00am Morning ritual
8:00am – 8:30am Meditate
10:00am – 1:00pm Meetings, Clients, Interviews
1:00pm – 2:00pm Lunch
2:00pm – 3:00pm Emails + social
4:00pm – Yin Yoga / Hike
5:00pm – Cook Dinner

	Monday	Tuesday	Wednesday	Thursday	Friday	Saturday	Sunday
THEME	Momentum & Money Mondays	Talkie Tuesdays	"WINsday" Wednesdays	Talkie Thursdays	Free Flow Fridays	Slow Saturdays	Self-Care Sundays
ACTIVITIES	Team Meeting; Cash Projects; Dance Class	Client Calls; Podcast Interviews	VIPs Big Picture Projects; Dance Class	Client Calls; Podcast Interviews; Writing Class	Personal Life Projects; Leisure Lunch; Bodywork; Movie Night	Family Activity; Solo Time	Couple's Meetings; Order Groceries

I designed my Weekly Workflow Plan around my daughter's school schedule, as well as the hours when I know I work most efficiently. Zoe goes off to school at 8:00 a.m., and then I meditate with George before starting my day. I try to schedule my client calls in the morning, when I do my best strategic and creative problem solving. After lunch, my energy wanes, so I take a nap for fifteen minutes. Then I devote the later hours of my workday to less demanding activities such as responding to email. I pick Zoe up from school at 3:00 p.m., and afternoons and evenings are spent catching up with friends, walking the dog, helping Zoe with her homework, and having dinner as a family.

The caveat is that my schedule is always changing. I've included an example of my ideal Weekly Workflow Plan, but in reality, no day is ever really the same for me, so I try to remain flexible while aiming for this schedule. The same will likely apply to you. What are the consistent scheduled commitments throughout your week? How could you let your work hours flow with the rest of your life? The objective is to map out your time in a way that supports your goals and is intentional.

I also like to theme the days of my Weekly Workflow Plan because it helps me protect my time and stay focused. Like time blocking or batching, breaking your day into themes gives your brain more context on what to focus on and when. What activities do you repeat each week? Could you work on similar tasks on a set day? If you don't set up how you want to spend your hours, someone else will find a way for you to spend them. Everyone else's to-do list will appear more urgent than yours. And then you'll be in reaction mode, putting out fires instead of prioritizing meaningful and profitable projects that will grow your business. Creating a structure can give you a sense of peace, because you know that if you follow the plan, you'll have time to work on everything that needs your attention throughout the week. Here's how I theme my days.

- **MOMENTUM AND MONEY MONDAYS.** I kick-start every week with a virtual team meeting on Monday morning. My team and I identify our priorities and build momentum for the week. After that, I focus on revenue-generating activities, or cash projects, which are projects that bring in money for the business. These include sending out sales offers, following up with potential clients, and looking at our profit-and-loss (P&L) report to see where we could save money. This is also when I focus on recurring activities for my company: reviewing newsletters to nurture my community, finalizing details for podcast episodes, and reaching out to past clients.

- **TALKIE TUESDAYS.** I call myself a social introvert, which means that I love people but I need downtime. This is why I batch all of my calls on Tuesdays and Thursdays. My team knows that if they are scheduling a call that I should be on, they need to schedule it on either a Tuesday or a Thursday between 10:00 a.m. and 1:00 p.m. This includes coaching calls with clients and podcast interviews. On some occasions I may need to break my calendar rule if somebody else's weekly schedule conflicts with mine. I'll make an Intentional Trade-Off on a case-by-case basis.

- **"WINSDAY" WEDNESDAYS.** The beautiful thing about batching my calls on Tuesdays and Thursdays is that it leaves my Wednesdays open for what the author Cal Newport calls "deep work."[1] This is where you have uninterrupted time blocks to focus on a project for a longer period. Wednesdays are when I work on my quarterly VIPs, or Very Important Projects. (I'll show you how to identify your VIPs in chapter 8.) This is the important work that will move the needle in my business, but it's not necessarily time sensitive. It's when I unleash my creativity and I think, innovate, and create. Can you tell I love WINSdays?

- **TALKIE THURSDAYS.** Same as Talkie Tuesdays!

- **FREE-FLOW FRIDAYS.** These are dealer's choice; I keep Fridays open for flexibility and fun. And sometimes focus. I might be co-writing to get my word count in for my manuscript or attending a monthly mastermind meeting with friends to talk about business, marriage, and life. Fridays are also when I can wrap up work projects so that I can unplug and be present for my family for the weekend. I also like to schedule personal appointments or have a fun "day date" with my husband on Friday.

My Saturdays and Sundays are less structured. Some weekends, I'm in my jammies all day and night. Other weekends, I'm hanging out with friends, driving to visit my ninety-seven-year-old grandma, or doing some work that I feel inspired by. Do you prefer to have more structure throughout your off days? Or does having fewer commitments on the calendar feel more nourishing? We'll explore your self-care style in chapter 11, but for now make sure that you schedule restorative activities for your body and soul that allow you to turn your work brain off.

As you develop your Weekly Workflow Plan, see if you can batch similar tasks and responsibilities on the same days and prioritize time for connection, play, and rest. This creates guardrails to make sure you have time for what matters most without ignoring the people and projects that matter to you. Keep in mind that you can change your schedule at any time. Use the Weekly Workflow Plan template in the appendix or download at shebuilds.com/resources. Keep things fluid and flexible, and readjust along the way as you gain insight.

Set Up Calendar Bodyguard Emails

You may struggle to put boundaries on your time. That makes sense; as women, we've been conditioned to make everyone happy, keep the peace, and be useful. We are rewarded with praise and recognition for overworking. But to stay sane, we must practice saying no with love to new opportunities that aren't right for us.

The goal is to come up with a clear and kind way of saying "No" with grace while noting your priorities. I hired someone to help me with this: my amazing right-hand, Michele. I call her my "calendar bodyguard." However, it's not necessary to hire a personal calendar assistant to do this. You can start by employing the following strategies.

- WRITE A "THANKS, BUT NO THANKS" EMAIL. Meet requests with gratitude, but say "No" to invitations that are distractions from your schedule. Here is an email template that Michele and I came up with, which we tweak as needed before she sends it out to decline requests that come in.

Hi, [Name],

My name's Michele, and I'm a part of Jadah's team; it's great to meet you! Jadah is committed to some pretty big projects right now, so I am personally following up because she cares so much about the people who take the time to reach out to her.

Thanks so much for inviting Jadah to be a guest on your podcast. Jadah is presently focusing on her book, speaking at conferences all over the world, leading retreats for her clients, and being a present wife and mom.

Her schedule is full, so we have to politely decline this opportunity. We really appreciate you contacting us and wish you the best of luck with your work.

Warm hugs,
Michele

- **SET UP AN AUTOREPLY EMAIL.** When you are in the middle of a big project that requires deep thinking, reflecting, and innovating (such as writing a book, redesigning a website, launching a podcast, or creating a new offer), set up an autoreply email to graciously let people know that you are declining new projects. I call this state, when I don't want to be disturbed, my "creative cocoon." To the outside world, it may appear that I'm dormant, but on the other side, I will emerge with creative work to share with others. I also schedule and edit the email each time I'll be away from my work responsibilities for several days. This public declaration is more for me than for anyone else. When I communicate my unavailability clearly, I give myself permission to not check my email or feel the need to respond in a timely manner. Greg McKeown, the author of *Essentialism: The Disciplined Pursuit of Less*, calls it "monk mode," and Jonathan Fields, the founder of the Good Life Project, has an autoreply email with the subject line "In Maker Mode." Here is an example of my personal out-of-office email.

Subject: I'm unplugging

Hello,

I'm on a solo writing retreat to work on my next book (if you're not on the waitlist, join here!). I'm unplugging from daily responsibilities, so I can FOCUS. #CreativeCocoon. I'll respond to priority emails on October 21st or later. If this is not urgent, please follow-up and re-send your email.

Of course if you're a close family member, a friend, or a part of my Dream Team, you know the best way to reach me with burning questions and love notes. And if you're a client and need immediate assistance, please reach out to my amazing right hand, Michele, at jadahsellner.com/contact. Here's to making dreams come true without distractions!

Warm hugs,
Jadah

Create a "Now Page" on Your Website

A "now page" is a section of your website that you update regularly to reflect your current priorities and work projects. I first saw this done by Leo Babauta at Zen Habits, who had been inspired to create a now page by Derek Sivers at nownownow.com/about. You can also link to your now page in the two strategies I shared: the "Thanks, but no thanks" email and your autoreply email. Set an alert in your calendar to remind you to update the page at the beginning of every quarter, when you may have newer goals, priorities, and events. Below is an example of my now page (you can also see my current page at: jadahsellner.com/now):

CONNECTION:

Taking care of my family and my body are my top priorities. My husband and I are on a 368-day meditation streak. I'm building a habit of reading a book 10 minutes a day.

MENTORSHIP:

While I write my book, I'm only serving my private clients. I support a handful of founders and have a waiting list. For business coaching, masterminds, and retreats, learn more here.

CREATING:

I'm in a weekly immersion writing class with a NYT bestselling author and writing my next book with Harper Business. I'm also creating a planner.

EVENTS:

I'm kicking off a virtual and global book tour in 2022, so I'd love to be on your podcast or stage. Contact my team to schedule. Or book me to speak at your event.

TRAVELING:

Staying #safeathome. Places I've been to: London, Paris, Italy, Spain, Costa Rica, Philippines, Australia, Fiji, Mexico, Japan, Cuba, China, Bali, Dominican Republic, Hawai'i, Canada, Iceland, Amsterdam, Brussels, Budapest, Prague, Munich!

PODCAST:

I recorded conversations on grief, healing, and reclaiming our lives on the *Lead with Love* podcast. Listen to "I'm not hiding, I'm healing" and "Behind the scenes of my next book."

These are my priorities. I must lovingly say NO to everything else (unless Oprah calls). ☺

These calendar bodyguard and "now page" strategies are permission slips that enable you to say "No" without guilt and to keep sight of what your priorities are. Saying "Yes" when you'd like to say "No" leads to resentment, an overcommitted calendar, and an overworked life. So take the time—even though you may have little of it right now—to put some calendar bodyguards in place to protect your time and mental well-being.

Now that you have a better sense of what you can achieve given your time limitations and priorities, and you have put guardrails in place to optimize your time and energy, we'll explore how to build up the support you need in your business and at home. In the next chapter, we'll get even more off your plate and design your Dream Team.

6

Design Your Dream Team

If you want to go fast, go alone.
If you want to go far, go together.

—Paraphrase of an African proverb

Do you find yourself asking "Why isn't my business growing more quickly?" If so, the reason could be that you don't have the right team in place. Often we put off building our teams because we are unsure whether we should hire staff now, as our business is growing, or wait until we've made more money. In this chapter, I'll address how and when to hire, along with the importance of having people in your corner to help you execute your vision for your company, take ownership of responsibilities and tasks, and lighten your daily workload. In other words, we're going to build your Dream Team.

In chapter 4, I talked about gathering your Support Squad, the people you lean on emotionally, intellectually, and spiritually throughout your entrepreneurial journey. Your Dream Team is different; these people are the key players you will need to hire for support both at work and at home to help grow your business and take things off your plate. Ultimately, this will minimize your overwhelm, freeing up your time for big-picture creative thinking and living the life that you want. Your Dream Team is made up of employees and independent contractors who will support you on logistical and operational levels. As your business grows and becomes more successful, the demands on your time will increase, but the hours in a day won't, which means that your Dream Team will be essential.

Making the Decision to Grow

Old ways of thinking and old patterns of behavior often make it difficult for us to outsource, delegate, and build our teams. As entrepreneurs, we may have trouble relinquishing control and trusting others due to perfectionism or past experiences when we've hired staff and things didn't work out. But if we want our business to grow, we must build, and then we must let go. Trying to do everything on our own beyond the early stages of our business will set us up for burnout and overwhelm. That was the case for my client Denise Bustard, the founder of the recipe site Sweet Peas & Saffron, when we began our work together.

I met Denise in 2019 at a food blogging conference in Utah. At the time, I had already left Simple Green Smoothies and was running my own coaching business. Denise had taken my Build Your Challenge course and created a Meal Prep Challenge for her community, growing her email list from 700 to 45,000 subscribers in two years. That was the public version of her story, but I later learned that she was exhausted and felt overwhelmed by the success of her business. On one hand, she loved that the Meal Prep Challenge brought in new website traffic and more money for her blog. With that income, she was able to work from home, spend more time with her two sons, have her husband leave his job, and buy her dream house. But she also started to resent the number of participants who signed up for her challenges, because she was working at a frenetic pace to keep up with the demands of her growing community. She felt 24/7 pressure to respond to emails and social media comments.

Denise was working forty to sixty hours a week, and she didn't know how much longer she could do so. "I feel like there's not enough time in the day," she told me. She was hosting free community-building challenges online, just as my company did with Simple Green Smoothies, but she didn't realize that I had an entire team helping me pull them off. Denise had done what many business owners do: emulate a strategy without understanding how it's being executed behind the scenes. At Simple Green Smoothies, I was able to accomplish what I did because of my Dream Team. In addition to my cofounder, Jen, being the visionary behind our visual brand, we had a project manager, three part-time community happiness specialists (our customer and social media team), a graphic designer, and a copywriter. What eight people were doing at our company, Denise was doing as a team of one, and she'd been doing it for two years! No wonder she was burned out. She was constantly in hustle mode, working nights and weekends, and her life and business had become one big blur.

As part of our work together, Denise and I strategized on how to build her Dream Team so that her business could keep growing, while taking the pressure off her to do everything single-handedly. Before hiring anyone, she examined how she was spending her time on a daily basis by using the Weekly Time Log in chapter 5 to track her time. Then we did an Energy Audit to identify areas where she needed help, based on the activities that were draining her energy. Through the Energy Audit, we discovered the following.

- Video editing, which did not energize her, was taking up a lot of her time.
- She was spending her evenings creating and scheduling social media posts. She justified working at night because she "relaxed"

and watched TV while she worked on mindless tasks. But that also meant she never got a break, which contributed to her burnout.

- She was spending eight hours a week writing content for her blog, but she wasn't enjoying her writing as much as she had in the past, when she'd had less of it to do.

She then made a list of how she would reallocate her time if she could find a way to off-load those draining tasks:

- Create a new meal plan book.
- Clean up SEO on her website.
- Do higher-level thinking about her company.
- Spend more time in the kitchen cooking (which she did enjoy).

With all of this information in mind, she made a wish list of future hires based on tasks she wanted to get off her plate:

- Content writer to write blog posts
- Social media manager
- Videographer to help record cooking tutorials and edit videos
- Kitchen assistant to shop, prep ingredients and props, help with recipe testing, take notes, and wash dishes
- Photographer to take recipe photos

However, she couldn't afford to hire all those people right away. We decided that she would fill the most urgent role first, then wait until she was earning more income to fill the others. Denise felt most overwhelmed by the constant pressure to create social media posts, so she hired a social media manager first. In the interim, until she generated enough income to fill her remaining Dream Team roles, she used the Weekly Workflow Plan in chapter 5 to batch and theme her days based on her repeated weekly activities to improve her focus and work more efficiently. And because she had gone through the process of tracking her time, she had a good sense of how many hours of support she would need from her new social media manager each week.

In addition to a social media manager, Denise hired two additional contractors (a virtual assistant and a video editor) to support her business over the next three years. She added each subsequent Dream Team member when she realized that she was holding projects up due to her own lack of bandwidth. With each new hire, she felt nervous about the financial cost, but she also knew that she couldn't afford *not* to hire more help. Have you ever felt nervous about making a new hire? Whether you have a huge team already or you're thinking about taking baby steps to building your team, hiring will stretch you as a leader no matter what stage your business is in.

To ease her anxiety, ahead of each new hire, Denise decided to put money into an emergency fund to cover the new hire's pay for six months. During our coaching sessions, I broke down the hiring process into four key phases—identifying the role she needed to fill next, writing a job description, interviewing applicants, and training the person—and she spread these phases out over a period of several months so that she had time to build her savings.

The last time I spoke to Denise, she was bringing in $450,000 in annual revenue, more than double what she had been making when we had first met. And she is now working with less hustle and more intention. By building her Dream Team and doing it at a pace that made financial sense for her business, she allocated more space in her days to high-level creative work. She is no longer drowning in busy work. She has also cultivated leadership skills by creating clear expectations for her team and training them to take ownership of the projects they handle for her.

Even better, she no longer works evenings or weekends, she has time for reading and creative writing, and she takes a daily walk to give herself a break between computer work and making dinner for her family. She also took a three-month sabbatical from her business to prioritize her family and mental health, while her team kept moving projects forward. She is no longer living in hustle mode, she loves collaborating with her team, and her business is thriving.

As Denise discovered, hiring support staff involves investing money, time, and mental energy. But if you commit to doing the work and designing your Dream Team with intention, the benefits down the road will be worth it. You will feel more energized and inspired to show up for your work, your team, and your loved ones. If all goes well, you may even feel a little guilty that you have so much free time while work is still getting done.

Think Like a Visionary CEO

To build your Dream Team and free up your time, you will need to embrace a new way of thinking. You will be able to pull it off only if you embrace the anti-hustle mindset shifts, allowing yourself to be fully supported in all areas of your life. You must give yourself:

1. PERMISSION TO TRUST. This is one of the most liberating decisions you can make as a business owner. Trust that you will be able to find someone who can do certain things better than you can, will enjoy doing the work, and will care just as much as you do. This isn't easy. When you've been doing everything on your own, trusting someone with the intimate details of your business can be a challenge. And if you've hired someone in the past who didn't work out, that experience may have made you hesitant to trust someone new. But you will need to move past this apprehen-

sion to grow. Instead of using a bad hiring experience to justify why it's okay for you to keep doing everything yourself, ask yourself this question: What's the gift and the lesson of someone not working out? Commit to letting that lesson guide you as you grow your team.

2. **PERMISSION TO LET GO.** The only way to create more time and space in your life is to release your grip on your to-do list and overcome your desire to manage every detail so you can focus on the work you love to do. As my friend Kristoffer Carter, the author of *Permission to Glow*, once told me, "Letting go is hard, but holding on is like falling on water skis and getting dragged around the lake." Many leaders hesitate to loosen the reins because they have high standards and don't think anyone else will be able to meet them. However, you will likely be surprised by your team's performance if you make your expectations, preferences, and boundaries clear and hold your team accountable for meeting them.

3. **PERMISSION TO LEAD.** I hear a lot of women business owners say, "I'm not a good leader. I don't like managing people." To grow your business, you'll have to leave that mindset behind and accept that you are the CEO of your company and your life. If you don't know how to articulate your vision, needs, and desired outcomes clearly and consistently, find a mentor or program to guide you to the point where you can. This isn't optional. No matter how good a job you do at hiring a team of employees or contractors, they will not do their job well if you aren't guiding the ship. Leading requires a shift from thinking like a highly paid task manager to a more visionary style of leadership. You are the talent scout, finding the best people to be in the right seats and then letting them do what they do best.

Design Your Dream Team with Intention

Once you've shifted your mindset to embrace growth, you'll be ready to design your Dream Team. Start by asking yourself: What am I spending my time on? What do I need support with? Who can help me? What can they take off my plate? What am I holding on to? Where can I start to let go?

Next, you are going to go through the same steps that Denise and I did so that you can determine how you are spending your time, where you need support, and exactly who you need to hire to get that support.

Review Your Weekly Time Log and Do an Energy Audit

Go back to the Weekly Time Log you completed in chapter 5, where you tracked how you spend your time in your business and at home. Now look at the Energy Audit that you completed, where you identified each activity in your calendar as "energizing," "neutral," or "draining." Also look for where you might be wasting time and could create more efficiency or reallocate that time. Identify patterns that will show you where you need support. One other big benefit of this time-tracking exercise is that it gives you a concrete sense of how many hours you are spending on various tasks each week. After you map this out, you will be at an advantage once you hire new staff because you will know exactly how many hours per week a particular role entails.

Create a Delegate List

Based on your responses in the Energy Audit, you are now going to decide whether you want to keep certain tasks on your plate or out-source them. Create a Delegate List of the activities that drain your energy, similar to the list that we created for Denise. You'll realize how much time and mental space you can free up if you delegate those tasks to someone else.

Denise's Delegate List

Activity	Frequency	Time	Action or Insights
Creating Pinterest pins	Daily	2½ hours	Delegate
Creating YouTube videos	2 times per week	16 hours	Delay (until find a faster video editor)
Creating new recipe blog posts	3 times per week	8 hours	Do now, delegate later
Doing grocery shopping	2 times per week	2 hours	Delegate (use an app to automate list)

Define Needs and Roles

Review your Delegate List, grouping activities and responsibilities that seem to fit together. These may be roles you already have in your business or home, or they may be potential future hires (for example, administrative assistant, bookkeeper, house cleaner, social media manager, nanny). This is an opportunity to make a Dream Team wish list beyond the people who are currently supporting you. As you look at each role, think about any additional tasks and responsibilities you'd like the person in that role to take on, even if you have time to do them now. Think about how to free up more time both at home and in your business to focus on the activities that only you can do (and love to do). To help you separate your immediate needs from your Future Vision, ask yourself: What support do I currently need in the business and at home? What support do I need to grow and free up even more time in the future?

Do a Roles and Responsibilities Review

When it comes to your business team, whether you are currently a team of one, wearing all of the hats yourself, or you have ten employees, it is important to assess whether you have the right person (including you) to handle each job and determine if you need to hire anyone. The following questionnaire will help. I was first introduced to these questions by my coach Christen Bavero at ThinkHuman. If you're running your business solo, answer the questions for yourself to assess how you're doing as the leader of your company. This will give you a better idea of what's working and what's not. You'll also gain clarity on where your strengths and enjoyment exist in your current roles. And you will identify gaps and opportunities for when you're ready to bring in additional support in the future. If you already have a team, give the questionnaire to each person, letting them know that it should take about thirty minutes to complete and giving them at least a week to answer the questions and send them back to you. Let them know that their responses will be confidential. As you review your team's answers, write down any clarifying questions you have, along with your insights.

Roles and Responsibilities Questionnaire from ThinkHuman

- What are your core responsibilities in your role? Include what you do on a daily/weekly/monthly basis.
- Who is the person you report to? Are you clear about who can give you the answers that you need to solve questions?
- Are you currently using what you believe to be your greatest talents to move the business forward in a powerful way?
- What unique talents and strengths are you not using in your current role?
- What do you do on a day-to-day basis that makes you most proud?
- What do you do on a day-to-day basis that you feel is a waste of time?
- What processes do you think are broken or could be improved?
- How supported do you feel by your manager and/or the company's leadership team (1: low level of support; 10: high level of support)?

- Where do you see yourself professionally one year from now? Ideally, what role would you have? What would you want to be doing more of? What do you want to be doing less of?
- What do you really love doing in the company?
- Do you have any other thoughts or comments?

As you review the responses, consider whether each member of your team is happy in their current role, is in the right position, or has untapped potential to take on more responsibility inside the business. Schedule a twenty-minute meeting with each of your team members to discuss their answers and any potential changes to their roles based on their needs and the way you want to grow the business. Don't make this a onetime exercise; doing it once a year is a great way to make sure everyone loves their work and is growing individually as your company grows.

Review Your Support at Home

Next, take stock of the support you are getting at home, which directly and indirectly affects the growth of your business. At home, support could be split (not necessarily evenly) between a spouse or significant other, children, roommates, and/or even parents. Begin by having a conversation with the members of your household about redistributing responsibilities. You may also want to consider outsourcing some of the work to someone outside your home to free up more of your time (such as cleaning or grocery shopping).

In my case, family dinners had become a time-consuming source of stress that I was ready to outsource. I wanted all of us to eat healthier meals at home, but I didn't have time to cook dinner. To complicate things further, we all have different tastes: Zoe is a vegetarian, George loves meat-centered meals such as chicken and steak, and I'm a foodie who loves spicy, flavorful ingredients. My husband initially resisted the idea of hiring someone to cook for our family, thinking that it would be too expensive. He volunteered to cook for us instead, but after several weeks went by during which we continued to face the "What's for dinner?" dilemma, ordering a lot of takeout and eating frozen pizza, I renegotiated with him. I added up the expense of eating out and ordering in, then figured the cost of hiring a personal chef who would buy groceries and make meals that worked for the whole family. Surprisingly, it turned out, we'd save money; it was less expensive to have healthy meals cooked by a personal chef than to eat out or waste money on unused produce in the fridge. We agreed to try it for thirty days to see if we liked having someone cook for us, and we ended up loving the meals! I had the chef make recipes that I was drooling over in cookbooks and on blogs, making sure that they also contained plenty of protein for George and that we also had a vegetarian version for Zoe.

Making a change may be met with resistance at first, but when you recognize that you are not getting the results you want, advocate for a new way of doing things and make sure you are getting the support you need. As I mentioned in chapter 4, sometimes that resistance is an emotional block, so honor a pace that works for your personal journey.

Define Your Dream Roles

Using what you learned above, it's time to define the roles you need to fill by writing a job description for each one. Once you have job descriptions written, you will be able to move on to the next phase: hiring, interviewing, onboarding, and training your team.

If you're resisting hiring someone, it could be that you aren't clear about exactly what you want that person to do. Sometimes, simply creating a job description can help you break free from inertia. Keep in mind that letting go of control and empowering others to take over some of the responsibilities on your to-do list will help you focus on higher-level projects that will increase your company's revenue, fine-tune your vision and strategy, and create balance in your life (time for rest, play, and fun outside your business). Let this be your motivation.

My client Denise had been eager to take some responsibilities off her plate to focus more on what she loved doing in her business and be more present at home. During one of our coaching calls, she said, almost as an afterthought, "I'm finding it hard to work while my kids are home. It's a frantic time of day. I'm pulled in all directions all the time."

She was resistant to the idea of hiring more support because she struggled with letting go and trusting people to do things as quickly as she could. During our next coaching session, I encouraged her to draft a job description for the role she needed to fill most urgently, which in her case was a social media manager. We started by writing a dream list of qualities, identifying what was essential for the role, what was optional, and what were nonnegotiables. Once Denise clarified what she wanted, she felt ready to bring someone on to help. She posted the job online, and when the responses came in, she chose her top five candidates and interviewed them. Here is the job description she came up with.

DENISE'S SOCIAL MEDIA MANAGER JOB DESCRIPTION

Are you passionate about meal prep and a healthy lifestyle?

Do you consider yourself a social media superstar and think it would be so cool to get paid to talk to people online?

This might be the role for you!

Sweet Peas & Saffron is expanding, and we have a position on our team—where managing our Facebook and Pinterest accounts is your core responsibility.

As the Social Media Manager, you will also assist in daily communication and engagement with readers and meal prep challenges.

We believe that with a little meal prep, even busy people can enjoy healthy meals made from scratch.

As part of the Sweet Peas & Saffron team, you'll be at the front of the lines interacting with our community and spreading the love for meal prep and healthy recipes. Think of yourself as the meal prep cheerleader—sharing recipe tricks, and providing ingredient tips and swaps.

Core Responsibilities & Tasks

- You'll spend most of your work hours managing and growing our Facebook and Pinterest accounts.
- You will create and schedule new pins, Web Stories, share engaging content, create graphics and respond to reader comments and questions. It's always a fun day with Sweet Peas & Saffron!
- You will analyze performance on social media accounts and stay up to date with current technologies and online marketing trends.
- You will assist in keeping our community excited and engaged during meal prep challenges.
- You will write positive and optimistic copy, so that Sweet Peas & Saffron readers feel like they can accomplish any meal prep recipe.

Required Skills, Strengths, and Knowledge

- Must have excellent communication skills and grammar
- Must be passionate about meal prepping and a healthy lifestyle
- Must be dependable and eager to learn
- An eye for graphic design, font pairing and food photography is an asset
- Experience using Adobe programs like Photoshop and Premiere Pro also an asset, but not essential

Details

- You'll work 15 hours a week to start (with the potential for more)
- Working hours are flexible

- Pay is $25 per hour with a 30-day trial period
- Training begins on June 1
- This is a virtual subcontractor position
- Must have your own computer

Currently only accepting applications from Canada (we still love our global community!)

If this sounds like you and you believe you're a great fit for this position, complete the application by May 10. APPLY NOW. We can't wait to hear from you!

XO, Denise

PS: If you know someone who may be a great fit for this position, please share this and tell them to apply. We truly appreciate it.

Now it's time to write job descriptions for the Dream Team roles that you need to fill most urgently.* Using Denise's example as a model, consider the following steps and prompts to write your own.

1. OUTLINE YOUR COMPANY'S MISSION. Explain what your company does, what your values are, and what it's like to work for your organization. Make this fun and enticing. It should read like a mini sales pitch on how amazing your company is.

2. DESCRIBE THE POSITION YOU'RE LOOKING TO FILL. This should include an overview of the job and the characteristics and strengths that you're looking for in an ideal candidate.

---

* If you'd like a template for how to write your own job description, visit shebuilds.com/resources to download a fill-in-the-blanks worksheet. It's like a Mad Libs for hiring your Dream Team.

3. LIST THE CORE RESPONSIBILITIES AND TASKS OF THE ROLE. These should include the typical tasks performed daily, weekly, and monthly in the role you are looking to fill. Reference your Weekly Time Log so you can be as specific as possible.

4. LIST THE REQUIRED SKILLS, STRENGTHS, AND KNOWLEDGE FOR THE ROLE. These could include educational level, years of experience, and the ability to use specific software you use in your company.

5. MENTION OTHER IMPORTANT DETAILS. These could include things such as application deadlines, hours required per week, hourly rate or salary, and start date. Also specify if the job is remote or in person and whether it is an employee or subcontractor role.

When it comes to recruiting for your position, I recommend looking for referrals from your personal and professional network first. Then if you don't find someone through a recommendation, here are a few sources to find help online: Hire My Mom, Indeed, Upwork, Freelancer, Fiverr, and UrbanSitter (for the most up-to-date list of my favorites, visit shebuilds.com/resources).

o o o

Don't put pressure on yourself to build your ideal support team overnight. It's a lot of work to hire and train team members, and it requires investing your money and your time. But ultimately, it's worth it because having a Dream Team will enable your business to grow and thrive while you maintain your peace. Take time to think about your vision for support, not only in your business but in your personal life. As your vision for your Dream Team takes shape, give yourself permission to trust, let go, and lead. Your team is waiting for you.

7

So often in life, things that you
regard as an impediment turn out
to be great, good fortune.

—*Ruth Bader Ginsburg*

As entrepreneurs, we love to think big and move quickly. We're typically managing a constant stream of new ideas that can make us feel like our businesses are operating in a state of barely organized chaos.

Do you find yourself coming up with new products and services for quick money injections when cash flow gets tight? Do you spring "brilliant" marketing concepts on your team at the last minute, leaving them stressed and overwhelmed as they scramble to execute your latest burst of inspiration? These are all signs of what I call an *entrepreneurial outburst*, where you have a fast and frenetic surge of ideas, with an urgent need for action, followed by exhaustion. You run out of steam, and fatigue hits you. Flying by the seat of your pants has gotten you to where you are, but you know it's not sustainable in the long term.

If you feel this way, you are not alone. With every business I've started—and I've launched four over the past fourteen years—there have been many times when I felt as though I was in over my head.

As though I'd sneaked into a private club and at any moment some-one was going to find me out. Entrepreneurial outbursts are common, but it's not the state you want to be in while running your business for the long haul. In this chapter, I'll guide you through the keys to streamlining your business sustainably, which I call "The Five S's of Sustainable Business Growth."

When I talk about scaling up your business, I don't mean scaling up on the level of the glorified unicorn companies that go public, have billion-dollar valuations, and are on the cover of *Forbes* magazine. I'm talking about scaling up on a level that is sustainable for *you*. A sustainable business needs to be profitable, and you need to think about marketing, sales, the customer experience, financial details, and operations.

You may be familiar with these foundational business concepts, but it's worth the time to re-examine with more intention. Even if you already have solid products and promotional strategies in place, I invite you to revisit your core offers through the anti-hustle lens. Your business may look successful on the outside, but if you feel depleted on the inside, you may have built on a foundation of achieving and doing more just for the sake of it.

My mission is to help you build your company in a way that honors your Intentional Lifestyle and your humanity as you level up. You have an opportunity to build differently, and to Build with L.O.V.E.

The Five S's of Sustainable Business Growth

Other entrepreneurs have often asked me how we grew Simple Green Smoothies to more than a million followers in two years without having any prior business experience. The simplest answer is that we became obsessed with community building. I call this approach "love over metrics," believing that when we put people first, the numbers (reach, revenue, and impact) will follow. With this strong foundation in community building, the Simple Green Smoothies recipe for success featured five key ingredients in the Five S's of Sustainable Business Growth: Share, Sell, Serve, Systemize, and Sustain.

THE 5 S'S OF SUSTAINABLE GROWTH

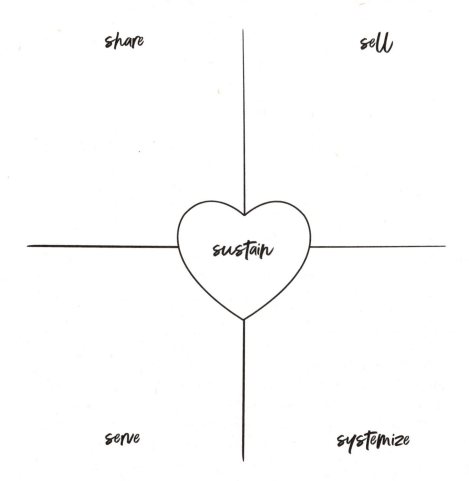

Share: Court Your Community

Share, the first element of sustainable business growth, is about demonstrating your expertise, attracting the people that you want to serve, and building trust over time. Too often, business owners make the mistake of skipping the trust-building process. I was initially guilty of that when we launched the Simple Green Smoothies website after building a fast-growing community on Instagram. We were eager to invite our followers to start getting their recipes from our blog, so we posted drool-worthy photos of green smoothie ingredients on Instagram with the caption "If you want the full recipe, go over to simplegreensmoothies.com." People asked, "Why can't you post the recipe right here?" Instagram was our primary platform, and they wanted to stay on it.

That was when I learned that the marketing and sales process is a lot like dating. Telling followers to visit our website was like inviting them to come home with us before they were ready. We needed to court our community and earn their trust over a longer period before they would be ready to move on to the next phase.

Look at the primary platform or medium where you're attracting your potential customers as though it's a "dance floor." It's a party with a lot of people, and you want to meet your people where they're already hanging out. Slow down, and don't try to take them away from the dance floor too quickly. Stay for a while, have some conversations, and allow people to get to know you, like you, and trust you. And don't expect everyone to turn into a customer. You want to share more of who you are and add value to people's lives before you invite them to your "house." Once they feel safe visiting you, focus on nurturing the relationship and building trust so they take the next step with you. From there, you can then invite them to your "bedroom," which means joining your email list. If someone gives you their email address, it means they'd like to maintain a consistent, intimate one-on-one conversation with you. Then the courting phase continues.

Breaking down my dating metaphor a bit further, here are the three distinct phases of courting a community around your business:

 THE DANCE FLOOR: ATTRACTION PHASE. Identify where your ideal customer is hanging out, and pick a primary venue for attracting the people you want to serve, such as a podcast, a video channel such as YouTube, a social media platform, or a speaker's circuit. Whatever platform you choose, it should be where you and your company really shine and feel the most excited to share your expertise and brand personality. Create, post, and share valuable content that your community is hungry for (this content can be educational, entertaining, or inspiring—or all three!). You will build trust that your product or service can help your followers in the future.

THE HOUSE: TRUST PHASE. Once you've built trust, create a welcoming environment in which your followers can learn more about you and your company. An ideal place to do this is on your company website, where you can express your company values and mission statement, communicate about your products and services, and demonstrate that you understand the problems, needs, and goals of your potential customers. As though you were having a guest over for a cup of tea, show the people you want to serve what you care about while also making them feel comfortable and well taken care of.

THE BEDROOM: INTEREST PHASE. Now it's time to take things one step farther. The bedroom is where potential customers become official subscribers by giving you their email address. They're showing you that they want to be in communication with you long term. Continue to build trust, and add even more value by offering them special perks in exchange. Don't make your business a one-night stand. Respect the opportunity, and court your community with care.

Where's your dance floor? Think about where your ideal customers are hanging out. Ask yourself how you can show off your moves and demonstrate your expertise, attract the people that you want to serve, and build trust with your community. Community is an expression of your love.

How will you share with your community to build your business? Grab a pen and your journal and jot down the answers to these questions.

- Who is the community you want to attract and serve? Who are its members? What are their likes and dislikes? What do they struggle with? What would make their life easier or more joyful?
- Where are they hanging out? Online or in person? Where will you focus on showing up to nurture the relationship?
- What can you do to build trust, share your expertise, and demonstrate that you are of value to your community?

Sell: Create an Intentional Buying Experience

Sell is about inviting the community you've built to give you money in exchange for a product. I believe that selling is service. Whether you are selling through an e-commerce or retail shop or you are a content creator who generates revenue through sponsorships, you are in the business of improving people's lives. Ask yourself: What is the one core offer or product my business provides that gets the best results for our customers? How can I think beyond the transactional when I'm promoting this core product?

With Simple Green Smoothies, the key offer was the free 30-Day Green Smoothie Challenge, where people committed to drinking one smoothie a day based on the recipes and shopping lists we shared through email. Then we invited those participants to take the next step and sign up for our *Fresh Start 21* meal plan (the one that led to the $86,000 launch I mentioned in chapter 3). We hosted the challenge four times a year with hundreds of thousands of participants to help promote our products in a fun way. That provided a transformational buying experience for our community members, demonstrating "love over metrics" in action.

The key to converting potential customers into paying customers is to continue to build trust and educate them. This way, you're selling with integrity (not salesy coercion), and they can make a confident buying decision because they have all the information they need. Ask yourself: What do these people need to believe, know, and feel to buy my product or service? Then your job becomes helping them decide if it's right for them. Next think about promoting your product in a way that generates an emotional connection with potential customers. How does your company want to make people feel about themselves when engaging with your brand?

How do you know which offer to focus on? You want to take the time to review your product suite. This is when you take inventory of all the products or services you offer to give you more insight into what's working for you and your company, as well as what's working for your customers. You then select the right model for you. My friend and mentor, Jonathan Fields, introduced me to the concept of "product-maker fit." Usually when starting a business, we talk about "product-market fit," which means you're on a mission to create a product that people will pay you for. Then, once you've validated your product to the point that customers are willing to pay you for it, you run with it. When you're building an Intentional Lifestyle, you want to find a product-maker fit where you, the founder and maker, are energized to deliver the product or service. It may take a little longer to find the sweet spot where people pay you *and* you are happy, but I promise that it's worth the wait.

Review Your Product Suite

Your product suite is the collection of all the products and services your company offers (and it's okay if you have only one core product right now or are still dreaming about it). It's important to make an intentional analysis of what you offer and how your products match your team's energy and output. Seeing everything you offer in one place will give you insight into opportunities for growth, as well as whether certain products may not be worth the time and effort based on revenue potential. You need to get a clear view of which products, services, and offerings perform the best and identify how much time and effort they take to deliver. Use the Product Suite template to write down your answers in the appendix or download at shebuilds. com/resources. I'll share an example from a product we created for Simple Green Smoothies.

1. **PRODUCT.** What's the name of your product?

2. **PRICE.** How much do you sell it for?

3. **REVENUE.** How much revenue did it generate in the last twelve months? What's the COGS (cost of goods sold) to make or deliver this product? What's the profit after COGS?

4. **RESULT.** What is the problem it solves, the pain it relieves, or the joy it creates for customers? What transformation will happen for them if they purchase this product?

5. **EFFORT.** How much effort and time does it take to create and deliver the product to the customer? What resources does it need from you and your team? Rate on a scale of 1 to 10. For example, rate something a 10 if it's a new product that you haven't created yet. Rate something a 3 if it's already been created and it will take minimal effort for your team to make minor updates to tweak existing marketing materials.

6. CROSS-SELL. What other products could a customer buy next as an additional purchase, or what would enhance the current product experience as an upgrade?

PRODUCT SUITE

PRODUCT	PRICE	REVENUE	RESULT	EFFORT	CROSS-SELL
Fresh Start 21	$59	August 2016 $86,000	Energy, quick weight loss, save time w/ meal planning, reset eating habits and cravings	It's new, will take a lot of time (but also exciting to work on). Need a lot of team members	Let's Eat Meal Plan, Recipe Card Kits, Affiliate blenders

How can you sell to your community while leading with love? Ask yourself these questions to get your wheels spinning, and jot down your answers.

- What products or services create the best results for your customers?
- What product or service is the most exciting and energizing for you to create and deliver to your dream customer?
- What is the transformation your customers will experience because they engaged with your product or service?

Serve: Delight Your Customers

Serve is about taking care of your customers beyond the transaction. Once people have purchased your product or service, how do you continue to surprise and delight them throughout their entire experience with you?

When you deliver world-class service, people will come back again and again, and they will spread the word, becoming your most successful sales team. Marketing studies show that word-of-mouth recommendations result in five times more sales, and customers are 90 percent more likely to trust suggestions from friends and family more than they do traditional advertising.[1] Pay attention to your own behavior. How do you make buying decisions? Think about the last three products you bought. What was your pathway to purchasing? For example, when I'm ready to make a purchase, whether it's buying an article of clothing or booking a hotel or restaurant, I read customer reviews. And when I want to hire someone, I crowdsource my friends and colleagues. People talk, so why not take the time to create moments worth talking about for your customers?

Be intentional, but also follow your impulse for generosity when a moment calls you to surprise and delight a customer in real time. At Simple Green Smoothies, we did this after a woman named Joanne posted a comment on our website about her upcoming breast cancer surgery. Our team was so touched by her story that we recorded a personal video for Joanne during one of our team meetings. We privately sent it to her on the day of her surgery to let her know we were thinking about her. We acknowledged her beyond a simple transaction by making a personal connection and making her feel as though she belonged. Because she felt cared for, she took the time to publicly share her feelings about our company. This is how trust in your business is built.

How can you better serve your customers by connecting to their journey from beginning to end? Jot down your responses to these questions.

- Who is your dream customer? How do you want to improve that customer's life?
- How could you surprise and delight the customer? How do you want them to talk about your company beyond the transaction?
- With your dream customer in mind, what's one thing you

could do to improve their experience when engaging with your product or service?

Map Your Customer Journey

Before we move to the last two S's of Sustainable Business Growth, we are going to create what I call your Core Customer Journey Map. Before you can scale up, these key elements of your core customer's journey must be clear to you, your team, and your potential customers. You need to know who you can serve, where you can find and attract them, and how you can help make their lives better through your paid offers. Think about the following questions. Write down the answers in your journal or use the blank version of this worksheet in the appendix. You can also access the Core Customer Journey Map at shebuilds.com/resources.

1. CORE CUSTOMERS. Who are they, what's their problem, and what do they want?
2. CORE DANCE FLOOR. Where are they hanging out? Where are you willing to show up and serve?
3. CORE LOVE MAGNET. What's a quick win tip, strategy, or resource you can offer them?
4. CORE OFFER. What product or service will solve a problem or bring them more joy?

Systemize: Design Your Repeatable Systems

Systemize is about identifying what you already do in your business. You may think you don't have systems, but you do; you just haven't put thought into what you do, how often you do it, and why you do it. Creating systems is about documenting your processes, communicating your preferences about how you like to get things done, and identifying shortcuts for repeatable activities and putting

CORE CUSTOMER JOURNEY

1 Core Customer

Work from home mom in her late 20's with two kids. She's tired and overwhelmed, and wants to have more energy for her family, and more purpose for her life.

2 Core Dance Floor

Share green smoothie recipes and health tips on Instagram. Include entire recipes in the captions to make their lives easier.

3 Core Love Magnet

In exchange for a potential customer's email address, they opt-in to participate in a free 30-Day Green Smoothie Challenge.

4 Core Offer

The 30-Day Green Smoothie Challenge becomes a sales tool to introduce and promote our Fresh Start 21 meal plan them into place. Once you organize the way you run your business, you can start to find ways to eliminate friction, save time, and create more ease in your daily operations. All worthy benefits if you want to streamline your business and keep the humans in it happy.

My past client Allie Van Fossen is the founder of Body Mind Soul Studio, which offers virtual yoga classes. When she came to me, she knew that she had been exhausting her team and herself, running her business at a nonstop frenetic pace. Allie's team was desperate for processes and structure because her business lacked systems. It was time to prioritize getting her business organized on the back end. We embarked on a mission to systemize Allie's company that we called "The Great Cleanup."

During "The Great Cleanup," Allie identified what was causing the most problems in her business. There was no intentional planning for either short-term or long-term projects, so she implemented weekly meetings with her team, along with a quarterly planning process (I'll walk you through how you can create your own Quarterly Plan in the next chapter). Then she took the following Business Cleanup Steps, which you can also implement to prepare for systemizing your business.

BUSINESS CLEANUP STEPS

1. CREATE AN FAQ DOCUMENT. Every company with front-facing customers has questions that get asked repeatedly. Create a "Frequently Asked Questions" document that you can share with customers in an automated email or on your website. If you have a team who responds to customer inquiries, create a shared document inviting them to edit it. This will become a resource for your team with specific guidance on how to respond to emails, social media, and website comments using your brand's voice. Once Allie implemented an FAQ document,

she was able to avoid frequent interruptions from her team because everyone could simply refer to the time-saving document. A customer-facing version of your FAQ document can also be added to your company's product sales pages to help answer common concerns that may come up for customers during the buying process.

2. **CREATE TEMPLATES.** Take time to identify repeatable activities in your business and document the process (you can reference your Weekly Time Log in chapter 5 and the Roles and Responsibilities Review in chapter 6). Allie hosted online events a few times per year to promote her studio. Instead of creating new promotional graphics from scratch every time, she hired a designer to create graphic templates that they could reuse and update each year.

3. **CREATE COMMUNICATION GUIDELINES.** One of the biggest time wasters is ineffective communication with your team. As you expand your Dream Team, it's important to establish a communication process. This is a set of guidelines about when to use specific communication tools and how often you want to meet with your team. Before cleaning up her business, Allie would frequently text her team, meaning that conversations would get lost and it was hard to reference past decisions that had been made. During cleanup, she made the decision to upgrade her team's communication tools: They started using Slack, an instant messaging software, for internal real-time questions instead of texting or emailing. Emails were reserved for external communications with people outside the company. They started using Asana to manage project workflows and deadlines. And if something wasn't time sensitive, they'd discuss it at their weekly team meetings. Creating those systems stopped Allie from being the bottleneck in her business, and the team could do its job with ease and efficiency.

As you systemize and organize your business, keep the words of Simon Sinek in mind: "Systems and processes are essential to keep the crusade going, but they should not replace the crusade."[2] Don't get so caught up in making everything perfect and pristine on the back end that you lose sight of the heart of your business. Your systems are fluid and ever changing, so don't spend too much time on creating processes; use just enough to create more structure and flow.

If the idea of systemizing your business makes you want to bury your head in the sand, don't worry. You do not need to create systems by yourself; in fact, I wouldn't recommend it. You can invite your team to help document and cocreate systems together. And if you don't have a team, you may benefit from hiring a business coach who can help you prioritize what to do first.

How can you systemize your business to strengthen its foundation? Consider these questions and jot down your answers.

- What systems do you need to put into place for the business to feel like a well-oiled machine?
- What activities in your business do you repeat over and over again?
- What templates and processes could be created and documented?

Sustain: Build Rejuvenating Practices

Sustain is about working in a way that works for our lives, honoring our humanity and our vitality. In this book, we're learning a slower, more sustainable way of growing a business that doesn't compromise our health or relationships. As entrepreneurs, we are engaging with and helping people all the time—our customers, coworkers, partners, children, and friends. When we experience burnout, it isn't because we are working too much; it's because we care so much about all the people we hold near and dear.

But we also hit walls because we feel the constant need to be productive all the time. If you feel this way as the founder of your company, you are modeling that behavior, which then trickles down to your team. That's why it is so important to identify your priorities now and to advocate for adjustments that are needed to get the job done without exhausting yourself or your team.

Think of building your business as if you're running a marathon—not a sprint—with refueling stations along the way where you can stop, drink some water, and catch your breath. Know what rest looks like for you and your team. This takes some self-awareness of what replenishes you when you're running close to empty. And as the leader of the company, take the time to identify how to take care of your team through employee benefits, vacations, team-building activities, and appreciation in the workplace. Here are some sustainability practices to get your wheels turning on what's possible.

- LEARN YOUR BUSINESS CYCLES. Become clear about what your company needs to do to thrive, and identify the best time of year to make that happen. If you've been in business for a few years, you should be able to spot patterns for your high-output months. Inform your team about those all-hands-on-deck seasons. At Simple Green Smoothies, we launched our challenges four times per year. To support our seasonality, we knew that the months of January, April, July, and October would be our busiest times of the year. Before we hired people, we'd let them know that we'd need them to work nights and weekends during those times, when there would be more community engagement and more sales. We'd use the month prior to each challenge month to prep behind the scenes. And we'd use the month after the challenge to rest, reflect, and rejuvenate for the next launch cycle.

- BUILD IN TIME FOR REST. Avoid overcommitting yourself or your team. Schedule time after big bursts of energy to slow down and reset. My client Meri Cherry runs an art studio where she hosts a ten-week summer camp for kids. This is her busiest time of the year, with the studio buzzing full of children and parents picking up and dropping off throughout the day. After camp, Meri closes the studio to the public for two weeks, allowing her staff time to clean up the space before the rush of the fall season begins.

- DECIDE WHAT REFUELING LOOKS LIKE. Take time to find out what your employees value and care about when it comes to rest and rejuvenation. You can design this on a big-picture level through company benefits. For example, Martha Shaughnessy, the founder of The Key PR, says her company values mind, body, and life wellness. In addition to unlimited vacation time and flextime, one of its employee benefits is a company nonprofit donation match. You can also think about how the day-to-day work environment supports your team's well-being. Perks such as flextime and work-from-home opportunities are enticing, but make sure psychological safety and compassion are built into the company culture as well. Notice when your team is doing well, as opposed to communicating with them only when something goes wrong or needs to be fixed. Make time for celebration, play, and connection. This can happen through off-site retreats and fun events to create team bonding that may have nothing to do with growing the bottom line but everything to do with nurturing the whole person and deepening relationships.

Taking care of yourself and your team while growing your business is essential. You have the opportunity to build a company culture in which burnout is not an option. How can you build a business that will sustain you and your team for the long haul? Consider these questions and jot down your answers.

- What do your employees value and care about? What makes them feel appreciated at work?
- What's the seasonality of your business? When can you preschedule intentional rest time to prepare for big output seasons?
- How can you avoid overcommitting yourself or your team, so you stay focused on the big picture priorities?

○ ○ ○

Which part of your business needs the most attention right now? Let's review the Five S's to determine where to prioritize and focus:

- **You are in Share mode** if you need to strengthen business development opportunities, create new content, or establish your presence on a platform.
- **You are in Sell mode** if you need to generate more revenue, build out promotional materials, or create a new offer.
- **You are in Serve mode** if you need to create a better customer experience and improve the product fulfillment process.
- **You are in Systemize mode** if you need to focus on your team, operations, and processes behind the scenes.
- **You are always in Sustain mode** because sustainability is at the heart of Building with L.O.V.E.

Now that you've established a solid foundation for your business, it's time to create a tangible action plan, called your Quarterly Plan, in the next part of this book, "Visualize." Note which mode your company is in right now: Share, Sell, Serve, Systemize, or Sustain. You will want to bring that insight to building your Quarterly Plan in the next chapter.

she builds with

Focus.

8

Build Your Quarterly Plan

Without leaps of imagination, or
dreaming, we lose the excitement of
possibilities. Dreaming, after all, is a
form of planning.

—*Gloria Steinem*

Nature has four seasons, and business cycles are seasonal, too. As you walk through your neighborhood or observe a vegetable garden, pay attention to how trees change and plants grow throughout the year. In spring, new leaves sprout and seeds are planted; in summer, flowers are in full bloom and fruit ripens; in autumn, leaves change color and fall off the trees and the crops are harvested; in winter, branches and soil are bare and dormant. Now consider the seasons of your business. In spring, you set intentions for new growth; in summer, you celebrate, ideate, and collaborate with others; in autumn, you review the year's accomplishments, gauge your future capacity, and prepare to conserve time and resources; in winter, you slow down, rest and reflect, and plan for the upcoming season or quarter.

There will be exciting times in your business when you experience new growth and profit. However, don't make the mistake of thinking you should stay in those seasons forever. Thinking that we should exist in perpetual growth mode is a by-product of hustle culture, which glorifies an endless summer in our businesses. When we constantly operate in growth mode, we neglect crucial moments for reflecting, restructuring, and letting go of what is no longer working during slower periods, and we skip over the germination of new ideas. We must learn to honor the inevitable shifts and changes, the highs and lows, the fruit and the dormancy of our businesses. There will also be challenging seasons when we face unpredictable setbacks. These are life's storms forcing us to shift our priorities and borrow from the abundance of previous seasons to sustain us.

As with the seasons, the one thing you can count on when growing a business is change. As Gary Zukav, the author of *The Seat of the Soul*, says, "We cannot stop the winter or the summer from coming. We cannot stop the spring or the fall or make them other than they are. They are gifts from the universe that we cannot refuse. But we can choose what we will contribute to life when each arrives."[1] It's important to plan and prepare as much as you can while still honoring the changing seasons of your business. Our plans create a structure for implementing our Future Vision, ideas, and dreams. But we also need plans to give us the room and flexibility to grow, expand, and adapt to the constant shifts of the industries we are in, as well as the changing seasons of our personal lives.

The Quarterly Planning Method

The Quarterly Planning Method is the system I have developed for building my business with both strength and flexibility, allowing for growth and change in alignment with its natural seasons. Quarterly planning entails mapping out my projects and priorities every three months, as opposed to just once a year, which means I gain greater agility, I keep my business relevant, and I am better able to adjust to the changing tides of my industry and my life. Having a Quarterly Plan prevents me from getting stuck in one way of doing things and gives me the opportunity to reflect and correct course throughout the year. As I am a visionary woman with big ideas, this process also allows me to map out my vision in a way that is strategic and detail oriented without losing sight of the bigger picture.

I have used the Quarterly Planning Method in my own businesses for more than ten years, and I want you to know that if you do nothing else in this book but follow every step in this chapter, you will see immediate results. You will walk away from this chapter with more clarity about what projects to focus on next, which is the foundation you need to achieve your business goals. Quarterly planning is at the heart of the work that I do with my clients, whether in an online workshop that lasts two to three hours or in an inspiring location with a group of women for two to three days. This process is about stepping away from your day-to-day responsibilities and prioritizing the future of your business with a solid plan.

I structure my quarters based on the standard calendar (quarter one begins in January, quarter two begins in April, and so on). I have friends and clients who prefer to work with nature, moon cycles, and the changing seasons. The exact dates you choose do not matter. You can also plan around important events or milestones in your business, such as school breaks or the start and end of the fiscal year. Regardless of your exact start dates, I recommend planning for each quarter one to two weeks before the quarter begins. The essential thing is to create a new Quarterly Plan every three months. This process provides clarity about what you want your team to focus on, gives you confidence in the direction you ultimately choose, and often eliminates overwhelm.

The five steps of the Quarterly Planning Method, which we will explore in detail throughout this chapter, are:

1. SET YOUR INTENTION. Review your big-picture vision, connect to your "why," and define your desired outcome for the quarter.

2. CELEBRATE YOUR WINS. Take a step back to acknowledge your progress, so that you can plan with confidence instead of doubt.

3. FILL YOUR DREAM BANK. Unleash the ideas swirling around in your head and give them a home on paper to free up mental space.

4. DETERMINE YOUR CAPACITY. Identify how much time, energy, and resources you have available to work on growing your business over the next quarter.

5. CHOOSE YOUR VIPS (VERY IMPORTANT PROJECTS). Prioritize which of your Dream Bank ideas you will turn into VIPs that you will pursue over the next three months.

You don't need anything fancy to create your Quarterly Plan, just a quiet space and a pencil (because the plan is adjustable).* I recommend writing your Quarterly Plan out by hand first, because research shows that when we think about our goals and then write them down, we increase the chances that we will accomplish them (a psychological concept known as the *generation effect*).[2] If you want, you can transcribe your plan and then type it up on a computer so that it's more legible after you complete the quarterly planning process.

Throughout this chapter, I will use my past client Nikki Silvestri as a running case study for the Quarterly Planning Method. Nikki is the founder and CEO of Soil and Shadow, a consulting agency that supports nonprofit organizations, for-profit environmental businesses, and social entrepreneurs. Her career highlights have included making presentations at the White House, negotiating with the Environmental Protection Agency, acting as a board member

---

*   You can review the Quarterly Plan template in the appendix or download at shebuilds.com/resources.

of Greenpeace USA, and being named one of the Root's 100 Most Influential African Americans.

When Nikki and I started working together, she had been running Soil and Shadow for two years and was fourteen weeks pregnant with her first child. She was already suffering from burnout, unsure of how she would juggle her growing business along with a new baby. She was also moving toward becoming the primary income provider for her family because her husband needed to take a health sabbatical, which added to her stress. She knew she had to work in a new way and build her business differently. She felt that she needed to shift from being a solo consultant to running a consulting firm, with a team and scalable products, but she questioned whether she could make the transition successfully.

Nikki and I talked about how she could benefit from the organizational techniques of quarterly planning, how it might reduce her feeling of exhaustion, and how it would ultimately give her greater freedom and flexibility once her baby was born. Then we embarked on the first step of the Quarterly Planning Method by defining her intention for her business.

Set Your Intention

Before focusing on what you want to achieve, it's important to connect with the "why" behind your goals. It is all too easy to skip intention setting when creating a strategic plan for your business. But keep in mind that when we plan without intention, we end up chasing someone else's goals. We cross the finish line and achieve flashy wins, but still feel empty inside. We end up losing our passion that inspired us to start in the first place.

To create your business plan from a place of intention, begin by returning to the Future Vision you wrote in chapter 3 and reviewing it. Imagine your business and your life three years from now. Think about what success and fulfillment look and feel like. If you and I were sitting down, clinking glasses filled with champagne or kombucha, what would we be toasting? How do you see yourself making a difference in other people's lives? What would have to happen to make your vision a reality? What obstacles might arise to achieving your Future Vision? What would you need to do differently to overcome those obstacles?

Remember that setting an intention for your business is not about the goals you want to achieve; it's about who you want to be and how you want to feel while in pursuit of your vision. To set your intention, first take a moment to connect to your breath by taking three deep inhales and three deep exhales. Next, place your hands on your heart, and tune into the wisdom of your inner voice. Then grab your journal, and ask yourself the following questions.

- Who do I want to be?
- What do I want to be doing?
- Why do I want to be doing it?
- What does success mean to me?
- What is my intention?

As you ask each question, allow whatever bubbles up to emerge, and jot down your answers without self-editing.

As a model for the way that you might respond to these prompts, these were Nikki's responses.

- WHO DO I WANT TO BE? I want to be a thought leader whose work integrates leadership development and self-care practices with environmental advocacy.

- WHAT DO I WANT TO BE DOING? My team and I will build a community of two million individuals who are committed to working on themselves, their relationships, their communities, and society at large. I will have a small team within my business dedicated to projects that are specific to zero-waste economies and sustainable development.

- WHY DO I WANT TO BE DOING IT? Many times, the spiritual infrastructure holding our species and our planet together is forgotten as we debate environmental policy. My calling is to remind people of that spiritual infrastructure.

- WHAT DOES SUCCESS MEAN TO ME? Mental, emotional, spiritual, and physical health, and solid revenue from a thriving business that's aligned with my calling.

- WHAT IS MY INTENTION? I want to cultivate pleasure, joy, and expansion in my business in a way that's good for my family.

Your intention for your business is not carved in stone. It is fluid and powerful, and it will guide your actions and decisions over the next three months. If you'd like a meditation where I personally guide you through the intention-setting process, you can download the audio file at shebuilds.com/resources. Above all, keep in mind that there is no such thing as a perfect intention. Setting the purpose for your business is not about reaching the destination; it is about making a commitment to enjoy the process of creation and leaning in to your ambition without becoming attached to specific outcomes.

Celebrate Your Wins

As entrepreneurs, we are problem solvers, which is a strength. But it also means that we can get caught in a fix-it mentality, constantly asking ourselves what we could be doing differently or better. This inner dialogue keeps us from appreciating the progress we are making and using that gratitude as fuel. However, when we make a point of celebrating our wins, we gain momentum and build our self-confidence.

In my quarterly planning sessions with clients, I make it a priority to reflect on their past wins and celebrate them before we create a plan. I ask my clients to pause and think of personal and professional wins they have experienced over the past year or so in their businesses and in their lives in general. Those wins could be big things such as hiring new employees, booking new clients, or publishing a book, or they could be smaller, such as attending salsa classes or walking on the beach at sunrise. Some of my clients share a long list of celebrations every time we plan, and some struggle to come up with even one. But I don't let them skip this step. If a client is struggling with this, I coach her through it with compassion and patience.

Nikki and I went through this exercise at a planning retreat that I held in San Francisco. When the retreat began, Nikki expressed frustration that she hadn't accomplished all the goals she had set for her business over the past year, including while she was out on maternity leave. My personal coach, Rebecca McLoughlin, was our mindset mentor for the retreat, tasked with supporting the group through the emotions that would inevitably surface while they were making plans for their big dreams. During a group coaching session, Rebecca asked Nikki, "Have you taken your vitamin V lately?" Everyone looked at one another, puzzled. *What's vitamin V?* Rebecca told the room that "V" is for "validation," and that "taking your vitamin V" is code for validating yourself and celebrating your past successes as you work toward your goals.

In response to the question of whether she had been celebrating her wins, Nikki said, "I struggle with the fact that I haven't accomplished what I set out to in my business since I went on maternity leave. However, I'm recognizing that if I start out with certain goals and end up accomplishing things that weren't in the original plan, these are cause for celebration, too! I'm going to commit to celebrating those unanticipated accomplishments as victories now."

I then asked Nikki to share her top personal and professional wins over the past year. Here are a few she listed.

- Delivering the keynote address at the Ellen MacArthur Foundation's annual summit in London
- Getting a new coaching client at $4,000
- Doing long-term planning with her operations director and hiring a new project manager
- Meditating thirty minutes every day
- Being there for a close friend who has stage 4 cancer

Then I asked her, "What strengths did you tap into to create those wins?" Her response was "I had to be kind to my body, trusting, and in flow." Through this exercise, Nikki gained confidence and direction by reconnecting with the bold, powerful version of herself who had created those wins.

Now it's time to take inventory of your wins. Grab your journal, think back over the past year, and write down the five to ten accomplishments, both professional and personal, that you are most proud of. As you record your answers, play a feel-good song. (Songs I like to play at my retreats include "All I Do Is Win" by DJ Khaled, "Run the World (Girls)" by Beyoncé, and "Can't Hold Us" by Macklemore and Ryan Lewis.) Keep writing until the song is complete. To jog your memory, you can look back at photos on your phone, review your calendar, and scan through planners and journals where you document your life. Once you have your wins written down, reflect on the question that I asked Nikki: What strengths did you tap into to create those wins?

Jot down your response to this question without overthinking, and then reflect on that response. You have just taken a dose of vitamin V!

You will need to bring that energy and confidence into the next step, where you'll let your inner dreamer shine.

Fill Your Dream Bank

I first heard the term *blue-sky period* in a podcast interview of B. J. Novak by Tim Ferriss.[3] B. J., a writer and actor on the NBC sitcom *The Office*, shared how he and the other writers came up with story ideas. They started each season with a blue-sky period that lasted between two and four weeks, when everyone in the writers' room would brainstorm "what-if" scenarios. As B. J. told Tim, "There's no penalty, there's no 'Maybe we can't,' there's no, 'But this one conflicts with that one.'" The blue-sky period is about generating as many ideas as possible and not questioning, editing, or shutting any of them down. At the end of the period, the writers choose which ideas they love the most for the show.

I take a similar approach to strategic planning with my clients, which I call "filling your Dream Bank." This exercise is about giving yourself permission to dream up as many short- and long-term business ideas as possible without self-editing. You are going to brainstorm these ideas for your business by asking "What if?"

- What if I write a book?
- What if I create a new product?
- What if I hire an executive assistant?
- What if I host a company retreat in Hawai'i?
- What if I work four days per week?

Grab your journal, write "My Dream Bank" at the top of the page, and set a timer for ten minutes. Write down all of the possibilities that you might want to explore over the next three years in your business. Frame these possibilities as questions, beginning with "What if . . ." If you need help getting ideas for your Dream Bank flowing, review your

Future Vision from chapter 3. Or skim notes from conferences and events you've attended (if you're like me, all your ideas live in a never-ending "notes" file on your phone). Don't get stuck on how to make these things happen. Don't think about when you'll do each thing or how much it will cost. For now, I want you to dream without limits until your timer lets you know that ten minutes are up.

If you identify as a big dreamer, this process may feel soothing to your soul. If you struggle to generate ideas, this exercise might feel like a stretch, and that's okay; lean into the discomfort, and write without judgment or overthinking.

Once you've filled your Dream Bank with as many ideas as you can think of, it's time to do an exercise I call "3–2–1." This is where you will review your Dream Bank and decide when you want to pursue each of your ideas. This time, set a timer for five minutes and follow your intuition. For each item on your list, put a "3" next to it if it's something that you want to accomplish in the next three years or more. Put a "2" next to it if it's something that you want to accomplish in the next two years or so. And anything that you want to accomplish in the next twelve months gets a "1." If, when you review your list, you discover that you don't want to pursue one of your ideas, simply cross it out.

In her Dream Bank exercise, Nikki came up with the following list, which includes her "3–2–1" ratings.

- Revise team infrastructure and solidify team's work plan while on vacation. (1)
- Create a budget. (1)
- Find a new CRM database software to manage clients and their emails. (1)
- Create a communication plan that can be scheduled ahead of time. (2)
- Be a founding board member of family's drug treatment center. (3)

- Build personal brand and add 1,000 new email subscribers. (1)
- Promote online course. (1)
- Plan fun and relaxing vacations over the summer. (3)
- Plan kid-free getaways. (1)
- Host live event. (3)

Now that you have your Dream Bank list, which may look similar to Nikki's, set it aside. We'll return to it in the "Choose Your VIPs (Very Important Projects)" exercise, where all of your 1's will become the VIPs that you plan to pursue over the next twelve months.

But first, let's take stock of what you have time to pursue in your Quarterly Plan based on your capacity.

Determine Your Capacity

To decide which of the projects in your Dream Bank you plan to pursue, you will first need to determine your capacity, in the same way that you explored and defined your capacity in chapter 5. This starts with reviewing the current commitments in your calendar and assessing your energy levels while filling out the Quarterly Planning Worksheet.

As you can see, I have divided each of the four quarters by season. You are going to start by reviewing your current commitments over the next twelve months and marking them on your worksheet, divided into the following categories.

- **PERSONAL COMMITMENTS.** Think of upcoming vacations, holidays, birthdays, and special life events. Mark their dates in each quarter of your worksheet, knowing that during those times you will be out of the office and unlikely to have time to work on business projects.

- **SEASONAL COMMITMENTS.** Next, I want you to consider how your capacity and energy vary during certain times of year. Pay attention to events that repeat themselves each year, such as kids being out

QUARTERLY PLAN

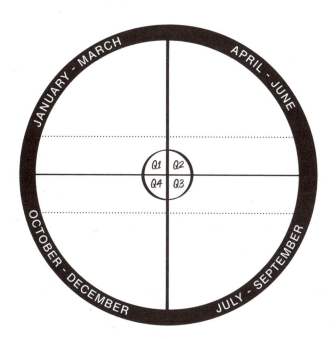

of school for the summer. This provides insight into when it makes sense to take on big projects in your business and when personal commitments will take precedence. Identify the seasons when your business has more sales and an increased influx of clients. Based on these patterns, block off time when it makes the most sense for you and your team to speed up, slow down, rest, and play.

- **BUSINESS COMMITMENTS.** Now you are going to add your business commitments over the next twelve months. Write down anything you have committed to including specific dates for business travel or offsite events. If you've done a Quarterly Plan in the past, review that plan and pull in projects that are still relevant. You'll update your plan every three months because you'll gain new insights and may want to adjust your plans accordingly.

Most of Nikki's clients were nonprofit organizations, many of them with a fiscal year-end on June 30. To honor her capacity and her company's natural rhythms, she knew that she would need to be available for the busy end-of-year period, and then she could plan for fun summer vacations in July and August, which were quieter months. She was also in her own personal season of growing a family. Once she became a mother, she wanted to work fifteen to twenty-five hours per week. Prior to having a child, she'd typically worked thirty to forty hours a week, so it would be a big adjustment. Her ambition and goals were still the same, but her time was not.

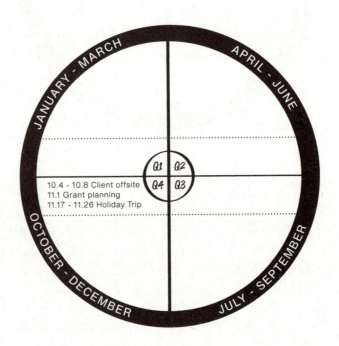

Nikki filled out Q4 (Quarter 4) with her out-of-office personal commitments, which included spending time with her baby and taking personal time off for the holidays (a seasonal commitment). Then she marked the business commitments that would take her out of the office, which included off-site client fulfillment. When she calculated the total personal and professional out-of-office days in Q4, she found that she would be taking a total of sixteen days away from in-office responsibilities. From October through December, Q4 has a total of ninety-two days, and when she subtracted sixteen out-of-office days and twenty-six weekend days, that left her with fifty days to devote to work projects. Writing those dates on her Quarterly Plan gave her a clear sense of what her capacity would look like at that time of year.

Choose Your VIPs (Very Important Projects)

In this last step of building your Quarterly Plan, you will decide on the VIPs you plan to pursue in your business. Grab your Dream Bank list, review your 1's, and follow these steps.

1. Decide which of your VIPs are most urgent. These are the projects you will mark in Q1 on your worksheet. You can place up to three VIPs in each quarter. If you have a very lean team or your team is only you, I'd recommend focusing on one VIP at a time.

2. Distribute your remaining 1's across Q2, Q3, and Q4. Since you'll do another Quarterly Plan in three months, these can be educated guesses. Look at the future quarters as placeholders for your ideas from your Dream Bank. Create some balance in how you spread out your projects. You don't want to overwhelm yourself with several challenging projects in a single quarter. Instead, aim for one VIP in each quarter that will take you out of your comfort zone and help you grow, and one VIP that's already in motion and you feel confident about completing this quarter. Then add one personal project, such as a kitchen renovation or a new fitness program or hobby you want to take up.

3. Fill out all four quarters, keeping in mind that certain projects, such as writing a book or designing a new website, may get carried over from one quarter to the next. Certain future quarters

might be empty, and that's okay, because you will gain more in-sight every three months.

It is common to front-load your priorities when you first do this exercise, overestimating what you can get done. But by the second or third time you do it, you will have a better sense of your true band-width and capacity. And if you're still stuck, here are some guide-lines and insights for helping you determine what should go on your Quarterly Plan.

- If you have four or more VIPs in a quarter, decide which one(s) you're willing to move into another quarter. Spread them out over the other three quarters.
- If you're unsure if you have the capacity to do a certain VIP and you really want to prioritize it, write it (in pencil) in that quarter, and see how it feels. You get to choose how full you want your schedule to be.

When Nikki reviewed her Dream Bank, she chose three 1's to add to the upcoming quarter as her VIPs:

1. Plan kid-free getaways.
2. Promote online course.
3. Create a budget.

Nikki marked each of those VIPs on her planning worksheet un-der Q4, then made her best guesses for placement of the remaining "1" VIPs, based on the order in which she thought she would want to pursue these projects. Following is an example of what her Quarterly Planning worksheet looked like for Q4.

Once your Quarterly Plan is filled out, consider whether you have any questions or uncertainties about pursuing your VIPs. Think

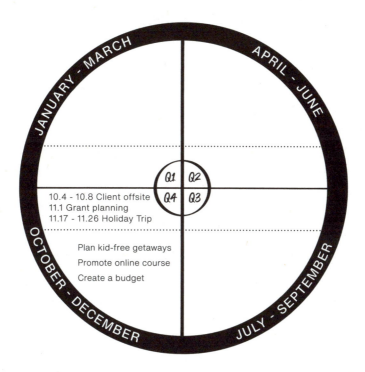

about where you might feel stuck or unclear or need feedback. Write those concerns down and take them to your coach, mastermind group, or another trusted member of your Support Squad. Sometimes, the act of writing a question down gets your gears turning and you will be able to come up with your own answers.

Once you've gotten the support you need on the questions you have and you're clear what your VIPs are for the next quarter, make them visible to yourself and your team. For my team, I list the current VIPs that we are focusing on at the top of our weekly team meeting agenda. Nikki writes her Quarterly Plan down on a large sheet of sticky paper and posts it in her home office so she can see it every day. To stay focused, we need visible cues to remind us of what our priorities are.

Once you have decided what your VIPs are and they are written on your Quarterly Plan, you have completed the last and final step.

Declare and Share

Now that you have a Quarterly Plan and a sense of what you want to focus on over the next three months, it's time to make some magic by speaking your dreams out loud and sharing and declaring your plan with someone else. Verbally share your VIPs with your accountability partner, your coach, or a trusted member of your team. It should be someone who understands what you are trying to accomplish and who will help you track your progress while holding you accountable for moving forward. By verbalizing your goals, you build more confidence about your plan and open more opportunities for support. The people you share with early on will also feel more invested in your journey and can help encourage you when you face setbacks and celebrate you when you reach the smaller milestones along the way. Here are some prompts to get you started.

1. Share what your business intention is for the next three months. This is the purpose for your plan.
2. Share what your business focus is for the upcoming quarter. These are your VIPs (Very Important Projects).
3. Share what actions you will commit to for the next quarter. These are the steps you plan to take (if you're not sure what steps to take yet, we'll cover that in the next chapter).

Looking Ahead

As you wrap up the quarterly planning process for the upcoming season, be sure to keep the goals of the process in mind: staying true to your intention and building sustainably. You may ultimately find that you have overestimated what you can accomplish in a single quarter, in a year, in three years. It's okay to change directions or extend your timeline. Let your Future Vision be your compass and your Quarterly Plan be your road map. You run your business; don't let your business run you.

When I checked in with Nikki a year after she began the quarterly planning process, she had seen life-changing results. She was working three to four hours a day and generating more revenue than she had while working thirty- to forty-hour weeks previously. That allowed her to spend time with her son, and it enabled her to shift her mindset from anxious and stressed to inspired and innovative. As of this writing, Nikki has two beautiful children, her marriage has never been better, and her business is set to hit mid-to-high six figures annually. Nikki continues to live the intention she set: "Cultivate pleasure, joy, and expansion in my business in a way that's good for my family."

After completing the quarterly planning process for the next quarter, give yourself some time to let your new plan settle. And whatever you do, don't try to rush any of the projects forward right away. Embrace the anti-hustle mindset. Dreaming and strategizing take a lot of energy, so you need to digest this work before jumping into implementation. Allow your nervous system to slow down. Unplug from work, go for a walk, take a bubble bath, watch a show, spend time with loved ones. Remember, you're a slow cooker. You have permission to build slowly and with intention.

When you clarify what you want, prioritize your focus, and declare your commitment, you solidify a plan that serves your greater vision. Now that you've identified your VIPs and have your Quarterly Plan in place, it's time to act on those ideas. In the next chapter, I'll walk you through how to create a Visionary Action Plan.

9

Take Visionary Action

When I dare to be powerful—to use
my strength in the service of my vision,
then it becomes less and less important
whether I am afraid.

—*Audre Lorde*

Now that you have identified your VIPs, the top projects that you'd like to focus on during the next quarter, you may feel one of two things:

1. EXCITED. "I got this! I'm so happy that I know what to focus on next. Woohoo!"
2. OVERWHELMED. "How am I going to get all of this done? Where do I even start? Help!"

There are two types of business owners. Some of us love making up a detailed action plan before getting any project started. Others, myself included, get overwhelmed by detailed plans and prefer to have the freedom to improvise on a daily basis. Whichever of these types you are—strategic type A planner or fly-by-the-seat-of-your-pants rebel—this chapter will provide you with a method for bringing your projects to completion.

In the previous chapter, you built your Quarterly Plan based on your Future Vision in chapter 3, and you identified the VIPs (Very Important Projects) you want to focus on over the next three months. But it's also important to think about what's happening now. My friend and member of my personal Support Squad, brand strategist Jen Kem, calls this WIN-WIN. What's now? What's next? You first figure out what you need to do now and then what you need to do next. Now it's time to bridge the gap between your big-picture vision and the steps it will take to realize your VIPs; this is what I call taking Visionary Action.

Visionary Action is about prioritizing the meaningful projects that will move you closer to your long-term dreams and goals. Meaningful projects are important to you, but they're not always urgent, and the challenge is keeping sight of the difference. As entrepreneurs, we deal with time-sensitive "emergencies" that demand our attention and an immediate response. But most of the time, putting those fires out is about moving someone else's goals forward, not our own.

When you're unclear about what projects really matter to you, other people's priorities will take center stage. Checking email frequently is one example of how this can happen. The constant flow of email puts us at the mercy of disruptive notifications and unsolicited pitches. Responding to our email distracts us from focusing on our important projects in favor of attending to other people's requests and priorities. We may also feel a sense of accomplishment when we tend to this kind of busywork, regardless of whether constant busyness is taking us where we want to go.

This is where your Visionary Action Plan comes in; it's a tool for keeping you focused on the big picture and moving you toward your goals, while giving you the ability to filter out the seemingly urgent nonemergencies that pop up throughout the day. If you were not checking and responding to other people's priorities all day, how could you use that time to work on your VIPs? That's what we'll explore in this chapter.

Your Three-Phase Visionary Action Plan

It is time to divide execution of each of your VIPs into a Visionary Action Plan with three distinct phases: Prepare, Produce, and Promote. Think of yourself as wearing a different hat and playing a different role for each of the three phases of this process. In phase one, you are the planner; in phase two, you are the producer; and in phase three, you are the promoter. Trying to play all of these roles at the same time can feel overwhelming, so you will need to dedicate a set amount of time to each phase.

As I mentioned in chapter 8, if you are running a business on your own, you will want to focus on one VIP per quarter. If you have a robust team, you can focus on up to three key projects at a time. Regardless of the number of VIPs you choose to pursue at once, you will need a separate Visionary Action Plan for each. However, to optimize resources and maximize efficiency, I'd recommend having your team prioritize one project per quarter so that everyone is pointing in the same direction.

Keep in mind that some VIPs may require more than one quarter, such as my website redesign, which took six months to complete, or writing this book, which took more than two years. Other VIPs require less time, such as launching the *Lead with Love* podcast for my coaching business, which took six weeks. I will use my podcast launch to illustrate the steps of creating a Visionary Action Plan later in this chapter.

The Prepare Phase (1 to 2 weeks)

This is usually the shortest phase of your Visionary Action Plan. In the Prepare phase, you will:

- Create a Project Brief to define what success looks like for your project (see the exercise below).
- Plot out the steps that you will need to take over the next quarter to realize your VIP.
- Decide on and finalize dates, and add them to your calendar or project management software (such as monday.com, Trello, or Asana).
- Identify what people, tools, and resources are needed to execute your project.
- Communicate with key players and determine their availability.

Create Your Project Brief

At the start of your Visionary Action Plan, a project can feel ambiguous. The Project Brief will serve to outline your overall goals, give structure to your idea, and inform each phase of completion. This also makes it easier for you to communicate your vision, along with your desired impact and results for a project, so that everyone on your team is on the same page. At the start of the Prepare phase, spend an hour creating a Project Brief by responding to these questions.

1. DEFINE DONE. What's your desired result? How will you know that the project is successful? What will you do to celebrate?

2. IDENTIFY THE RESOURCES NEEDED. How much time and money do you need to complete the project? Who can help you? Does this energize and excite you?

3. CREATE SPACE. How will you need to reconfigure your calendar to take action on the project? What do you need to say "No" to, eliminate, or take off your plate to make it possible?

4. IDENTIFY THREE KEY STEPS. For the Prepare phase of your project, write down three essential actions to move this phase forward. As you go through each phase, you'll add the essential actions you need in that phase as well.

The Produce Phase (2 to 6 weeks)

The main goal in this phase is to bring each of your VIPs from "thinking" to "doing." This is usually the longest phase of the process because it has so many moving parts. In this phase, you will:

- Update your Project Brief with your three essential actions for this phase.
- Ensure that everyone involved in a project knows what their responsibilities are and when items are due.
- Execute action items for this project, such as producing content, writing and recording key marketing materials, and updating online resources.
- Oversee vendors and contractors as needed (e.g., communicating with a designer to deliver graphics).

The Promote Phase (2 to 6 weeks)

This phase involves making the project public, such as promotion of your product or service to your customer base or sharing with your team if it's an internal project (e.g., creating company values). The time you spend on this phase will vary depending on how much time you want to dedicate to a promotional period. In this phase, depending on the nature of your VIP, you will want to:

- Update your Project Brief with your three essential actions for this phase.
- Publish and share marketing content with potential customers, including via social media posts, emails, product pages, brochures, and promotional outreach with partners.
- Host workshops, in-store events, or online webinars to promote your service or product.
- Share completed project with your team during a company meeting.

Revisit your Project Brief to stay on track and use as a guidepost throughout each phase. As you move through the phases, you'll keep reviewing your list to make sure that you're reaching your milestones. You can use a project management tool to keep track of your action items on a checklist that's shared with your team. If a new action item pops up that you hadn't anticipated, add it to the list.

My Visionary Action Plan:
Launching the *Lead with Love* Podcast

In late 2017, I decided that I wanted to implement a strategy in my coaching business to attract new clients. Talking comes easily to me, and I love having conversations with people, so launching a podcast seemed like the perfect VIP to build into my Quarterly Plan, one that would enable me to build trust with my audience and demonstrate my expertise as a coach.

Before mapping out my Visionary Action Plan for the podcast, I had to decide on a launch date and create a schedule, working backward from that date. My team and I chose February 14, Valentine's

Day, because it seemed like a memorable date and it fit our podcast title, *Lead with Love*. Then we created a three-phase Visionary Action Plan to give the project the momentum it needed to move from concept to completion. Here are the steps we mapped out.

The Prepare Phase: January 1–12 (2 weeks)
- Draft a Project Brief and determine our three essential actions for this phase: decide on podcast name, purchase website domain name, and discuss at next team meeting.
- Research and choose podcast editor.
- Announce February 14 date to my community on January 3.
- Send survey to subscribers and ask to submit topics.
- Draft ideas for podcast introduction script.
- Have meeting with designer about cover art.
- Watch Pat Flynn's Power-Up Podcasting course.
- Reach out to friends with podcasts to get tips.
- Brainstorm a list of potential guests.
- Brainstorm solo episode topics.
- Schedule interviews for January 22 to February 2.

The Produce Phase: January 15–February 9 (4 weeks)
- Add our three essential actions for this phase to our Project Brief: write email to invite guests on show, create podcast graphics for social media, and register podcast name.
- Research and purchase song for podcast introduction.
- Record podcast introduction and outro.
- Record first three episodes.
- Design and review cover art.
- Write newsletters; share behind the scenes; vote on cover art.
- Create podcast post template for website.
- Pick podcast keywords and categories.

- Write podcast and episode descriptions.
- Submit podcast to Apple, Google Play, Stitcher, and Spotify.

The Promote Phase: February 12–23 (2 weeks)
- Add our three essential actions for this phase to our Project Brief: be a guest on three podcast shows, post "new podcast coming soon" on social media, and email promotional graphics to guests to share with their audience.
- Update email signature line with podcast link.
- Publish podcast episode and promotional graphics on website.
- Submit *Lead with Love* to Podcast Directory.
- Post on social media: Facebook, Instagram, Livestream.
- Post in relevant online groups and communities.
- Update social media bios with link to podcast.
- Post promo audio teasers.
- Update website navigation bar with podcast category.
- Send email to subscribers announcing that the podcast is live.
- Reach out to friends and ask to share.

There were some ideas we brainstormed at the start of the project that we never moved forward on, especially in the promoting phase, including paying to boost social media posts that linked to podcast episodes; reviewing podcast survey responses from my community on what type of topics they'd like to hear; and hosting a free give-away to be coached by me in exchange for a podcast review. I created a list called "Future Action Items" where I parked those tasks to return to later, once the podcast was better established. Remember, it's okay to pace your ambition. You don't have to get everything done on your to-do list.

My *Lead with Love* podcast has truly enhanced my business as a vehicle for gaining new clients and nurturing my existing community, giving me the opportunity to interview *New York Times* bestselling authors, creative entrepreneurs, and business leaders. And by mapping out its execution with my Visionary Action Plan, I could identify a structure and next steps without being too rigid, making it also a joy to create.

Clearing Roadblocks in Your Visionary Action Plan

There are four common roadblocks that I have seen come up time and again for my clients and in my own business: overwhelm, distractions, low energy, and self-doubt. Over time, in my own work and in working with my clients, I have developed the following strategies to overcome them.

Strategies for Minimizing Overwhelm

The greatest perk of being your own boss: You control your time. The greatest pitfall of being your own boss: You control your time. Sometimes without the structure of working for a larger company and without a supervisor looking over your shoulder to make sure projects get done, it can be difficult to prioritize tasks. If you feel too busy to get your important work done, block off dedicated time in your calendar to focus on it, and protect that time. And if you feel as though you're always working and never have time for yourself or your loved ones, schedule time in your calendar for that, too. There are two ways I do this: (1) I set a time to unplug from work and use prescheduled bookends to start and end my day, and (2) I dedicate at least one day a week to my VIPs.

I've been guilty of letting my work overflow into my personal life. "Just one more email," I'd say to my husband. Creating prescheduled activities and agreements to bookend my days helps me unplug from my work. I first set up office hours from 9:00 a.m. to 3:00 p.m. Then, around 3:00 p.m., I schedule a walk 'n' talk with a friend, I pick my daughter up from school, or I attend a dance class. Knowing that I have an appointment and someone is relying on me to show up makes it easier for me to step away from my work. Additionally, although I have the ability to work from home, I choose to rent office space to help safeguard my focused work time and keep my family time sacred as well.

Once I'm home with my family in the evening, we have a tech-free policy starting at 7:00 p.m. on school nights (Sunday through Thursday). As a family, we have agreed to turn off all devices (TV, smartphones, laptops, iPads, etc.) and to keep them off until 9:00 p.m. That's when Zoe starts winding down for bed. Sometimes we make an exception to watch a show or movie together. The unstructured time away from devices allows us to rest, facilitates impromptu conversations between us, and leads to unplanned activities such as reading or playing a board game together. I also find that many of my best ideas and thoughts come when I'm screen free. As I like to tell my daughter, boredom leads to creativity.

You identified your VIPs in the last chapter, but there are also other, smaller life tasks competing for your attention that may be contributing to your feelings of overwhelm. To combat this feeling, I like to use a decision-making tool called the Eisenhower Matrix, popularized in the book *The 7 Habits of Highly Effective People* by Stephen Covey.[1] This model helps us identify what tasks and actions need to be dealt with when, by breaking them down into four categories:

- **TASKS THAT ARE URGENT AND IMPORTANT.** These tasks are time sensitive and need your immediate attention, such as filing taxes or enrolling your child in school by a certain date.

- TASKS THAT ARE IMPORTANT BUT NOT URGENT. These tasks are connected to your long-term goals that have a more fluid timeline, such as meditating daily or launching a podcast.

- TASKS THAT ARE UNIMPORTANT BUT URGENT. These tasks need to get done, but you don't need to be the one to do them, such as uploading and scheduling blog posts or cleaning your house.

- TASKS THAT ARE UNIMPORTANT AND NOT URGENT. These tasks distract you from your personal and professional goals, such as checking social media several times a day and watching an endless stream of adorable puppy videos.

The Eisenhower Matrix, called the "Urgent Important Matrix" in Stephen Covey's book, gives you a visual tool to see your workload and organize your priorities. You can use this tool to break down your tasks into four boxes so that you can prioritize what you should focus on first, what to schedule for later, what you should delegate to someone else, and what you can delete from your to-do list.

DO IT NOW Urgent and important (focus on first)	DEDICATE TIME TO IT Important and not urgent (schedule a time to do it)
DELEGATE IT Urgent and not important (find someone else or delay)	DELETE IT Not urgent and not important (eliminate from your list)

Your VIPs should go into the "Dedicate Time to It" quadrant, and you should identify a day of the week and time of day that will be your dedicated VIP time. I do the tasks for my quarterly VIPs on Wednesdays from 10:00 a.m. to 1:00 p.m., and I call this my

"WINSday" in my Weekly Workflow Plan. I block off this time in my calendar, and my team knows not to schedule calls or meetings on that day unless they are related to a priority project for that specific quarter. Is there a one- to four-hour time block in your calendar where you can schedule a time to work on your VIPs consistently? When will your Visionary Action Day be?

Now that you have your quarterly VIPs, you can align priorities and work on the most impactful tasks first. For the smaller, less urgent tasks, you can try a few things: wait until they become more urgent and important (these rise to the top when they really need to get done). Or decide they're not important and delete them from your list. Do a "brain sneeze" like the one I described in chapter 1 and batch similar tasks together. For example, you can batch calls to make all of your appointments, pay all of your bills, and run errands in town that are close in proximity. Estimate how much time it would take, and when you see an opening in your schedule, dedicate that time to addressing those tasks. Designate a "power hour," when you tackle a bunch of smaller tasks on a specific day each week or time of day. For me, Mondays and Fridays or late afternoons are great times to work on this.

Strategies for Eliminating Distractions

Anyone who works from home knows the temptation of the laundry that sits unfolded in the basket, taunting us. Or, when we're in the office, the constant pings of incoming text messages or the lure of social media, threatening to take us down a rabbit hole during the workday. We can't help but react to the barrage of information, invitations, and notifications constantly vying for our attention. These distractions eat away at our time and attention, leaving us with fewer resources to devote to our VIPs. Here are the strategies I use when I know that it's time to work, to prevent myself from being distracted by shiny objects.

- ELIMINATE TECH DISTRACTIONS. During designated deep work time on my VIPs, I set my phone to airplane mode (unless I am expecting a call) and turn off the vibration setting. I do this only when I've communicated with my husband that I'll be offline, so he can be available for a family emergency. I have also assigned special tones for calls and texts that come from my husband and daughter, so if they do contact me, I'll know it's them, and I can ignore any other alerts. Right before I start my deep work time, I also turn off all sounds and pop-up notifications on my laptop and set my status to "Do not disturb" for messaging programs such as Slack.

- USE THE POMODORO TECHNIQUE. In the late 1980s, an Italian student named Francesco Cirillo came up with a time management approach to help him study in college. He would focus on one task for twenty-five minutes and then take a five-minute break before starting his next focused work sprint. He called this the Pomodoro Technique, inspired by the tomato-shaped timer he used (*pomodoro* means "tomato" in Italian).[2] I follow this method when I have a task I need to focus on without interruptions. In fact, I have fourteen minutes left on my pomodoro as I type this sentence right now. If I'm in the flow, I can go three to four pomodoros before taking a break. Then I take a thirty-minute break to get up and dance to a song, refill my water bottle, eat a snack, or check my messages. I also find that writing down the time I start each pomodoro helps me see the visual progress of my work.

- WORK WITH AN ACCOUNTABILITY PARTNER. I set up coworking dates with friends. Social accountability is one of the most motivating and effective ways for me to get work done. I schedule coworking times for one to four hours where we meet on an online video conference or in person at a local café with good Wi-Fi.

We tell one another what we're working on, set the timer for a twenty-five-minute pomodoro to focus on that specific task, then take a break and share how we did.

- LISTEN TO MUSIC TO IMPROVE YOUR FOCUS. A group of studies, including on the "Mozart effect," has found that listening to music is an activity that stimulates both sides of the brain. This helps with memorizing and thinking through long-term solutions. I play instrumental music when I'm working, such as Japanese Lo-Fi, classical music, nature sounds, and HemiSync. If there are no words in it, the right side of my brain is entertained by the sounds while the left side of my brain moves a big project forward, since the left side's function processes new information sequentially.[3] Check out my "InstruMENTAL" song playlist at shebuilds.com/resources.

- ESTABLISH A WORKSPACE ROUTINE. When I'm at a desk doing creative work, I have certain rituals that tell me it is time to focus: I light a candle, pour myself a glass of water or hot tea, and turn on music. I also tidy my desk, throw away old sticky notes, close my fifteen-plus open computer tabs, and organize folders and documents on my laptop. I think better when I've decluttered my physical and digital space. Consider the workspace rituals that help you focus, and make them part of your routine.

Strategies for Increasing Your Energy

Have you ever read the same line in a book over and over? You look as though you're reading, but you're not able to process the words on the page. That happens to me when I'm working. There are times when I feel physically and mentally stuck. I struggle to concentrate. I stare at my computer screen, but nothing flows out of me. I'm like the spinning rainbow wheel on a Mac computer. When you see that wheel, you must force quit all the open apps, turn off your computer, and restart it. Here are a few things I try when I'm feeling stagnant and need a brain and body reboot.

I step away from my work, and I . . .

- Drink a glass of water or a green smoothie.
- Step outside and stand in the sun for five minutes or walk around the block for fifteen minutes.
- Play one to three songs and dance.
- Take a thirty-minute nap (I set a timer and charge my phone away from me, so I don't accidentally turn nap time into mindless scrolling time).
- Put my headphones on, play meditation music, close my eyes, and lie on the floor with my legs elevated on the couch.
- Take a shower and get dressed (on the days when I have rolled out of bed and started work in my pajamas).
- Have a long lunch without checking my phone.
- Call a friend or family member and do a walk 'n' talk for up to an hour.
- Watch a TV show that will make me laugh or cry (crying releases oxytocin, which helps ease both physical and emotional pain, and laughing produces serotonin, which stabilizes our mood and releases feel-good chemicals).[4]

There are also times of the month when some of us may have less energy due to hormone fluctuations or our menstrual cycles. If you know that this is the case for you, be gentle with yourself during those times. Don't force yourself to be productive if your body is screaming for rest.

Strategies for Overcoming Self-Doubt

Several years ago, I flew to the Dominican Republic, prepared to deliver a TEDx talk, and as my plane touched down, I found myself praying that I would get sick. TEDx Santo Domingo was covering all of my travel expenses, and I would have the opportunity to meet and mingle with a fascinating group of speakers. So why was I ready to throw in the towel before the event began?

I delivered my talk at 4:30 p.m., and an enormous sense of relief followed as I stepped off the stage. Then I went to the after-party with my new friends. Shortly after enjoying a good meal and getting ready to dance and celebrate, I had to go to the restroom. As in *go* go. I told my new friends and fellow speakers that I was sick and took a cab back to my hotel, hoping I wouldn't throw up on the way. I had manifested food poisoning one hour too late.

What was going on with me? The truth of the matter was that I had been battling self-doubt for several months leading up to my talk. I had hired a coach to help me prepare for my keynote presentation. But I struggled to finish my assignments to flesh out my talking points. This then led to my not having enough time to practice and memorize my speech. Eventually, I got the speech done and committed it to memory, but I was ignoring the emotional fears that immobilized me. My avoidance surrounding the event came from a deeper place.

When I delivered my TEDx talk, it was exactly one year after I had left Simple Green Smoothies. Looking back, I realize that I had tied a lot of my self-worth and self-confidence into being associated with that business because we had hundreds of thousands of followers across our social media channels. I hooked my self-worth to my net worth. I didn't give myself space to grieve and acknowledge the loss of a business that had been a part of my daily life for five years. Who was I if I wasn't in that business anymore? I had thoughts that kept me awake at night, such as: No one wants to hear from me. What if I can't build something as meaningful and successful? What if I'm a one-hit wonder? People cared about me only when I was with Simple Green Smoothies; now I'm a nobody.

Had I tended to the part of me that needed to be seen and heard and acknowledged that I was doing something scary, I might have been able to take the Visionary Action I needed to feel more confident when I gave my talk. And I might not have been forced to skip the after-party. At the time, I was compartmentalizing my emotional life and my strategic business projects, unaware of how one affected the other. Today, I understand that nothing happens in a vacuum and that business *is* personal. Now if I'm stuck in business, I'll bring that to both my life coach and therapist, and I'll work with them on the "Heart of the Question" prompts that I outline for you next. If you are struggling with self-doubt or emotional resistance, I recommend that you do the same.

Quiet Your Inner Critic and Get Unstuck

Oftentimes we get stuck because there are feelings or experiences that we haven't fully processed, and they're creating an emotional block or causing our inner critic to get very loud. If you feel blocked or mired in self-doubt as you work on your Visionary Action Plan, use the strategies below to get unstuck.

Sometimes writing out what you are struggling with and what actions you've already taken is enough to get your gears turning to come up with solutions on your own. Other times, especially when you are feeling overwhelmed, it helps to strategize with someone you trust: a coach, a team member, or mastermind partner. Respond to each of the prompts, either on your own in writing or verbally as you discuss them with a member in your Support Squad.

Heart of the Question Prompts

- CONTEXT. Share some background. Why is this project important to you professionally and personally? What actions have you taken so far to move it forward?

- CURRENT CHALLENGE. Where are you feeling stuck? What challenges or roadblocks are you facing? What do you feel fearful or uncertain about?

- DESIRED OUTCOME. What results do you hope to achieve in pursuing this opportunity? What's the big-picture goal you ultimately want to accomplish?

- REFLECTION. Based on your answers, what is the primary experience, emotion, or roadblock that is getting in the way of executing your Visionary Action Plan? What do you see as the best way of moving through this obstacle?

Now that you have mastered the three key phases of the Visionary Action Plan and cleared any roadblocks that may have gotten in the way, you can prioritize your VIPs with focus. Follow the plan you've built, but hold it lightly. Challenges that you hadn't planned for will come up. Ideas that you had mapped out in detail may go onto the back burner if you don't have the time and resources to complete them, and that's okay. Meet yourself with grace and compassion.

You can be highly committed to a project but unattached to the way it will unfold. As you prioritize ideas worth implementing, continue to take small, incremental steps to move your VIPs forward. Let your failures be building blocks of something greater, and allow detours to take you into surprising and rewarding territory.

10

Sometimes, you have to look
back in order to understand
the things that lie ahead.

—*Yvonne Woon*

One Saturday morning, my daughter, Zoe, and her friend Ava scurried ahead of my husband and me as we entered a building emblazoned with a bright orange Q-ZAR laser tag sign. Once inside, we smelled sweat and buttered popcorn, and a chaotic symphony of sounds blasted from each game.

"Ava, have you played laser tag before?" I asked.

"Yeah, I had my eighth birthday party here two years ago. 'Member, Zoe?" Zoe nodded her head.

"So you both know how to play, then?" I asked. "I haven't played laser tag in years, so I have no idea what I'm doing."

We made our way into the pregame briefing room, where we met our opponents. On the left side of the room, the orange team had already gathered, all tween and teen boys. We headed over to the green team's side, populated by inexperienced parents and their young kids looking for a fun weekend activity. The orange team was all elbows and high fives, and you could tell they had played this game many, many times. I saw their contorted smiles as they readied themselves to annihilate us with their unfair advantage. My competitive edge was awakened. *Not fair!*

"Welcome to Q-ZAR!" our laser tag host, also known as the marshal, greeted us and then played a video explaining the game's safety rules, which included:

No running.
No physical contact.
Hold laser with both hands.
No climbing.

The TV screen faded, and the marshal said, "All right, time to suit up! Enter the doors to your left, where you'll find your vests. Good luck!"

We awkwardly dressed in vests that resembled the heavy shoulder pads that football players drape over their upper bodies. The marshal ushered us out into the dark arena, and as theatrical fog-machine smoke filled the air and galactic sounds played through the overhead speakers, I saw the red numbers turn from 15:00 to 14:59. The game had started. The orange team huddled, then assembled themselves for battle, hiding strategically in nooks and crannies throughout the dark maze. Our green crew looked like lost mice in a labyrinth, dashing back and forth.

"What are we supposed to do? Does anyone know where to go?" I yelled above the laser beam sounds and high-pitched screams. I wanted to win. But I couldn't remember a thing the video or the marshal had said. I realized at that moment that it's one thing to know how to play the game and another thing to actually play it.

I stayed close to the people I knew: George, Zoe, and Ava. I tiptoed with my infrared laser gun cradled in my hands. Then I broke away from my crew and just went for it. My eyes targeted every orange vest sensor. I pulled my trigger multiple times and watched the LED lights flash at the speed of fireworks. Then the pack vibrated against my chest. I looked behind me. Two boys lasered in on my vest. I'd been shot. Vulnerable and exposed.

Dangit! I had to "energize" my gun to refuel.

I scooted-jogged-galloped to our home base. Because . . . *no running.* And I saw at least five of the orange team having a field day shooting at our home base.

Dangit! We had left our home base completely unprotected. We were supposed to defend our home base and simultaneously attack the opponents. We had done neither.

A loud siren went off. The red digital numbers on the clock went to zero. The game was over. We left the room panting. We followed the sound of tweens howling. The final scoreboard read:

ORANGE TEAM: 342
GREEN TEAM: 168

The orange team had more than double our score. Still reeling from the adrenaline rush, the four of us stepped outside for some fresh air.

"Well, that was fun! Y'all ready for the next round?" George asked.

Zoe, slumped over, replied, "Dad, we suck at this game. I don't want to play another round if we're just going to lose."

I said, "Remember, Zoe, we win, or we learn, but we never lose. Do your best and—"

"—forget the rest," Zoe finished my sentence with an eye roll.

Then I did what I knew best: I gathered our crew and came up with a new strategy based on what had just happened to prepare for our second game.

We went back inside for another round, and the teams were the same. We were again up against the rowdy group of tween boys. But this time, we huddled with our green team, and George, Zoe, Ava, and I presented our plan for earning more points faster. Some of our team players would have to sacrifice their individual points to protect the shooters who would attack the opponent's home base. We chose who would be the main shooter, suited up, and went back into the arena with an intentional strategy.

This time, our team stayed together, and we stuck to the new and improved plan. When the game was over, we exited the doors sweaty and out of breath. We rushed to the scoreboard. Zoe jumped up and down and exclaimed, "Oh, my gosh—we won!"

The Power of Reviewing, Reflecting, and Realigning

There is a popular entrepreneurial saying: "Slow down to speed up." Living by this expression means making better business decisions by pressing pause, reflecting on the past, and learning from mistakes in order to recalibrate for the future. This is what my family and I did when we played laser tag that Saturday morning. We stepped out of the arena, we *reviewed* what had happened and what had worked well for us, we *reflected* on what we wished had gone differently, and we *realigned* with a new strategy for improving our game. You can do the same. Reviewing, reflecting, and realigning creates a consistent feedback process in your business, enabling you to double down on what is working and eliminate what is not.

Professional athletes (and laser tag pros) not only make time for postgame rest and recovery, they also make time to review, reflect, and realign. They huddle on the field to adjust their game plan based on what is or isn't working. They sit down with their coaches for post-game review sessions where they watch the video and learn from past performance. Big corporate companies use a Strengths, Weaknesses,

Opportunities, and Threats (SWOT) analysis; some businesses call this an after-action review. The term I use for this review process is *Retrospective*, which was popularized by the author and consultant Norman Kerth in his book *Project Retrospectives: A Handbook for Team Reviews*.[1] The Latin root of "retrospective," *retrospectare*, means "to look back."

Use the Retrospective Process

As each season of your business draws to a close, it is important to pause and reevaluate before moving forward with your next phase. This means making your Retrospective a part of your quarterly planning process. Just as you create a future plan for your business every three months, look back at the previous quarter and do a Retrospective before you solidify your next Quarterly Plan. You can host your Retrospective a week or so before your quarterly planning session, or include it as part of the session itself. Either way, you will want to devote an hour to this exercise.

Whether you are a solopreneur or leading a team, schedule a Retrospective each quarter even if things are going smoothly. If a problem arises that needs an immediate resolution, don't wait for your Quarterly Review; gather your key players and use this process to strategize and problem solve. Here are some red flags that signal that it's time to do a Retrospective.

- You (or an employee) feel overwhelmed, burnt out, and depleted because you are doing everything in your company. Processes and projects stall out or slow down because there's a bottleneck (and sometimes you're it).
- You want to make updates in the company, such as redefining roles and responsibilities, reworking a product or service, or improving the customer experience.
- You've hit a plateau in revenue or growth. You're not getting traction using your current methods, and you can't pinpoint why.

- You're facing a roadblock because something specific went wrong in your company and you need a plan to resolve it before your next Quarterly Review. Some examples could be that a team member is not performing their role well, a project fails, or you lose a big client.

Begin your Retrospective by stating an intention (in the same way you did in chapter 8). Then discuss the following three questions with your team to identify obstacles, as well as opportunities for growth and improvement. Ask each question and set a timer for five minutes, asking everyone on your team to write down their answers. When the timer goes off, move on to the next question and repeat. After you've gone through all three questions, gather the answers and read them out loud so that everyone can hear the collective feedback.

- REVIEW: WHAT'S WORKING? Write down what you are doing well that's bringing you closer to achieving your vision.

- REFLECT: WHAT'S NOT WORKING? Write down where you're getting stuck or the approach or strategy that is no longer effective.

- REALIGN: WHAT MIGHT WE DO DIFFERENTLY? Write down what you could start doing that would improve effectiveness and efficiencies. Describe any changes you'd like to consider to help you move closer to your bigger dreams and goals.

Planning for the Future

Once you generate insights from answering the three questions, decide what actions you can take to improve your approach. Keep the following tips in mind.

What's working?

What's not working?

What might we do differently?

- You will want to schedule a Retrospective at least once a quarter, *before* you do any strategic planning. Identify a block of time (thirty to sixty minutes) that works for everyone on your team.
- If you are a team of one, you can follow this same process for assessing your individual performance.
- If you are doing a team Retrospective, circulate the topics you'll be reviewing ahead of the meeting via a shared agenda, giving team members the opportunity to add discussion topics and questions. This makes everyone feel invested in the process and better prepared to share honest feedback in a group setting.
- Schedule a follow-up meeting within two weeks after the end of the Retrospective to check in on progress made. This helps you see if anyone needs additional support or if there is a potential roadblock that might hinder your plan from moving forward.

If this is the first time that you have implemented a review process in your company, it might be beneficial to bring in an outside coach or consultant to moderate. This might be especially helpful if there is conflict or tension between employees and the leadership team, as having a coach facilitate the exercise enables everyone to feel safe sharing without fear of backlash. The coach can then create a summary report and share the results anonymously. If you opt not to bring in a coach or consultant, I recommend that you designate a member of your team to guide the process and keep track of time.

The Retrospective in Action

A Retrospective empowers you and your team members to be thinkers, not just doers; to be strategic, rather than reactive. Many founders I've worked with say they don't have enough strategic thinkers on their teams. I tell them that this is because we haven't modeled what strategic thinking looks like or cultivated this quality in our teams. You'll be amazed at what you can accomplish when you give people the opportunity to think about what's working and what's not and to suggest potential adjustments to your company's way of operating.

There are three ways to use a Retrospective:

1. Review your whole business.
2. Review a process, project, or product.
3. Review an individual's performance.

Here are some real-world examples in each category that you can use as models for conducting a Retrospective within your business.

Review Your Whole Business

Martha Shaughnessy is the founder of The Key PR (the client I mentioned in chapter 7 who provides unlimited vacations and flextime benefits to her team). Her agency serves mostly early-stage tech companies and has grossed millions of dollars each year while taking no outside funding. She manages all of this while prioritizing being a parent of school-age children.

Martha was committed to building a company culture that could sustain itself for the long haul. One year into business, the company had a team of ten full-time employees, and Martha wanted to be more intentional in how she built her team. She also wanted more efficiency and optimization, including how tasks were assigned and clients were onboarded. She hired me to support her leadership, middle management, and junior teams to identify how The Key could reach its goals and grow while being openhearted and human.

Martha wanted the middle management and junior teams to feel more empowered in their personal development and leadership, so I partnered with one of my previous clients, La'Kita Williams at CoCreate Work, since she had a background in organizational design. Together we led the employees of The Key through a companywide Retrospective, summarizing the consistent patterns we saw and identifying action steps for moving forward. Below are "Review, Reflect, Realign" goals that her team identified:

Review: What's working?
- The team is happy and grateful for the new office space
- Flexible work hours and unlimited vacation policy
- Senior-level attention for all clients and treat as people first (acknowledge birthdays, send cards)
- Business development and increased visibility in the market

Reflect: What's not working?

- Lack of clarity on expectations, goals, and role responsibilities
- Not enough time for ideation, time spent putting out fires
- Lack of teaching, coaching, and positive feedback
- No clear growth path in the company and no process for up-leveling team members

Realign: What might we do differently?

- Establish shared company agreements on how we approach our work
- Develop set meetings that are value added (all hands, stand up, 1:1's)
- All principals provide open hours to ask questions and provide mentorship
- Structure a review process of performance for all team members including positive feedback

The Action Plan

Here are the top action steps we came up with for The Key.

- CULTURE CHANGES. Develop guiding values for The Key that indicate who to hire and how to move people into and out of roles with more intention.

- WORKLOAD. Clarify role expectations and responsibilities, identify how many team members are needed, and plan for critical hiring areas.

- CLIENT PARTNERSHIPS. Review how the client experience starts, how account teams interact, and how to ensure that everyone can access important information and is looped in as needed.

- EMPLOYEE DEVELOPMENT. Create employee-based trainings on being entrepreneurial, taking ownership for individual career growth, and developing key skills and strengths.

Martha committed to doing periodic Retrospective Reviews across her business to identify what was working and making an implementation plan to bring those ideas forward. And she saw immediate results: in 2021, The Key was named number 51 on the *San Francisco Business Times'* Top 100 Fastest Growing Private Companies list. Even though her team had doubled in size since the time of the first Retrospective and the company's revenue had increased, she wanted to "focus on building better versus bigger." Throughout the COVID-19 pandemic and the "Great Resignation" that followed, The Key was able to avoid laying employees off while prioritizing stability and well-being over profit margin.

Once Martha took a step back and looked at the bigger picture of how her business was doing, she was able to be more thoughtful about the direction she was moving in and correct course. This also meant improving her team's work environment on a day-to-day basis.

Review a Process, Project, or Product

You can also use the Retrospective questions when you want to focus on one specific area of your business. Meggan Hill, the founder of Culinary Hill (she made the Intentional Trade-Off in chapter 2), grew her team from a one-woman food blog to a team of four full-time employees and several creative contractors. I met with her team every three months to guide them through a Retrospective Review and create a Quarterly Plan.

At the time of our first Retrospective, Meggan's team was experiencing growing pains with communication and workflow. Tasks were being assigned in a variety of places, from long email threads to personal text messages sent during off-hours. It was a challenge to remember who said what and where. That chaotic process made it challenging for Meggan's team to stay focused on the tasks at hand during work hours and prioritize what to work on next.

We began by setting an intention for Meggan's team: focus on improving team communications and workflow, brainstorm ideas, and stay curious. Then we asked the three big questions, and each team member contributed responses.

Review: What's working?
- Weekly editorial calls on Mondays
- Each team member keeping an "ideas" list over the weekend to bring up on the next team meeting call
- Using project management software instead of text and email

Reflect: What's not working?
- Content writer on the team emailing frequently with questions about their tasks
- Meggan texting the team at odd hours and on weekends
- Using their project management software for recipe-testing communication and getting lost in the process

Realign: What might we do differently?
- Add content writer to project management software, so she can add specific tasks there instead of emailing
- Designate a place for Meggan to leave random thoughts for her team, to avoid interrupting the team's work during office hours and disturbing their weekends
- All managing supervisors could be crystal clear when giving direction and not assume someone on the team knows what to do

The Action Plan

- Meggan assigned a specific person on the team to onboard the content writer on their project management software to effectively communicate tasks and deadlines.
- Set up instant messaging software (like Slack) during working hours and created channels to organize conversations such as #lovenotes, #testkitchen, and a #idea channel for Meggan to share her random thoughts and ideas for future meetings.
- A team member was added to the weekly content-planning meeting, so that person could be consistently informed about the projects the others were involved in.

Ultimately, Meggan's team reported that they were relieved and energized to have this action plan and to feel more settled in their roles. As we can see from the example of Meggan's team, a consistent review process in the form of a Retrospective supports team building, collaboration, and engagement, too.

Review an Individual's Performance

From macro to micro, you can also zoom in and use the three questions to review how a specific member of your team is performing. This is especially helpful if you've done the Roles and Responsibilities Review in chapter 6 and you see that a person's role needs to expand or shift.

Art studio founder Meri Cherry (in chapter 7 I shared that she closes her space to the public to build in time for rest) had a growing team, and one of her studio teachers, Trinity,* was stepping into the role of studio manager. However, as Trinity took on management responsibilities, she became overwhelmed by all that she had to juggle. Trinity was the one at the studio with all the answers, but she was

---

* The employee's name has been changed to protect her privacy.

having trouble keeping up, and she was constantly stressed by the fear of letting the team down. Meri reached out to me to schedule a coaching session with her and Trinity. Our intention was to figure out if the manager role was a good fit for Trinity and, if so, identify what needed to change to make it work.

We began by listing the responsibilities of Trinity's role, which included overseeing special projects and keeping staff on track, hiring and training new teachers, supporting operations and communication, developing curriculum, and teaching five classes a week. Her plate was full. Then we asked the three Retrospective questions, and Trinity shared her answers.

Review: What's working?
- Proud of the finished products for art kits and downloadable art classes
- Hiring and training new art teachers—they all feel supported, curriculum is good, and Trinity enjoys doing it
- Trinity has a good relationship with other team members to bounce things off and loves seeing the bigger picture

Reflect: What's not working?
- Juggling vendors, fitting into teacher's schedules, and reshoots for art kit and video production
- Lack of communication with art kit production which also includes needing Meri's review and approval
- Not enough time to create curriculum, train new hires, and teach when managing all the teachers' schedules

Realign: What might we do differently?
- Explore more lead time and create an SOP [standard operating procedure] for art kit and video production, and hand off to someone else on the team to manage

- Schedule production meetings with Meri upfront to get on the same page and receive feedback on new ideas, clarify priorities, and discuss team's capacity when making last-minute changes
- Create studio manager job description with clear roles and responsibilities, delegate art classes to other teachers

The Action Plan

- Create SOP timeline with another team member for art kit and video production, use project management tool to oversee tasks and deadlines
- Have teachers complete roles and responsibilities questionnaire and Trinity schedule one-to-one meetings to identify opportunities and streamline processes
- Meri and Trinity clarify studio manager job description and discuss pay

At the end of the Retrospective, we clarified the key responsibilities of the on-site studio manager so that Trinity knew what was expected of her. She was now the point person for training and supporting teachers and communicating with families. She also identified some tasks she was doing that did not fit into the new role, such as overseeing video production, handling payroll, and managing birthdays and events. Based on the clarity achieved, Meri and Trinity were able to define the job description for the studio manager. They also came up with a manageable weekly schedule for Trinity so she could get to a place where she no longer felt overwhelmed.

Instead of waiting until you or someone on your team hits a wall and wants to throw in the towel and quit, be proactive like Meri and Trinity were and use this process to support you.

Doing a Retrospective at Home

You can also apply the Retrospective process to your personal life. Once a year, my husband and I do a couple's retreat, where we rent a cozy cabin in Lake Tahoe for a long weekend to dream and plan for our family's year ahead. At these yearly retreats, we do a version of the Retrospective for our personal lives, and we do personal versions of the "Imagine Your Next-Level Vision" and "Quarterly Planning" exercises (in chapters 2 and 8).

Once we get home, we keep the celebrations and reflections going. As I've mentioned, we schedule a weekly meeting together, usually over a meal or in a hot tub. It's an opportunity for us to stay connected and identify ways we can support each other's personal goals and dreams. We also discuss the practical stuff, such as upcoming appointments, financial review, and meal planning. We use the Retrospective process for these meetings too. Here's how we organize our conversations.

- REVIEW: WHAT'S WORKING? We appreciate one another and share what we noticed the other person did over the past week: "I noticed you took the trash out without me asking" or "Thank you for taking the dog for a walk so I could sleep in." We note what we accomplished in the past week that we're personally proud of: "I finished writing chapter 10 and sent it to my editor" or "I ran three miles this morning when I didn't feel like it."

- REFLECT: WHAT'S NOT WORKING? This is an opportunity for both of us to communicate where we need more support. For example, George might mention that we're spending too much time on our devices and should trade screen time for family time. I oversee our end-of-year taxes, and in the past, I've made a request for George to hire a bookkeeper for his business to make our personal tax filings easier.

- **REALIGN: WHAT MIGHT WE DO DIFFERENTLY?** We then look at our calendars and start to make decisions for our week based on what we've learned from the previous week. This includes updating screen time agreements, hiring outside support, and communicating upcoming travel and commitments we made with friends. We also apply the three Retrospective questions to specific issues we may be working on, such as homeschooling our daughter.

o o o

Now that you understand the power of using the Retrospective process to review, reflect, and realign, you can transform setbacks into growth opportunities. A failure becomes feedback, losses become lessons, and mistakes become momentum. What was once an obstacle is now an open invitation to grow and deepen your roots. You have a solid foundation to build on. In the last part of this book, "Expand," you will learn a holistic approach for scaling up your business (and your life) that feels sustainable. It's time to pull together all the pieces you've created up to this point and follow the path that was designed uniquely by and for you.

she builds with

strength.

11

Refill Your Well

Even though you have learned
the skill of running on empty, now
is the time to learn the art of
breathing deep all over again.

—*Morgan Harper Nichols,* All Along You Were Blooming

In the first three parts of this book—"Lead," "Optimize," and
"Visualize"—you built a solid foundation that will enable you not
only to survive but to thrive, moving you toward sustainable growth
and expansion. With this new clarity, you can be more calm, centered, and confident about making decisions that will take your business and your life to the next level, on your terms. None of this will
be possible, however, unless you are willing to invest in your most
important asset: *you.*

There's a saying, "You can't pour from an empty cup," meaning that if we want to give of ourselves and serve others (our family, friends, coworkers, community, and clients), we must first have
something to give and "pour." You can't give what you don't have.
As entrepreneurs, sustaining our businesses and our families at the
same time, our "cup" must hold a lot; it's closer in size to a well. And
it's essential that we don't let our well run dry. When we're drained,

we become disengaged and unmotivated, and we're not fun to be around at work or at home. Everyone else gets the short end of the stick when we're mentally and physically exhausted. We need to figure out how to fill our well and keep it full. And the first step toward doing that involves redefining self-care in a holistic way that considers our whole lives.

Rethinking Self-Care

Self-care has become a trendy term equated with bubble baths, facials, and massages, which often leads us to minimize its importance. But true self-care is about much more than spa treatments; it's about being brave enough to advocate for our own physical, mental, and emotional needs, and it is an essential part of filling our well. The way in which we practice self-care is unique to each of us; depending on what we know, it can energize or drain us. For some of us, self-care can mean spending a few hours alone, lost in a book; for others, it might mean meeting a friend for coffee to rejuvenate.

WHAT FILLS YOUR WELL?

It's important to identify your self-care style so that as soon as you start to feel your well running dry, you know how to replenish. True self-care is about honoring your unique needs and reconnecting with your mind, body, and soul. What recharges your spirit and moves you from feeling exhausted to energized? What grounds you and makes you feel calm, centered, and alive? Review the following categories to determine your self-care style. You may be drawn to one, or you may recognize yourself as a combination of two, three, or more. You can also pull ideas and inspiration from each category depending on what is going on in your life.

THE SOLO LOUNGER. You love being alone with your thoughts, and your battery is easily drained by conversations and people (even if you love them). You need unstructured downtime away from stimulation and action to recharge your batteries. You may lean toward solo self-care activities such as hiding away with a good book, journaling, or watching several episodes of your favorite show from a cozy couch. Your dream is checking yourself into a hotel for a night with a "Do not disturb" sign on the door. If you know that this is your style, practice saying "No," avoid overcommitting yourself, and schedule activities in your calendar with plenty of time in between for breaks.

 THE INSPIRED ARTIST. You don't feel fully alive unless you are connected to creativity in some way. You crave artistic inspiration to awaken your spirit. You are inspired by activities such as going to live concerts, plays, poetry readings, and musicals; visiting museums or galleries; or taking a writing or painting class. Carry a notebook around with you to catch inspiration when it strikes. Make time to engage with art through reading literature, watching movies, and listening to music. Prioritize attending events and shows at least once a month to keep the muse fed.

THE SOCIAL BUTTERFLY. You thrive when you share experiences with other people, and too much solo time may leave you feeling lonely or drained. Conversations and interactions with other inspiring humans leave you feeling ready to take on the world. Invite the people who light you up to join your everyday adventures or even simple errands. Keep in mind that even if you are a Social Butterfly, you still need downtime. As much as connecting with others fuels you, enjoy restorative activities such as a spa day or a hike with a friend where you can chat but your body and spirit can rest for a little bit, too.

THE TIDYING FAIRY. You are inspired by your surrounding environment and feel most at peace when your space is clean and organized. Your physical space can reflect what's happening inside your mind. So if it's messy, you can feel unsettled and restless. Prioritize a few minutes each day to tidy one area of your home. And when you're done with your workday, put extra care into resetting your desk for your next work session. Whether you're at your office or at home, give yourself permission to declutter as an act of self-care. Every few months, spend several hours decluttering a whole area, leaving only things that spark joy.

THE NATURE SEEKER. You feel most alive when you are outdoors, and you feel drained and disconnected from the world around you when you face screens more than you do the sun. You feel a sense of peace, awe, and wonder when you are surrounded by trees, high in the mountains, or near bodies of water such as a lake or ocean. Make nature a part of your routine by scheduling daily or weekly walks, relaxing on a bench after a hike, or laying out a blanket on which to sit and listen to the birds chirping, the wind blowing, and the leaves rustling. Do activities that immerse you in nature.

People sometimes say "Only the strong survive," but I believe that those who nurture themselves survive and thrive. Now that you have cultivated awareness of your self-care style and what replenishes you, let's explore four ways you can sustain yourself as both a business leader and a whole person.

1. Celebrate yourself.
2. Listen to your body.
3. Make time for connection and play.
4. Tend to your emotions and protect your boundaries.

Let's discuss some strategies for filling your well in each of these four categories.

Celebrate Yourself

In chapter 8, I told you that my life coach, Rebecca McLoughlin, talks about the importance of taking "vitamin V" to validate and celebrate our successes. Taking vitamin V regularly is essential, and it is especially important to take an extra dose when you notice that your reserves are low (in the same way you might add elderberry syrup to an immune-boosting smoothie when you feel a cold coming on).

A few years into running Simple Green Smoothies, I learned the importance of vitamin V firsthand. Running an online business meant that I was constantly comparing myself to the competition, measuring my progress based on what other businesses were up to on social media and how many followers they had versus our following. I became obsessed with the metrics, and I continually moved the finish line. First, my goal was to reach my enough number, which was $180,000 per year. Then, once I reached my desired income goal, I didn't pause to celebrate the accomplishment; I just moved the goalpost forward to multiple six figures, then to seven figures. Those success markers were based on what others were doing rather than my own internal goals, and chasing numbers constantly left me feeling inadequate. I fell out of love with my business because my heart wasn't driven by numbers. Yet I was the one leading the charge to grow the company faster, because that's what society defines as "success."

Eventually, after leaving Simple Green Smoothies, I recognized that to sustain myself as an entrepreneur, I would need to keep my well from running dry by celebrating all of my wins (not just business achievements). That is why today, as a regular part of my quarterly planning process, I take a moment to celebrate my wins both personally and professionally, and document my progress before setting new goals. As soon as I started doing this, my relationship with goal setting changed. I no longer felt that I was chasing numbers; I fell more in love with the process than with the outcome.

Think about the times when you have felt that your self-worth was tied to your net worth. When have you relied too heavily on recognition and validation by the outside world? If you are going to adopt an anti-hustle mindset, you must relight the spark from the inside. It doesn't matter how much money you are making or how many followers you have; if the work you are doing doesn't nourish you, sooner or later you will burn out.

What if we were to stop looking for external validation and instead fill ourselves with vitamin V? What if we were to start making decisions from our hearts even if they didn't always make sense on paper? We could follow Rumi's wisdom "Let yourself be silently drawn by the strange pull of what you really love. It will not lead you astray."

My coach, Rebecca, taught me the following practice for making celebrations more tangible. She recommends creating a "vitamin V jar" as a visual representation of how far you've come. Start with an empty Mason jar, and every time you do something that you're proud of, add a pebble to the jar; watch it fill up. You could also write down each of the wins that you achieve on a slip of paper, put them into your jar, and then reread them at the end of the year.

A celebration does not have to be for an external accomplishment that someone can see (more money, more followers, more media mentions); it can also be for the intangible qualities of your growth as a person. It's the invisible transformation that's happening on the inside when you become a more authentic version of yourself. A way to get closer to these unseen characteristics is to write down the accomplishments that you are most proud of *and* the challenges that you've faced. Then ask yourself: What strengths did I draw on to create those wins? Who was I being to overcome those setbacks? Answers I've written in the past in response to these questions included: "I was being bold and unapologetic." "I was taking care of myself." "I was open to having courageous conversations."

Practicing gratitude is another essential part of celebrating ourselves. Studies show that those who keep a gratitude journal, for example, tend to feel better about their lives, are more enthusiastic about the future, and are more likely to make progress toward goals that are important to them.[1] If you're a Solo Lounger, some alone time at a park or library would be the perfect time to grab a pen and write down what you're grateful for.

Think about who and what supported your big and small wins—the people and the things in your life that sustain, support, and nourish you. Find ways to reward yourself that align with your primary self-care style. If you're a Social Butterfly, invite a group of friends for dinner and toast the special occasion (or throw yourself a "Business Shower" to celebrate a big milestone in your company). If you're an Inspired Artist, go see your favorite band or purchase an art print to hang on your wall. If you're a Tidying Fairy, get rid of some old items that no longer bring you joy and purchase beautiful office supplies. And if you're a Nature Seeker, spend a weekend in a cabin in the woods to fill your spirit.

You can also be grateful for the difficult and challenging times in your life and the lessons that accompanied them. Slow down, acknowledge yourself, and thank others who are supporting you on your journey, especially in difficult seasons. It's so easy to praise others for their accomplishments; make sure you do the same for yourself. Be your biggest cheerleader and a compassionate friend to yourself when you fall. When you allow yourself to express gratitude and celebrate how far you've come even during life's chaotic storms, you build the strength, resilience, and fortitude to keep moving forward with love.

Listen to Your Body

Our bodies send us signals when we are not adequately caring for ourselves, telling us that something needs to change. That was what happened to the American gymnast Simone Biles, who has a total of thirty-two Olympic and World Championship medals.[2] She disrupted the Beijing Olympics in 2021 by advocating for her own body and mental health. In the middle of the vault competition, she experienced the "twisties," where she didn't know which way was up or down. As soon as she landed, she told her coach "I cannot continue" and withdrew from the team competition. In a later interview, she was asked if she would go back and change anything, and she said, "No . . . I learned a lot about myself—courage, resilience, how to say no and speak up for yourself."[3] She showed her resilience when she came back a few days later to compete in the balance beam finals, where she won a bronze medal. She gave herself permission to rest, not quit.[4]

Give yourself permission to rest, not quit.

Listen to your body when it's telling you that it needs a break. Don't ignore its signals and attempt to power through at the cost of your well-being. When you've been at your computer for an extended period and your shoulders start to tense, your eyes are glazing over, or you're feeling early signs of a headache, don't ignore these signals and try to push through. Listen to what your body is telling you: *It's time for a break.* Then give yourself a quick recharge based on your self-care style. Here are a few methods that I use and that I highly recommend trying for yourself.

- I put on my "Feelin' myself" playlist and have a ten-minute solo dance party before returning to work.
- I step outside and stand in the sun for five minutes to soak up some vitamin D.
- I set a timer for twenty minutes and take a power nap. Even if I don't fall asleep, taking a break from working helps.

If you're a Solo Lounger, get quiet enough to hear your body's needs. Find a video you love and do a slow stretch in the privacy of your home in the early morning or late at night when everyone else is asleep. If you're an Inspired Artist, explore activities that get you out of your head and into your body, such as taking an improv class or taking a walk around a neighborhood that has street art and murals. If you're a Social Butterfly, find ways to be active with friends, sign up for a sports league, or invite friends for an outdoor boot camp at your local park. If you're a Tidying Fairy, you might tune in to your body best when your kitchen cabinets, drawers, and fridge are in order. Take some time to make sure your kitchen feels organized for a fresh start. If you're a Nature Seeker and live in a climate with changing seasons, find ways to immerse your body in the elements. Take a polar dip in the lake in the winter, sunbathe in the summer, take long walks to observe fall leaves, and hike a special trail to see blooming flowers in spring.

In addition to taking a break when your body rebels, you can build self-care time into your schedule. Here are a few things you can do.

- **TAKE LUNCH BREAKS.** If you don't already have a lunch time scheduled in your work calendar, add that right away and communicate with your team, especially with whoever is your calendar bodyguard. I have a one-hour time block for lunch scheduled in my calendar at 1:00 p.m., Monday to Friday. That way my team does not schedule any calls or appointments during that time. I also step away from my desk and phone while I eat—sometimes to a different area in my office, onto my balcony for fresh air, or out to a lunch date with my husband or a friend.

- **SCHEDULE BUFFER TIME.** Look at your Weekly Time Log, which you completed in chapter 5. Is there any place where you'd like more time to transition from one activity to the next? Update your Weekly Workflow Plan to include space for that in your calendar. I used to have client calls scheduled back to back, which left me rushing from one call to the next without even having time for a quick bio break. I was always running behind for the next call. At first I scheduled calls for fifty minutes instead of one hour to help fix the always-behind feeling, but a ten-minute buffer was still not enough time to transition. I then tried putting a thirty-minute space between calls. But finally I realized that the optimal gap between calls was one hour. As an introvert, I need more time to recharge and mentally prepare. That's another reason why I have Talkie Tuesdays and Thursdays, so I can have recharge days between call days. That's an act of self-care to preserve my energy.

- **SCHEDULE SELF-CARE APPOINTMENTS.** Choose one nourishing self-care activity you could do once a month, and put it on your calendar as a repeating appointment, so it's blocked off in your schedule. I schedule at least one type of self-care activity for my body each week, rotating among acupuncture, a massage, and a soak in a hot tub at my local hot tub rental spot. I also schedule my next appointment right after my self-care activity ends, so it's already blocked off in my calendar for the following month. You can find lower cost options like community acupuncture where you are seated in a room with other people. Or trade your time. For example, I have offered child care to a friend who is a massage therapist in exchange for a one-hour massage.

- **PLAN MOVEMENT DATES.** Make time to move your body. You can walk, hike, run, or stretch. You could also take a fun class in-person or watch a free tutorial on YouTube. Look at all the activities you want to do or try for the upcoming month, then check which days and times work for your schedule. And if you like to move your body with friends, invite them to join you for extra accountability. I go back and forth on how I like to work up a sweat. This is the biggest challenge for me because "daytime couch time" is my favorite thing. Twice a week, I go to an all-women's dance class to sweat and reenergize myself. As the end of the month approaches, I look at my calendar and schedule all of my dance classes for the next month.

Beyond moving, a simple and quick way to stay connected to your body is breathing. Box breathing calms your nervous system when you're stressed or anxious: you inhale for four seconds, hold your breath for four seconds, exhale for four seconds, hold your breath for four seconds, and repeat three times). Throughout the week, I look for ways to reconnect to my body and get out of my thinking brain. Most mornings, I meditate with my husband to help bring awareness to my breath. We use the Insight Timer meditation app to track our progress; some other great apps for meditation are Calm and Breathwrk. Our longest streak together was 437 days, but I try not to focus on hitting a certain number. Instead, my goal is not to miss more than one day, which James Clear talks about in his book *Atomic Habits*.[5]

You may struggle because you feel you don't deserve to step away from your work or you don't have the time. If you have trouble slowing down and building self-care into your routine, look for guided support to do so. A friend or coach can help you dig deep to find out what makes it challenging to take a break. How can you take care of your body in a way that your activities don't feel punishing but instead replenish you? What activities feel restorative to your body? Pay attention to the signs that let you know that your body needs to take a break and rest.

Make Time for Connection and Play

As busy as our lives are, when we make time to be surrounded by loved ones, deepen our friendships through play, and build a compassionate relationship with ourselves, we experience the simple pleasures in life. When we devote time to connection and embrace our playfulness, we're able to weather life's storms with more grace and ease. I'll share the various types of connection that keep our wells full and our lives fed.

Connecting with Others

According to a study conducted by the Health Resources & Services Administration on the "loneliness epidemic," loneliness and social isolation can be as damaging to a person's health as smoking fifteen cigarettes a day, and the lack of strong social ties increases a person's risk of stroke by 32 percent.[6] Nurturing our connections with others and finding ways to play with people who energize us can help reduce the risk of developing certain diseases and enable us to recover more quickly when we do get sick.[7] Play also strengthens our connections with those we love and keeps us close.

Whether traveling with loved ones or having a cozy evening at home with friends, make time to play with people who fill your well.

I have the best belly laughs when I schedule time with my girlfriends. This can be as simple as having a "girls' night in," when we watch an old romantic comedy such as *When Harry Met Sally*, drink hot apple cider, and make cinnamon rolls. Or we might go for an adventurous girls' trip. Like the time a group of friends and I took a Pink Jeep Tours on a backcountry excursion of Sedona's famous red-rock landscape. If you identify as a Social Butterfly, connecting with others energizes you, so make sure you have social activities on your calendar. If your primary self-care style is Nature Seeker, try scheduling a weekly hike with a close friend for a nourishing conversation outdoors.

Connecting with Ourselves

Create space for personal downtime and inspiration. What does rest look like for you? What inspires you? When are you able to hear your own voice? Julia Cameron's *The Artist's Way* is a book that I love, and Julia encourages us to do two things to facilitate this.[8] The first is to schedule a weekly "artist date" with yourself, which is a solo activity intended to spark creativity and playfulness. Nurture your Inspired Artist side by taking time away from home to attend a weekly guitar lesson or pottery class. When you make time for hobbies that bring you joy outside your business, you will return to work feeling energized, creative, and productive.

Julia's second suggestion is an activity called "Morning Pages," which is a writing exercise that helps you to process whatever is in your subconscious mind.[9] The idea is that as soon as you wake up in the morning, you jot down all the thoughts running through your head, stream-of-consciousness style, until you have filled three pages. Once you fill up three pages, you're done for the day and can throw the pages away (though I choose to keep mine). This exercise is a way to connect with yourself without having to feel the pressure of perfection.

Connecting with Our Senses

Also, remember the importance of pleasure—a sensory exploration of play. Find ways to unplug from technology and reconnect to your body by adding simple things to your life that awaken your senses. Indulge your taste buds by eating a sweet treat slowly or sip hot tea with your hands wrapped around a warm mug. Dig your toes into the grass at a park or into the sand in the ocean. Observe nature, from sunrises to sunsets to the stars and the moon. Light a scented candle or play some jazz music. Slow down and enjoy life beyond your work.

If you identify as a Tidying Fairy, a clean environment brings comfort to your soul, so designate a special place in your home that's just for you. What would happen if you gave yourself the space to tune in to your senses and be present for a few minutes?

THE VALUE OF PLAY

Play increases our connection to ourselves and others. It's an easy and quick way to nourish our mind, body, and soul from the inside out. When we remember to prioritize play, we can access our sense of wonder, joy, and lightheartedness. Though we all recognize the benefits of play for children as they grow and develop, what we may not be aware of is that play is also important for our mental health as adults. Play not only releases feel-good endorphins, but it improves our strategic thinking and stimulates creativity.[10] It helps us think outside the box in our businesses and counteracts stress in our busy lives.

There is plenty of research that documents the importance of play for adults as well. "It offers a sense of engagement and pleasure, takes the player out of a sense of time and place, and the experience of doing it is more important than the outcome,"[11] says Dr. Stuart Brown, the founder of the nonprofit National Institute for Play. "Play is a basic human need as essential to our well-being as sleep, so when we're low on play, our minds and bodies notice." This means that if you feel yourself becoming cranky, rigid, or stuck, it's time to play.

What does staying connected to our joy look like in the context of our busy adult lives? Play is not just about booking a special vacation filled with activities that we enjoy, although this certainly counts if you can make time for it. Play should be part of our everyday life. What was your happy place as a child? What did you love to do when you were ten years old? Getting back into touch with this childlike "happy place" is key to identifying the type of everyday play that will excite you as an adult.

As a kid, I loved riding my bike with friends and playing card and board games such as Uno, Rummikub, and the Game of Life. So today, I make time for play by riding my bike with my family and hosting couples' board game nights with friends. My primary self-care style is Solo Lounger, so at home, play looks like taking a bubble bath with a candle lit and music playing while reading an inspiring book, such as **MORE MYSELF** by Alicia Keys or **UNTAMED** by Glennon Doyle. Maybe you loved horseback riding and being in nature as a kid, and the idea of bringing this sort of play back into your life lights you up. You could take monthly horseback riding lessons or buy a local hiking guidebook and work your way through it over a year to keep you outdoors in your happy place.

It is also important to recognize the people in your life who can remind you to play. This also strengthens your connection with others, so accept invitations to get out of the comfort of your home and your daily routine. For me, this person is my husband, George. I call him the CPO (chief play officer) of our household. He not only reminds me of when it's time to eat, but he is the one to pull me away from my computer with an invitation to walk to the park, sit on a blanket, and read together as a family. He also loves to browse discount travel sites to find flight deals and vacation packages. Often when he presents ideas to me, I'm resistant because all I see are the calendar logistics and the fact that I'll have to take time off work to go. But some of my favorite memories and experiences have come from my husband's last-minute travel ideas and deals, because I gave myself permission to take a break from work and explore the world.

Who could be the CPO in your life? Can you give yourself permission to listen to this person when they encourage you to get out there, experience the world, and make time for play? It is essential to find ways to enjoy life beyond your business so you can come back recharged, more productive, and creatively stimulated. Prioritizing play enhances your connection with yourself, with others, and with the world around you.

Tend to Your Emotions and Protect Your Boundaries

At times I struggle with anxiety regarding my business, which can affect my mental well-being. When something goes wrong, I tend to turn a molehill into a mountain. I lose sleep replaying the scenario in my mind and imagining how it might have gone differently. Then I'm exhausted the next day. Logically, I may know that what happened is not the end of the world, but I still worry and imagine worst-case scenarios. When I find myself doing this, I know that I must tend to my emotional needs.

As women, it's important to nurture a connection with our emotional selves and to acknowledge our disappointments, worries, and fears, rather than suppressing them or using distractions (including our work) to numb our feelings. We grew up with the message that women are too emotional, a stereotype that has been debunked many times because men experience the same highs and lows. Neuroscientists have acknowledged that emotion is what drives intelligent thought.[12] Emotions are our superpower. It's a basic human need for us to be seen and understood even when what we're feeling doesn't make sense. When we take time to notice and honor our full range of emotions, we can come up with strategies for moving forward in a more loving, compassionate way. This kind of work is not easy to do on your own, so I highly recommend finding a skilled therapist or a life coach with a therapeutic background to safely guide you through the process. There are affordable therapy options such as Open Path Psychotherapy Collective, starting as low as $30 per session, Therapy for Black Girls, and National Queer & Trans Therapists of Color Network, along with the Loveland Foundation, which provides financial assistance for Black women and girls who are seeking therapy. (You can access a full list of recommended therapists at shebuilds.com/resources.)

A crucial part of tending to and safeguarding your emotional needs is establishing clear boundaries about what is reasonable, acceptable, and comfortable to you and what is not and communicating these limitations to others.[13] Poor boundary maintenance in our business and personal lives can lead to resentment, disappointment, and anger, causing emotional and physical fatigue and ultimately burnout. If you experience these emotions, it is a clue that a line has been crossed. When you identify your limits and communicate them clearly to others, reinforcing them from a place of power instead of guilt, you are better able to protect your energy. Following are some general guidelines for establishing healthy boundaries in your life and protecting them.

Communicating Your Needs

Articulate your desires so that people know to treat you and your time with respect. You first must understand your personal needs and wants, and communicate them clearly. If there's a conversation you are avoiding or you find yourself complaining about something or somebody repeatedly, it's time to communicate your boundary with clarity and kindness. Identify what you want and articulate it, even if you're unsure of how the other person will respond. To practice radical self-care for yourself, you must advocate for your needs and wants even if it feels selfish.

When you're ready to set a boundary and make your request, say so from a calm and firm place. You don't need to overexplain yourself. As the novelist and nonfiction writer Anne Lamott puts it, "'No' is a complete sentence." Don't say you're sorry or try to justify your decision. To establish a clear limit, be respectful, but avoid sending mixed messages by apologizing. Sometimes we're wishy-washy with our boundaries because we are not clear with ourselves about what we want or need. Before you can communicate clearly to others, ask yourself: What do I want? What don't I want? What am I available for? What am I not available for? You will uncover what you are not willing to tolerate. Then you can describe how you would like your needs to be met or the request you would like to make. Our boundaries are invisible to others, so we must be explicit about what we want. It's okay if your boundaries and preferences change over time. You have permission to change your mind and update your boundaries according to what works best for you.

A limit you might set at home is asking your partner to put the kids to bed a few nights per week so you can have more time to rest or work on your business. This reminds your partner that your dreams and downtime are just as important as theirs. Another limit you might set to protect your mental health is unfollowing certain accounts on social media that trigger you or that don't represent your values. A boundary you might set in your business is to not respond to clients or coworkers after 5:00 p.m. or on weekends.

Asking for More Time

Guilt and blurred boundaries between your business and home life can make you take on more than you have capacity for. So it's important to communicate your boundaries on your time, energy, and priorities. Look at the big picture of your life so you don't overcommit yourself. Don't cram your personal life into the small pockets of time left over after you work on your business. Make sure you have enough time to do your VIPs each quarter, connect with the people you love, and refill your well.

A powerful way I've learned to avoid overcommitting myself is to ask for more time, whether before replying to an invitation or extending a timeline for something I promised to deliver. This respects other people's time boundaries as well as your own. Get into the practice of not replying to a request right away to do a project that will take up a big chunk of your time in the future. If you're used to answering people quickly, you can say, "I need more time before I make a decision. I will get back to you on such-and-such a date." Then check your calendar, check in with important people who may be impacted by your decision, and sleep on it for at least one night. Likewise, if you promised you'd deliver something by a certain date and you know you're not going to make the deadline, communicate with the person involved as soon as you know it's going to take a little longer and let them know the updated timeline.

Sometimes you will create self-imposed deadlines, and you won't make them. You then become your harshest critic and head down a shame spiral. This is when you must ask for more time from yourself. Don't give up. Take a beat, then assess why you didn't make the deadline, adjust your approach as needed, and reset your pace. Don't put a timeline on your dreams. We are human, so we won't always get the timing right for how long things will take us. Find graceful ways to extend the timeline and create more space in your decisions and deliverables.

Reinforcing Boundaries

If someone does push back after you communicate a boundary, make sure to stay consistent. People are not trying to violate your limits;

they currently aren't aware of what those are, or they have their own agenda they're trying to push forward. Don't leave anything open to interpretation. Clarify your boundaries and reinforce them when someone else oversteps them. Expect people to test you and feel disappointed by your responses. It is not your responsibility to manage their reaction to the boundary you have communicated. Even if you think they won't approve of your request, you must stay firm while still respecting their humanity.

Don't put a timeline on your dreams.

What do you do when someone violates your boundaries after you've clearly communicated them? First, pay attention to your internal alert system to know when a boundary has been crossed. You may receive a response from someone and feel dismissed, annoyed, or anxious. You may even feel physical sensations such as sweating and shaking or feel your chest or throat tighten. Use these physical and emotional signals to let you know that something is off and needs to be addressed. Next, create a loving narrative in your head that reminds you that you are worthy and deserving of having your needs met.

Give yourself permission to guard your boundaries with that

fierce mama bear kind of protection. Your time is as valuable as anyone else's. Staying quiet only leads to more stress, wasted time, toxic relationships, and overwhelm. If you strengthen your ability to set boundaries, you will experience less stress because you are protecting your time and most important relationships, including your relationship with yourself. You're not a doormat, you're a magic carpet.

Audre Lorde said, "Caring for myself is not self-indulgence, it is self-preservation, and that is an act of political warfare."[14] Prioritizing your emotional needs is a revolutionary act of self-care. If you are a Solo Lounger, you might enforce boundaries by saying "No" to a social engagement so you can stay home and recharge. If you are a Social Butterfly, communicate your need for in-person connection to the people closest to you. If you are a Tidying Fairy—and a clean, organized environment makes you feel more at peace—ask the members of your household to do a collective cleanup session right after dinner, and throw on some music to make it fun. If you are a Nature Seeker, when you feel overwhelmed or stressed, step outside and walk for ten minutes to calm your nervous system. Enforcing boundaries is not only about having hard conversations, it's about protecting your peace and making powerful requests to meet your needs and nourish your soul.

Create Your Self-Care Menu

Now that we've discussed the importance of prioritizing self-care in your business and your life, it's time for you to identify what fills your well and make a personalized self-care plan. This plan shouldn't become a rigid, daily to-do list. Instead, think of it as a menu that you can choose from, depending on what is going on for you at any given time. If you know that you lean toward one particular self-care style, don't be afraid to explore activities in other categories as well. Experiment to discover what nourishes you.

SELF-CARE MENU				
	NOURISH AND RELAXATION	**MOVEMENT AND ENERGY**	**CONNECTION AND PLAY**	**EMOTIONAL PROCESSING**
SOLO LOUNGER	Stay home with a good book or movie, or relaxing bath.	Take a nap, stretch your body, or do a walking meditation.	Invite some close friends over for a "girls' night in."	Journal feelings, cancel plans, watch a show that makes you laugh or cry.
INSPIRED ARTIST	Attend a concert, play, or art exhibition.	Take an improv class or have a dance party at home.	Take a painting, knitting, or pottery class.	Write "Morning Pages" or listen to your favorite feel-good songs.
SOCIAL BUTTERFLY	Organize a picnic at the park or soak in a hot tub with friends.	Go on a recurring hike with a friend or play a team sport such as pickleball.	Host a wine night or book club meeting with friends.	Unplug from social media, call a friend, or snuggle with loved ones.
TIDYING FAIRY	Clean up a designated area of your house and then lounge with a cup of tea.	Take a calming yin yoga or tai chi class.	Host a clothing swap with friends.	Make a mental declutter list or engage in a breathwork exercise.
NATURE SEEKER	Hike with a friend for nourishing conversation outdoors.	Swim in nature or try an outside activity that aligns with the seasons.	Get away for a weekend in a cabin or at a campsite with friends.	Step outside for a ten-minute walk to clear your head.

Grab a journal and pen, and spend fifteen minutes generating ideas about what helps you feel rested, calm, and centered. Based on the self-care style(s) that you identified for yourself at the start of this chapter, create a Self-Care Menu of practices that refuel you by answering the following questions.

- When I feel depleted, what activities and people nourish me?
- How do I want to fuel and move my body?

- What current habits, practices, or rituals do I already do that fill me up?
- What activities typically help me process my emotions and big feelings?
- If I had a full day for pure relaxation, how would I want to spend it?

Once you've created your Self-Care Menu, here are a few things you can do to help turn these nourishing activities into daily practices.

1. SCHEDULE TIME FOR SELF-CARE. Think about the frequency of each of your listed self-care practices that would be most beneficial (daily, weekly, or monthly). Instead of waiting for the next dip to happen, proactively schedule self-care in your calendar. Pick the top three items from your Self-Care Menu and add them to your calendar as recurring events. Also add them to your Weekly Workflow Plan from chapter 5. Try out your new Workflow Plan for a month with practices from your Self-Care Menu built in, and notice how different you feel.

2. GIVE YOURSELF PERMISSION TO SAY NO. As you build your Self-Care Menu, are there times when you need to say "No" to things that are draining your well? What are they? Make agreements with yourself on what you will not do. Some examples: I will not work on the weekends; I will not work past 6 p.m.; I will not be away from home for more than five consecutive days. Then identify what you will say "Yes" to. For example, I will schedule one social or self-care activity on the weekends; I will take a lunch break every day; I will take a vacation without my laptop.

3. IDENTIFY A QUICK, SIMPLE ACT OF SELF-CARE, AND DO IT. What is one act of self-care that you could do in fifteen minutes to feel a

quick recharge? This could be taking a nap, taking a quick walk around your neighborhood, doodling in a sketchbook, or making a call to check in with a loved one. Or maybe you need an entertaining mental break such as listening to a heartwarming audiobook, flipping through magazine pages, or embracing *Dolce Far Niente*, which is an Italian phrase that means "the sweetness of doing nothing." Take time off. Rest. Just be. Set a timer and do it today.

Remember, burnout is not an option. Revisit your Self-Care Menu when you're feeling depleted, overwhelmed, or exhausted, and practice self-compassion. As former first lady Michelle Obama put it, "We need to do a better job of putting ourselves higher on our own 'to do' list."[15] You are learning and becoming more aware of your needs, so that you can better show up for yourself, your business, and your loved ones.

There is a whole woman behind your business. It's important to respect your needs by prioritizing self-care, filling your well, and keeping it full. As we lead our companies, we have an opportunity to bring our whole selves to work. We no longer have to compartmentalize what matters to us. We no longer have to put ourselves at the bottom of our to-do lists. Building sustainably requires self-care as a business strategy. We need rest, play, and rejuvenation to stay in it for the long haul.

Building sustainably requires self-care as a business strategy.

You may be torn among filling your well, being present for loved ones, and showing up for your work, feeling as though you're never doing enough in any area of your life. Sometimes the greatest act of self-care is to show yourself compassion. What if, each day, you were to say to yourself, "I am doing my best and I am enough"? How would you feel?

Building a business is hard work, but your business won't work if you're running on empty. Self-care is a necessity not an indulgence. Prioritizing your mental health and wellness helps you to build a better business. Now that you have a Self-Care Menu to refer to when your energy feels low, it's time to build at a pace that works for you and the season of life you're in.

12

you will be lost and unlost. over and
over again. relax love. you were meant
to be this glorious. epic. story.

—*Nayyirah Waheed*

My husband, our daughter, and I run a 5K a few times a year, including our neighborhood Turkey Trot. None of us is an avid runner.
We alternate between sprinting, walking, and stopping to catch our
breath and drink some water. Each of us has a different pace, but we
all make it to the finish line. So we came up with a family motto to
honor everyone's unique tempo. As we run, we chant together, "My
race. My pace. My personal best." It's the same in your business: *you*
choose when to speed up, slow down, or stop.

As you learn new ways to avoid overwhelm and end burnout, you
will still hit roadblocks along the way and be forced to shift your
priorities. Plans will change, unexpected things in life will happen,
and your energy and focus will ebb and flow. This chapter will help
you learn how to navigate your pace, especially when you're not sure
what direction to move in next.

How do you know when it's time to slow down in your business,
accelerate a project, or move in a completely different direction?

There are three decisions that you can make at any time to help you honor the totality of your whole life as you run your business: pause, push, or pivot. We're going to discuss how to identify and act on each of these.

- PAUSE. When something unexpected in your life comes up and you must slow down or halt progress in your business while something else important takes center stage.

- PUSH. When a project or initiative in your business needs an extra level of effort, focus, and energy to get to the finish line.

- PIVOT. When you need to find the courage to change directions because you recognize that a shift is necessary, or when you realize that something is no longer working.

Let's take a closer look at each option, exploring what to consider in each phase and how to make each of these shifts without putting unnecessary stress and pressure on yourself.

Pause: Give Yourself Permission to Build Slowly

You are not operating your business in a vacuum. You are not immune to unforeseen personal challenges that impact how you are able to show up for your work. You must take your whole life into account. You are more than just your business. As an entrepreneur, you may not have the same options that someone working for a big company with paid sick or family leave has. You're the boss, and at times, it's hard to give yourself time off.

When life is demanding your attention and you are forced to turn toward it, do not resist. Instead, give yourself permission to slow down and tend to what is needed. Put your business on hold so you can focus on your life. Be still, take a break, and surrender to the unknown. This can feel counterintuitive to productivity. For some people, pressing pause might feel like a relief, like a long exhale when you didn't realize you were holding your breath. For others, a pause can feel very stressful and uncomfortable. Filling space is easy to do; creating space is not as easy.

As I mentioned in chapter 5, a big life change, such as becoming a parent, losing a loved one, or managing a health diagnosis, can affect our ability to focus 100 percent of our attention on our business. We need the time and space to adjust to our new responsibilities, tend to our grief, and do the deep healing work.

I often see women struggle when they ignore what's happening personally and push themselves to hit a deadline or berate themselves for being behind because life happened. When life delivers hardship and loss, taking an intentional pause to redefine your priorities is the bravest thing you can do. And often it's the best thing you can do for yourself and for your business.

In 2019, I lost my fifty-nine-year-old father and my sixteen-year-old brother unexpectedly within the span of six months. I found myself in intense waves of sadness and exhaustion. Not only did I have to process my grief, but there were also the logistics of things to be done after losing loved ones: hopping on planes to Las Vegas and Kaua'i, talking to lawyers, and planning memorial services. And I was still running my own business. At the time I was publishing weekly episodes on my podcast, working on my book proposal, and leading a mastermind program. It was not ideal or convenient to hit pause on my business, yet taking a pause was the most human thing I could do.

I decided to stop publishing new episodes on my podcast for the rest of the year. I let my book rest and told my book coach I didn't know when I would return to it. I brought in mentors to support my mastermind program so I could be fully present with my family. On the outside, everyone understood, but inside, I was torn. I resisted pausing at first. I felt I was letting my clients down and putting the future of my business at risk.

It's moments like this when I did not want to be strong and resilient. Yet hustle culture celebrates strength and powering through. It's a survival mechanism to keep going even when it hurts. Where in your own life do you need to give yourself more space and grace to be present to moments of loss, grief, and heartbreak? Remember that even though you're the "strong one," you don't have to pick up right away and carry on.

I had to trust that everything would work out in time if I tended to my heart. And the timing did work out. Of course, it wasn't the timing I wanted; money was tight, and my energy was low. It took years to feel like myself again. But I prioritized my healing so I could rebuild my capacity to show up for work again. The following year, during the COVID-19 lockdown in northern California, I filled my coaching practice with a waiting list, recorded season three of my podcast, and finished my book proposal, ending the year with a multiple-six-figure book deal with my dream publisher.

Do You Need a Sacred Pause?

This is a time to turn inward. It's a time for deep rest, healing, and focusing on what's most important, including anything that affects your personal life and calls you to adjust to a new normal. Jot down your answers to the following questions to determine whether it may be time to pause.

- What needs your attention most right now? What do you want to focus on?
- Are there current commitments in your life and business that you would prefer to put on hold to make space for what you want to prioritize?

- What VIPs on your Quarterly Plan would you prefer to put off due to your current capacity or priorities changing?

VANESSA'S PAUSE: REMEMBERING WHAT REALLY MATTERS

One of my previous clients, Vanessa Raderman, is the founder and director of Greenleaf Mindful Montessori. The daughter of a renowned pioneer of education in Caracas, Venezuela, Vanessa grew up in the Montessori system, and she combined her love of this education philosophy with her meditation practice when she opened a preschool in Sherman Oaks, California. When I met Vanessa, she was in the growth stage of her business, with a full roster of children, generating over $20,000 in revenue per month and ready to expand into new classroom spaces and take on more teachers.

On Vanessa's Quarterly Plan for January 2020, her VIPs were to find a new space, hire and train a new teacher, and update her website. Her personal commitments included visiting colleges on the East Coast with her son, who would be graduating from high school in May. Vanessa's plate was already full, and she was trying to balance her time to avoid overwhelm and burnout. Then, in March 2020, the COVID-19 pandemic hit, and she had to close her preschool to in-person learning. She tried to provide an affordable online alternative, but her enrollment decreased to 35 percent, causing her income to drop significantly. There was little indication of when she would be able to reopen fully and get the enrollment back up. Then her teenage daughter had a mental health crisis. Vanessa didn't know where to focus her energy. She wanted to be there for her daughter, but she was also worried about keeping her business afloat. She felt like a rope in a tug-of-war, constantly being jerked back and forth. She was concerned about her daughter, exhausted, and constantly worried about money.

In the past, Vanessa had taken a grin-and-bear-it approach to overcoming obstacles and dealing with challenges. She prided herself on her work ethic and her ability to thrive amid change and constant reinvention. But this season of her life took it to another level, and even she could not cope; she became increasingly unmotivated, disconnected, and disheartened. None of the strategies she was experimenting with to refill her own well to keep her business alive was working. She had tried shutting down on the weekend to watch her favorite shows and baking bread to give her mind a break, to no avail. She was stressed out, burnt out, and unsure of what to do next.

What Vanessa needed to do was pause. She couldn't make grounded decisions while she was in survival mode. Initially, she admitted that taking a step back from her business felt like giving in or admitting failure. However, I advised her that she needed to take a sabbatical in order to take care of herself and her family. Rather than continuing to do business calls with me, I recommended that she work with my life coach. I transferred my sessions that Vanessa had already paid for and had my life coach support her instead.

Through working with my life coach, Vanessa determined that she needed to focus on what really mattered during that season: her children. She stopped promoting her online program and decided to close her preschool doors, instead tutoring a few students on one-to-one calls, two hours per week (and she committed to only one week at a time, so she could stop if she needed to). Although it felt scary, she prioritized her family and rest. Because she took out business loans to get her through the "pause" period, she reminded herself that she was okay, she was safe, and her family had a roof over their heads.

Taking a break from work was hard for Vanessa. Without the structure of a full-time work schedule, she felt untethered and unfocused. So I asked her, "What would a dream day look like for you if you had all the time in the world?" Here's what she came up with: "I would wake up and do 'Morning Pages,' fill out my gratitude journal, meditate, work on art pieces, eat a yummy plant-based lunch, and dance. I would connect and play with my kids, do a yoga challenge with them, dress up and make silly TikTok videos, and cook dinner for my family."

That became her Self-Care Menu that she could pull from while she was on sabbatical. I had her choose the top three things from her dream day that she could make time for right away. She chose filling out her gratitude journal, reading **THE ARTIST'S WAY**, and doing daily yoga sessions with her kids.

What happened when Vanessa took a break? After the six-week pause turned into six months, she went back to work fully rested, with a clear mind and still in love with her business, the one she had almost closed permanently. She was able to reopen her preschool with a full roster of families. Because she had taken a break from the business frenzy, she was able to prioritize what really mattered to her. She readjusted her schedule, so she could focus on helping her son and daughter. Her basic needs were met, so even as new ideas for her business popped into her mind, she would say to herself, "So exciting! Not essential." The undivided quality time she'd given her kids while on sabbatical had been invaluable, with her son going on to enroll in the Berklee College of Music and her daughter now working to support others who are struggling with mental health issues.

Instead of continuing to push hard, Vanessa needed to embrace the anti-hustle mindset. She needed to rest and to reimagine her business and her life in order to move forward. She had to be courageous enough to trust the process so she could lean into the mystery of discovering her next right step.

There will be certain seasons when you need to give yourself permission to build slowly. If you're not as visible or productive during these periods, remember that you're not hiding, you're healing. It takes time to recover from adversity and setbacks, including not having access to economic resources such as loans or savings. You may have to cut your expenses or live with family members, as I did after closing Little Sprouts. Give yourself the space and grace to pause and recover. Sometimes you might wish you could warp speed to the end of where you want to be. But we must learn to trust the timing, trust the process, and trust ourselves.

You're not hiding, you're healing.

Push: Move Past Perfectionism and Procrastination

There will be times in your business when you hit a plateau and are not moving forward. There are numerous reasons why you may have stalled, including perfectionism, and you may need to give yourself a push to make meaningful progress. Pushing and hustling in our business for a limited period of time does not mean that we have opted in to hustle culture; it simply means that we are accelerating until we achieve certain goals and get things moving again.

Getting yourself into "push mode" is beneficial at certain crucial moments in your business, such as when you need to get a big project off the ground. Or when you are trying to get something completed and over the finish line based on external deadlines. When you know that you're about to enter push mode, it's helpful to inform your team, your family, and any other key players to let them know that the project you are working on will take priority over everything else for a while.

I went into push mode when I was in the early stages of writing this book. I had to follow the advice of *The War of Art* author Steven Pressfield, who says, "Put your ass where your heart wants to be."[1] When I first began writing, I dedicated an hour every weekday morning to working on the book, and I also blocked off Fridays as my superfocused writing days. I was doing everything I talked about in chapter 5 to prioritize book writing as my VIP—or at least I initially thought so. But after four months of writing every day, something was not clicking, and I was not able to get chapters turned in to my editor.

With the final deadline looming and feeling like an inadequate everything—wife, mom, entrepreneur, and author—I booked a call with my coach, Rebecca, and we got to the heart of the resistance I was experiencing. I named the shame. "I keep telling myself that I can't get this book written because I don't have time," I said. "But the truth is, I'm worried that I'm not going to be able to write a good enough book." My daily writing habit looked like progress on the outside, but it was a sneaky cover-up for my perfectionism. Every time I faced a page, I felt stuck, but I didn't know why. I didn't need another extension from my editor. Before I did anything, I needed to clear my emotional blocks, honor my workflow, and make writing the book my number one priority. It needed to take center stage in my business and my life. Everything else would have to come behind it for a short period of time.

I went into push mode and strategized with Rebecca on ways to give the project the additional momentum it needed. She suggested scheduling some solo writing retreats so that I could deeply immerse myself to work on the book. I was willing to try anything at that point, so I discussed the plan with my family and the fact that it meant that George would need to pick up more responsibilities at home for a time. I also had to rearrange my client calls to free up several consecutive days to write. Ultimately, for three consecutive weeks, I stayed in a different hotel for three to four nights at a time, and then I returned home for a few days before going to another hotel to write some more. With my fierce focus and by clearing my calendar, I was able to complete the draft of my book.

Do You Need to Do a Strategic Push?

You've started something, and you know it's worth putting time, effort, and resources into. You've been talking about it for years, yet it's not complete. Acknowledge your resistance, and get whatever support you need to push the project to the finish line. Answer the following questions, and consider whether it may be time to push.

- What project on your Quarterly Plan needs more time, effort, and energy to complete?
- What obstacles and fears are preventing you from working on your VIP and accomplishing your goals?
- What has been your approach to overcoming these obstacles so far?
- What logistical or emotional support do you need while you go into push mode in your business?

ENRIKA'S PUSH: SHIFTING THE FOCUS

Enrika Greathouse is a cofounder of Small Gorilla, a brand and marketing agency that helps entrepreneurs tell stories through in-person and digital training experiences. Enrika is also a creative with a huge heart. She became a teen mom at sixteen, traveled as a professional dancer and choreographer, and brought her empathy and creativity to everything she did.

When I first started coaching Enrika, she considered herself a big dreamer who was generating ideas on a whiteboard with nothing ever getting finished. She felt scattered and like a failure. She knew she had the strategy, skills, and expertise, but she lacked confidence and was indecisive.

The Quarterly Planning Method helped Enrika organize and prioritize her ideas so she could start taking action and not just dream about it. She got realistic about how much (or how little) time she had to take care of all of her commitments, including the winter vacation she was getting ready to take with her family. In her Q4 (Quarter 4) plan, she had three priorities: promote her agency's "Beast Your Brand" New Year Workshop; finish up systems and processes to make client work a breeze; and plan her upcoming trip. If Enrika was going to reach her $100,000 revenue goal for the year and take time off to be present with her family while traveling, she would have to push to get her projects to the finish line.

Enrika broke down her VIPs into clear action steps with deadlines that would enable her to complete her projects before her family trip. She scaled back her school commitments to the minimum required and asked her husband to take the lead on homeschooling their daughter and cooking. She also stopped taking on new clients and design work. She didn't want to overfill her schedule with helping people with their brands and not have enough time or energy left over for her own. This allowed her to focus on one priority project as opposed to trying to split her attention across many. She also identified her fears, saying "I don't want to get it wrong. I want all of my ducks to be in a row so I won't let people down or disappoint them." But, she said, she was hopeful and ready to do whatever needed to be done.

Being in push mode with a set deadline in mind for when her vacation would start, Enrika created and promoted her workshop event in only five days. She was shocked when she shared how quickly something could come into form. "But the material has been living in me for sooooooo long," she added. She put the sales page up and connected with people who were interested in working with her. With an email list of only 105 people, she had ten people join her branding workshop, offered two scholarships, and generated $1,000.

For the rest of the year, Enrika carried that momentum forward while integrating time for self-care and rest. Before I started coaching Enrika, her business made zero, and by the end of the year, it had generated over $100,000.

By Enrika taking a leap of faith, asking for help, and becoming more action-oriented, her husband was able to resign from his six-figure job, take full responsibility for homeschooling, and cook at home (which she said he's really good at). But more important, Enrika became more confident in standing up for herself and her goals. She stopped volunteering so much, stopped saying yes to everyone and everything, and stopped feeling guilty for not overserving.

Pushing is not about powering through; it's about setting a clear intention and directing your time, energy, and attention toward a project that has a lot of meaning for you. It's the work you can't *not* do. You know you would feel more yourself and more fully expressed if the project came to completion. If you take steps to prioritize your VIP, you can enter a flow state where you're able to focus for longer periods of time and putting in the effort doesn't feel like hard work. The psychologist Mihaly Csikszentmihalyi defines flow as "when a person's body or mind is stretched to its limits in a voluntary effort to accomplish something difficult and worthwhile."[2] In chapter 2, we talked about Intentional Trade-Offs, or saying "No" to one opportunity to free up time and energy for what matters most right now.

Make an Intentional Trade-Off that you're willing to prioritize in this season of your life, and embrace your flow.

Pivot: Follow the Direction of Your Heart

"I want to exit the company," I said to my business partner, Jen, over the phone. My palms were sweaty and shaky. It felt like a breakup. We were consciously uncoupling as cofounders. I had built a business with my friend from zero to more than a million followers in a few short years. Was I stupid for walking away? Was I crazy?

But I had found the answer to these questions (which was no!) buried in a journal where I had written out my Future Vision three years earlier. As I explained my decision to Jen, I read some of my Future Vision out loud to her. In that three-year-old document, I had described the business and life I *really* wanted: I wanted to coach and guide women entrepreneurs to build world-changing companies while raising a family. That Future Vision still held true for me, and it did not align with my company's current business model.

Making the decision to leave the company wasn't easy. I met with a lot of internal resistance and self-doubt. My inner critic got loud: *Who do you think you are? This business changed your life. You're a commitment-phobe. You're lazy. You're a quitter. Just do the work and be grateful.* But a conversation with my mentor, Jonathan Fields, reassured me. I asked him, "Am I crazy for leaving?" "That's not the question you're really asking," he answered. "The question you're asking is 'Can magic strike twice?' and the answer is *yes*!"

There will be many crossroads in your business and your life where you will be faced with the decision of whether to stay or to pivot in a new direction. When the hustle and grind of your business don't feel congruent with the peace, joy, and fulfillment you want out of life, that can be a sign that it's time to take inventory of what's working and not working and make a change. You could keep doing what you're doing and maintain the status quo. Or you could choose to leave the safety of your comfort zone and take a chance. Jim Carrey delivered a commencement speech at Maharishi International University, saying ". . . you can fail at what you don't want, so you might as well take a chance on doing what you love."[3]

This doesn't mean that you need to blow up everything in your life to make your expanded vision a reality. You can honor what you've built, the people you care about, and your responsibilities while still staying in touch with your truth in the process. For example, when I was leaving my company, I still followed through with all my deliverables even though my heart was no longer in the work. My cofounder and I also had a coach to help us navigate the more challenging conversations that come up when selling a business.

A pivot can come in many forms. It may involve removing a certain product to create space for something new; letting go of a team member to support your company's changing needs; canceling an in-person event due to weather or a global pandemic. Or it could be something bigger, such as closing or selling a company, as I did.

Do You Need to Make a Purposeful Pivot?

You're in transition, and you know that something is no longer working. You want to move in another direction, but you're not sure what the next thing should be. This is the time for reinvention—to test, explore, and try things on. Consider the following questions to help you decide whether it may be time to pivot.

- What's no longer working in your business? What are you tolerating that is no longer sustainable? What have you committed to that no longer feels true to pursue?
- What obstacles and fears are preventing you from making this pivot?

- What has been your approach to overcoming these obstacles so far?
- What logistical or emotional support do you need to have in place while you pivot in a new direction?

**NIKKI'S PIVOT:
CREATING WHAT WANTS TO BE BORN**

I've mentioned my close friend and member of my personal Support Squad Nikki Elledge Brown in previous chapters. She created an online training called A Course About Copy in 2014, to help entrepreneurs communicate online with confidence. In her first launch, she welcomed more than fifty students from all over the world (and over $50,000 in revenue). A year later, she had more than three hundred paying customers and was building a six-figure business with her toddler by her side.

Once she realized what was financially possible, she set her sights on her first million-dollar year. She got pregnant with her second child and continued to grow her business while her husband was deployed on a submarine with the United States Navy. Everything seemed great on the surface, but once the baby was born, she felt a jarring shift in her values. Now with two little ones under five and a husband under the sea, she realized she was tired of running on the hustle hamster wheel, spending so much time with her head in her laptop. She felt torn between being present with her family and scaling her course-based company to the next level. She reluctantly slowed things down, and within a year, she launched the **NAPTIME EMPIRES** podcast to have honest conversations on the realities of parenting and entrepreneurship.

At a mastermind dinner in Sedona, Arizona, Nikki had a conversation with me and two other female CEOs that led her to ask the question "What do I really want?" Her heartfelt answer was: "Having a third child and writing a book would mean more to me than reaching a specific financial goal." She knew she had to pivot. Growing her family was more important to her than any business strategy. Her heart was no longer invested in promoting and teaching her online course. What she truly wanted was to spend less time online and more time with her family. She also wanted to publish a book and coach other women on how to navigate running a business and raising a family.

The next year, she found the courage to close the doors to her course, drafted a 94,000-word manuscript for her **NAPTIME EMPIRES** book, and recorded a fresh season of conversations for her podcast. Months later, she gave birth to a healthy baby girl. She finally traded the guilt and anxiety she'd felt for falling out of love with her business for gratitude that she was able to live life on her terms. And now she helps others do the same. Sometimes a pivot is quick and clear, and you know exactly what you want to do next. Sometimes it's a little more ambiguous, and it takes a lot of patience and trust.

You need to make a pivot when you're clear that something is no longer working and something else is ready to be born. Making a pivot is not easy. It's a lot easier to keep pushing. But you must listen to your instinct when it tells you that something isn't right. If you decide to make a pivot, know that even if you lose money, followers, or some of your self-confidence along the way, you're bringing the essence of who you are and the insight you've gained to wherever you go. Tune in to your heart's whispers; there's a lot of wisdom in there.

How to Embrace Your Pace

It is natural that the energy we have available to put into our business will ebb and flow throughout the seasons of our lives. The stories I shared may seem as though they are tied up nicely in a perfect ending. But we are all fighting for our lives when we're in the messy middle. It's brutal, uncomfortable, confronting.

Not everyone has financial resources such as savings, access to credit or loans, or an option to live with family members (as I did after closing Little Sprouts). When you're living paycheck to paycheck, sometimes pausing or pivoting isn't possible. And cutting expenses or getting an additional job is still not enough. Remember, providing for yourself is the priority. You may have to make hard choices to pause your business so you can honor your well-being and sense of security. Do what you need to do to get your needs met.

Oftentimes, you will not know the answer right away. And even if you know the answer, you can't make a move until you have the resources to do so. The important thing is to learn to tune in to these shifts and listen to yourself while keeping sight of your Future Vision and goals. Now is the time to decide whether you need to pause, push, or pivot.

Explore Embodied Decision Making

Are you in a place where you need to pause and take a break? Do you need to push and accelerate? Or do you need to slow down and pivot in a different direction? If you find yourself stuck and uncertain about which direction to go in, you can talk to someone you trust who can help you sort out your thoughts, such as a coach, a mentor, a business peer, or your Support Squad. Ultimately, however, it is up to you to decide which move is right for you.

Once you check in with outside sources, don't forget to take some time to tune in to yourself, your truth, and your inner wisdom. One way to do that is through a decision-making process I use for myself and with my clients called Embodied Decision Making. It enables you to look with an open heart at the possible options you might pursue. This process engages your body and your intuition. Work your way through the prompts in the following exercise, and jot down your responses. Be honest with yourself as you assess the pace that is needed in your life at this current time.

- Look at your Quarterly Plan. Based on the season of your life and your current commitments, where do you need to pause, push, or pivot?
- Whether you want to pause, push, or pivot, what big decision do you have to make right now? Write it down.
- Based on the decision you want to make, what options are you considering? Choose up to three possible scenarios, and write out each option. For example, Vanessa needed to decide if she would keep her preschool open during the pandemic, promote her new online program, or take a sabbatical. Enrika needed to decide if she would continue to homeschool her daughter herself or ask for more help at home. Nikki needed to decide if she would continue her successful copywriting course or change directions and focus on writing a book and making space for a third baby.

Once you've written down each option you're considering, have a courageous conversation with yourself. Say each option out loud, one at a time, as if you've already made the decision. After each option, close your eyes, take a deep breath, and then read the next one.

As you say each option out loud, observe how your body feels. Does it feel relief, regret, or resistance? Does your body contract and feel caved in and small, or does your chest open and feel expansive? What's the tone of your voice? Does it feel like a reluctant "no" or a resounding "yes"? If you can have a friend or coach listen to you, that person can usually hear the difference in your voice, too. Jot down any answers or insights that come up as you say each option.

Based on which of the options feels like a full-body yes, move forward with that option. Then, instead of looking for evidence that you should have made a different choice, do everything in your power to prove that you made the right decision.

Here's the truth: on some days, you will feel that your energy levels are low, you will feel overwhelmed and behind, and that's okay. And here's another truth: on some days, you will have to work harder and put in longer hours than you normally would to meet a deadline or push a project forward. But when you're building your business differently and with L.O.V.E., you can balance that rigor with being real with yourself.

The key is learning to be intentional about how you move through pauses, pushes, and pivots so you feel a sense of focus, flexibility, and flow in your business. This doesn't happen by accident; it's a process, and it takes practice. You must be willing to constantly reassess what your true priorities are. You must be committed to building at a pace that is sustainable and that works for you, your vision, and your life. Allow your business and your life to support each other, not be in competition.

When we honor the pace that works for us based on the season of life that we're in, it becomes impossible to hustle as we did in the past. We can't go back to the old ways. We need to build our business with intention and in a way that is regenerative and long-lasting. In the next chapter, we'll explore what it means to deepen your roots so you can flourish in your business and your life.

13

And the day came, when the risk to
remain tight in a bud was more painful
than the risk it took to blossom.

—"Risk" by Anaïs Nin

I'm from northern California, where redwoods abound. On hikes, I often think about how these great trees represent the ideal of how we want to build our businesses and our lives. Since I was a child, I've been visiting the Muir Woods National Monument, which is only a forty-mile drive from my current home. Each time I visit, the trees feel just as towering. I follow the trail to Cathedral Grove, with its sign that says ENTER QUIETLY. I stand among the giants, surrounded by the tallest, oldest redwoods. On the ground, I see the cones that carry tiny seeds no bigger than a tomato seed. To gain perspective, I tilt my head toward the sky. The sunlight sparkles through the tree-tops, and I'm in awe every single time.

Redwoods can grow to over three hundred feet tall, equivalent to the height of a thirty-seven-story building, and their roots can extend as far as twelve feet below the ground and a hundred feet wide. Redwoods are rarely knocked down in heavy winds because their root systems keep them stable. Although the roots may be out of sight, they need to be nourished so that the tree they belong to can continue to grow and stay anchored in the ground. Redwoods also thrive through their connections with other redwoods. Each tree's roots are intertwined with the roots of trees nearby. They lean on one another to live long lives and weather storms. The trees in Muir Woods are six hundred to eight hundred years old, the oldest being twelve hundred years of age. The beautiful part is that they've only lived half of their life span. With the right support, they will continue to grow to even greater heights.

In the previous chapters, you learned how to sow and nurture the seeds of your business and your life in a way that will enable you to thrive both personally and professionally. But that's not enough. Like redwoods, we want to build and grow our business by cultivating roots that will sustain us for the long haul—because only expansive, strong roots can withstand the inevitable and unpredictable droughts and storms of our business and our life.

What does it mean to deepen your roots? It means taking action that will nurture and protect the future of what you have built. It means building strategically and with focus while keeping sight of your Future Vision. As leaders and entrepreneurs, we are responsible for establishing a strong root system below the ground of our companies. Our businesses become stronger when we collaborate and grow together as redwoods do so that we can support our teams and communities. It also means pacing yourself as you scale your business up to avoid burnout. You need to slow down before you speed up to create more breathing room as you build with continued compassion and grace.

To build your business differently—to Build with L.O.V.E.—you must build in a way that enables you to level up without sucking all the joy and fun out of your life. Scaling your company up does not have to equate to working late nights, ignoring your body, and neglecting your most important relationships. You don't need to have a long list of goals, as you had in the past. You don't need more things to do; you need less. You don't need to be more; you are already enough. As you emerge and prepare to grow on your terms, let the next season be about deepening your roots below ground, where others may not see them but you know that they are there.

In this chapter, we will explore the three essential pillars of deepening the roots of your business: staying grounded in your truth; allowing life's storms to strengthen you; and scaling up with love. Having a strong root system means being deeply connected and in tune with your business, your life, and yourself, both now and in the future.

She Feels: Stay Grounded in Your Truth

Once we emerge, we are ready to grow our business to the next level at a pace that works for our lives. To build, grow, and expand takes a deep level of self-awareness and a heart-centered strategy, which you now have access to, given the anti-hustle tools you've acquired in the previous chapters. But Building with L.O.V.E. is about more than intentional planning; it's about remembering to trust the process, trust the timing of life, and, most important, trust yourself.

I have a recurring monthly call with my bookkeeper to review my company's P&L statement. We discuss revenues, expenses, and profits, and while looking at those numbers together, we strategize on how I can make future decisions. These calls are incredibly helpful, but sometimes, if profits are down, I can be hard on myself. I can recall a conversation we had a few years ago when I found myself feeling, momentarily, like an irresponsible business owner.

"I know you're capable of earning a lot more," my bookkeeper told me candidly after we'd reviewed the P&L together. "A large percentage of your expenses isn't matching up with revenue growth."

She feels.
She knows.
She builds.

I know, I know, I thought.

Normally, I loved his straight talk, using it as motivation. I would listen patiently before going back to my Revenue Map to crunch numbers. But that time, something was different. Something was brewing inside of me.

"I know what I'm doing," I blurted out. "I'm not trying to do a quick, flashy launch. I have a bigger vision, but it's going to take about three years for it to fully unfold. I'm making investments now for a long-term strategy in the future, which won't make me money right away. But I have a plan. I just need more time."

In that moment, on the phone with my bookkeeper, I spoke my truth. I was scared to speak my dream out loud, but my intuition knew that money wasn't my only goal. I needed to do work that fed my soul, too. My business is a vehicle that moves me toward my next-level vision. I had to be honest about what I truly wanted, even if there was no way to reflect it on a P&L statement. As leaders, we must stay grounded in our truth by listening to our inner wisdom and embracing our personal power. We can live our lives and lead our businesses the way we want to: no more choosing our work over our health; no more sacrificing time with our loved ones to complete our to-do lists; no more searching outside ourselves for answers; no more outsourcing our decision making to "experts."

Our intuition is our best business advisor. We know ourselves better than anyone else.

Sometimes your plans will go off track as life's curveballs disrupt your intention to grow to the next level. In a season of expansion, you must continue to take imperfect action, trust your moneymaker, and extend the timeline. You must be unshakable even amid uncertainty. Instead of pushing yourself to exhaustion, give yourself permission to slow down, hibernate through the winter, and stay in your creative cocoon. Trust that spring will come again, when you can plant new seeds and grow your business on your own terms. Your feet are firmly planted in what matters most to you.

When you commit to growing a business from your heart, when you know your work is more than a paycheck or a title, you may have to zig left when everyone else zags right. Your business is your art, a full expression of who you are and how you want to serve. You choose to lean into the discomfort and challenges that will push you to grow in all areas of your life. You will take the road less traveled. Trust that the path you are on is not about becoming an overnight success but about listening to your intuition. Learn to trust the voice deep inside you that points you in the direction of your heart.

She Knows: Allow Life's Storms to Strengthen You

What does it look like to let life's storms bend and change our limbs without breaking us? After a storm, once the sky clears, if our roots are strong and deeply planted, we emerge with more awareness of our strength, more resilience and grit, and more experience and wisdom. As visionary leaders, we will grow not only our companies but our capacity to show up more wholeheartedly. We remember how creative and resourceful we are.

In the last chapter, we explored when it's time to pause, push, or pivot when you feel an internal desire to shift gears or the unexpected curveballs of life force you to adapt quickly. Sometimes it's unclear how to move forward. This is the messy middle, the dark winter. Sometimes it means trusting yourself enough to sit still in the discomfort of not knowing what to do next. This is the call to get quiet and listen more deeply to what's being asked of you. But it does not mean giving up.

You were called to entrepreneurship for a reason. Do not throw in the towel when things get hard (and they will). To build differently, you must do the brave work that no one else will ever see. This is the brave work of facing your fears, leaning in to discomfort, and giving yourself the space to transform from the inside out. Things may break, but you will not. As Maya Angelou said, "We delight in the beauty of the butterfly but rarely admit the changes it has gone through to achieve that beauty." In these darker seasons, we realize that we can hold and do so much more than we thought was possible.

Samar and Gabriela Nassar, first-generation Lebanese Peruvian sisters and the cofounders of Hipline, had to do just that—not give up—to ensure the survival of their company through the global pandemic. Hipline opened its doors in 2008 as a brick-and-mortar dance studio in the San Francisco Bay Area. The studio is a safe and fun place where women and marginalized genders come to sweat and stay connected to their sensuality. Each class is illuminated by a disco ball and set to music by artists such as J.Lo, Britney Spears, and Lizzo. For years, one of my favorite activities was attending in-person classes at Hipline two to three times a week.

Then COVID-19 hit, and Hipline, like many other small businesses, had to pivot quickly when stay-at-home orders were issued. In March 2020, Samar and Gabriela sent an email to the community explaining their decision to close the physical studio and begin livestreaming their classes. They were committed to dreaming, even when the future remained uncertain. They found a way to recreate the magic of in-person classes while keeping their community connected through incredibly challenging times (an uprising for racial justice and a climate crisis, in addition to the public health crisis). The Hipline community members not only continued to sweat together, they maintained hope and recognized how agile and flexible we are not only in our bodies but in our hearts.

The Hipline owners could have thrown in the towel, but instead they took a step back, surveyed their community, and dreamed up new ways to serve their customers while preserving the integrity of their mission. When you build on a strong foundation and deepen your roots, you can lead with love. Hipline's owners' online space became an extension of their dance floor. Even as they struggled, they found ways to support their community by adjusting their pricing downward to help offset the financial hardships of the pandemic. They introduced a "For My Sis" program, which was designed to serve Hipliners in financial distress by matching them with fellow Hipliners who wanted to pay for their classes. They also hosted Black Girl Magic sessions, which included choreographed routines led by their Black instructors. Dancing to music by Black artists was cathartic for me as a multiracial Black woman who wanted to channel my rage, frustration, and sadness after the events surrounding the tragic deaths of Ahmaud Arbery, Breonna Taylor, and George Floyd.

As a small business operating off small margins, Hipline was able to sustain the financial hardship by welcoming more than two hundred new Hipline members, including from as far away as Greece, Antigua, and Taiwan. In 2021, it was voted Best Virtual Dance Studio in the *East Bay Express* best-of list. Most important, Hipline, whether in person or online, stayed connected to its mission as a business founded on love.

She Builds: Scale with Love

What does it mean to scale? In business terms, scaling is about having a strong foundation, team, and systems in place to sustain growth even as demands increase. For example, if your company was featured on the television show *Shark Tank*, with more than 3 million viewers learning about your company, would you have the infrastructure in place to fulfill a sudden influx of orders efficiently and maintain excellent service? Or would something in your company (perhaps even you) break?

Scaling leads to increased revenue, more employees, and more customers. You might think that growing quickly would inevitably put your company on the path to success, but a study done by the Ewing Marion Kauffman Foundation and *Inc.* magazine revealed that two-thirds of the fastest-growing companies in the top five thousand lists had failed just a few years later.[1] The owners of slow-growing, self-sustaining companies may take the longer road to achieve the results they desire, but they survive the ups and downs because they are strategic *and* intentional at every turn. They focus on simplicity over complexity. They spend more time clarifying their vision and mission, renewing their dedication to company values and a love-based culture, and attracting a team they trust to go the distance.

Building an anti-hustle business does not mean that life will get easier; it does mean that you will have to redefine scale on your terms so you don't burn out. You need to have systems in place that take care of you at the center of your business while also taking care of your team and customers. It's about leading with love. Scaling does not have to mean hustling if you do it mindfully. Consider the following questions. As you answer, think in terms of revenue, reach, and visibility. Be clear about the pace that works for you in this season of your life. This is an invitation to expand your thinking and see what's possible for you and your business.

- How big do you want to get?
- How fast do you want to grow?
- What relationships do you want to nurture?
- What skills do you want to strengthen?
- What opportunities do you want to pursue?

The important thing is not getting big; you can keep your business simple and lean. It's not speed; you can build slowly. It's not the number of people you know; you can focus on quality and depth. It's not being and achieving more; you can remember that you are enough and have enough.

Sometimes scaling means going deeper into what you've already built rather than chasing the hottest new trend or idea. Build a business that is compassionate and that cares about the humans that are its heart and soul. It is possible to scale with love by putting people first without sacrificing metrics—but you will have to shift the way you work by designing a company culture that will grow with purpose, grace, and love.

There are companies that have scaled and chosen to lead with love as their company ethos. It is not impossible to grow and keep love at the center of your business. My team and I have used a tool called Canva for many years. It's a free software program that anyone can use for design purposes, from social media graphics to promotional brochures to slide presentations. What I didn't know at first was that the company was founded by an Asian Australian woman who is the perfect example of choosing love over metrics. Melanie Perkins is the cofounder and CEO of Canva, which she launched from her bedroom in Australia in 2013.[2] She had a vision to give everyone the ability to design, no matter their skills, experience, or socioeconomic status. "You have to believe in yourself and your vision for a very long time before anyone else will," she said in an interview.[3]

Choose love over metrics.

In the start-up days of Canva, Melanie heard "No" from more than a hundred investors. While she was trying to raise money for her company, she slept on her brother's living room floor. After many rejections, she wrote a note to herself: "Mel, you're extremely tired. You are in a challenging situation, though you can pull through. Nothing bad is really happening, you're just feeling depressed because you are used to achieving things quickly. It's a hard environment. There is no doubt you will succeed and you will find the team you need, get the investment you need and build the company you have always wanted."[4] She used rejections as fuel to deepen her roots.

Melanie spent three years improving her pitch deck and building a team of cofounders and developers to support her, even though she had no idea how to run a company. But she knew she had to expand her support system if she was going to survive. She also had to create a product that people would use. She saw that users weren't clicking or creating designs in the way she had envisioned. She was disappointed to see that people were apprehensive about using Canva. She had to think outside her industry box if she wanted to stand out. She came up with a fun challenge to help people build their confidence in their own design abilities through gamification. It worked. She raised $3 million in seed funding to help her get to that next level.

Today Canva has more than 60 million users each month, and the company reached a $1 billion annualized revenue run rate in less than ten years. Getting rich for the sake of it was empty, Melanie said in an interview.[5] Instead, she made a public commitment through the Pledge 1% movement to donate 1 percent of the company's profit, equity, product, and time to the charities of its choice. Since Canva's giveback plans were formalized, the company has worked with 60,000 schools and 130,000 nonprofits. "If the whole thing was about building wealth that would be the most uninspiring thing I could possibly imagine," Melanie said on the *Forbes* financial website. "It has never felt like our money, we've always felt that we're purely custodians of it."[6]

My bonus dad Michael shared a similar piece of wisdom with me on a recent visit to Kaua'i: "We do not take our money with us when we die. We are only custodians of it while we're here on Earth." That was what he had learned from his grandfather: to pay it forward, enrich our loved ones, and set up a foundation of growth for the next generation. That's what Building with L.O.V.E. looks like: to learn how to be good custodians of our time, energy, and wealth; to build in a way that sustains us and contributes to the greater good at a scale that feels inspiring and regenerative. We don't need to have a billion-dollar dream to make a difference.

It's essential to dedicate time and thought to dreaming about your long-term vision. Your goals for your business and your life will evolve and change as you do. In certain seasons, you may need to pause and be in your own winter; in others, you will want to expand in summer's full bloom. It is crucial to honor each of these seasons of your life, pace yourself, and stay connected to your mission. Revisit and nurture your Future Vision through seasonal planning to keep the roots of your business healthy and strong and to remove any weeds that won't allow you to flourish.

Write a Letter to Your Future Self

It's time to remind yourself why you started your business in the first place by writing a love letter about your business to your future self. Here's the story of how I led this exercise on a retreat.

I walked through the woods with fifteen women ahead of me, pine needles crunching under our feet as we approached an outdoor amphitheater. It was the last day of a three-day retreat I was leading for my clients in the Santa Cruz Mountains. We had celebrated our wins, filled out our Quarterly Plans, and written and shared our Future Visions out loud. We had held mastermind sessions around the fire pit and prioritized rest and self-care in nature. Our brains, hearts, and bellies were full.

The women found seats beneath the canopy of majestic redwood trees. "Our final exercise will be to write a letter to your future self," I explained to the group. "This is a love letter to yourself. An opportunity to impart any wisdom, gratitude, and reminders to keep going." Each woman received a sheet of paper and a prestamped envelope on which I had her write her address. Then they began writing. They wrote down their hopes, wishes, and dreams, drawing strength from the trees surrounding us. They then folded their letters and sealed them in their envelopes. That was a conversation for their eyes only. One year later, I mailed the letters to the women so that they could read and reflect on their truths and how far they had come.

Now it's your turn to write to your future self. Grab a piece of paper and an envelope. Write today's date at the top of the paper. Then start with "Dear Future Self." Here are some questions to get you started.

- Describe your dream scenario one year from today. What are you celebrating? How will it impact your life if your hopes, wishes, and dreams come true?

- What do you feel is your biggest opportunity in your business right now? How do you plan to overcome obstacles that may try to hold you back?
- What matters more than anything else? What are you most grateful for? Do you have any memories of times when you showed resilience and strength?
- What's the biggest insight that you're taking away from this book that you can carry forward with you?
- Is there anything else you want to share with your future self?

This can be a deep, reflective process, or it can be light and full of humor. Write whatever pours out of you. Once you've completed the letter, seal it in the envelope and put it away. On the envelope, write a future date when you'd like to reread the letter. Look back at it a year from now or once you've worked through the plan that you created while reading this book. Then when it's time, check in with your past self to see how far you've come.

Deepening your roots involves implementing strategies in your business and your life that sustain you now and into the future. This is about honoring the messy middle and letting life's big storms transform you but not uproot you; sitting in the unknown and trusting the bigger picture of life even when uncertainty meets you; staying grounded, staying strong, and Building with L.O.V.E. at the center of everything you do for yourself, your team, your loved ones, and the world.

It's wild to think that the business you have right now was once just a seed of an idea. Celebrate yourself for how far you've come. As you continue to grow and deepen your roots, stay right where you are. Bloom where you're planted. Nurture what's right in front of you, and trust that you are on the right path. You have an opportunity to build your business into something innovative and unconventional at a pace that works for you.

There will be hard times when you'll want to flee. But I invite you to stay, to trust the process, and to trust yourself. You can have a high intention for what it is you are being called to create and a low attachment to how it will all unfold. Surrender to life's plans. Commit to building your business your way and Building with L.O.V.E.

She Feels . . . She Knows . . . She Builds

Work is love made visible.

—*Kahlil Gibran*, The Prophet

I stared out at the Golden Gate Bridge from the window of my hotel room. My laptop was open on the desk in front of me next to a green juice. I was locked away on a writing retreat, working to finish this book. No family, no distractions, just room service, occasional dance breaks, and Cheryl Strayed's "Write like a motherfucker" to fuel me.

For years, my biggest fear had been slowing down. I believed that if I took my foot off the hustle pedal, my business would fail and the life I had worked so hard to create would crumble. However, at that moment in my hotel room, I knew otherwise. I knew that the hustle was a lie and that there was another way to live. I picked up my phone and texted my past client Julie Santiago:

Just checked into the Cavallo Point hotel for a solo writing retreat. They booked me in the same room where I hosted our retreat six years ago! I remember you writing your three-year Future Vision in this room.

Julie replied:

What an incredible wink from the universe! I'm at home, watching the sunset outside and I just put the baby to bed. Feeling so grateful for the life I now have, which was only a vision all those years ago.

Julie is a friend and member of my personal Support Squad, and she is living proof that the strategies in this book work. When I started coaching her six years ago, her goal was to double her income. Today, she has far surpassed that goal—to well over seven figures in annual revenue—while running a thriving leadership coaching company of ten full-time employees that empowers professional women to avoid burnout. And she is doing all of this while raising a family in her dream home. This is Building with L.O.V.E. in action.

When I checked out of the hotel at the end of my writing retreat, I had a draft of my manuscript. I had also accomplished something even bigger: I had remembered to pace myself and to make time for play and connection with others while writing my book. I was fully supported by my Support Squad, my Dream Team, and my husband of seventeen years. I was not just leading with love, I was receiving it, too.

Because I had designed my schedule to prioritize what mattered most to me in that season of life, I had the time and space I needed to create something new: my book. Rested and nourished, I could serve in a bigger way without draining my energy. By sharing the Build with L.O.V.E. principles in a book, I knew I could reach so many more people than I had been in my private coaching practice and retreats. I had listened to that voice from within telling me that I could not continue to operate in my old way.

Like me, you may have questioned your lack of motivation or drive to be and do more. You may have felt conflicted about not creating, producing, achieving fast enough—as if that were a sign of weakness. You've been so busy that you might not realize there's a deeper calling for you, too. Or you already know what you want to build next and that's part of your stress—because you can't answer the call.

You may have felt too old or too late, too feminine or too lazy, too behind or too slow. When people think you are *too much* of anything and you feel less of yourself, you lose your muchness. What if being too much is the antidote to hustle? What if the goal is to be much more of yourself?

At the start of this book, you may have felt discouraged that your current business wasn't where you had envisioned it to be. Or that scaling, building teams, and expanding were beyond your reach. On the other hand, you may have felt nervous about growing too fast, thinking that more growth would bring more responsibility. You feared that the bigger your business got, the more it would take you away from the life of freedom you had been hoping to create when you started it.

But now you have the anti-hustle guide to growing your business and nourishing your life. When you do what matters most to you, not what you think you *should* be doing, motivation meets you in perfect timing. You can create space in your life because you have the tools and self-renewing strategies to evaluate your business time and again. You can choose Intentional Living rather than the fast-paced hustle lifestyle that leaves you burnt out.

After reading the stories throughout this book, you may feel inspired and ready to change the world in your pajamas. And at the same time, a part of you may be rolling your eyes at the movie-esque "you can do it if you try hard enough" endings. But the reality of entrepreneurship is there will be celebratory highs and there will be setbacks (even if and especially if you reach a level of success). Business is not linear. Sometimes we have to go back to basics and feel like we're starting over.

The women whose stories I've shared, myself included, have had to make tough choices at times. Paying our team members and not ourselves, dealing with a lack of motivation, questioning our own integrity when pulled toward a new passion, reevaluating spending, and cutting team hours to reduce expenses. It's not always easy.

Sometimes we have to scale back to go forward. But stepping back isn't a failure; it's a strategy. Sometimes you're not a start-up, you're a re-start-up. We don't just build, we rebuild, reimagine, reinvent our business and our lives.

It will take even more resilience, resourcefulness, and recharging our batteries to Build with L.O.V.E. You will take inventory of how you feel and trust your intuition more. But that doesn't mean burn-out won't happen again. It means you have more tools and strategies to navigate the dips with more grace and compassion. Building with intention takes time. And let me tell you that you're worth the wait.

As you integrate your work and life in a more fulfilling way, remember that you are still healing and there are times when you will have to resist the urge to slip back into hustling. It is easy and normal to fall into patterns of working that lead to overcommitting, people pleasing, and comparing your progress to others. But now you have more self-awareness and self-compassion to build a sustainable business on your terms. You're celebrating how far you've come, taking better care of yourself, and giving yourself a break as you identify the next steps along your journey.

And even though you still have a million things to do, you were resourceful enough to carve out time to read this book and reconnect to your inner strength; to turn inward and answer the call of what wants to be created next. You know you don't have to stay stuck in the cycle of fear, burnout, and hustle; it's okay to build *your* way.

Your race,
your pace,
your personal best.

This is your life. Tend to it with care, reverence, and deep gratitude. You are right where you need to be, no longer defining what's enough based on other people's goals. You are capable and deserving of creating the life you have envisioned for yourself, just like the women at my retreats. They have now built their own support networks, expanded their vision for their lives, and focused on building a business they love.

Imagine feeling more peace and inner freedom because you take a few days to step away so you can have a clear vision of how you want to build your business. Maybe you'll host your own solo retreat, as I did, plan a getaway with your partner or friends, or I'll see you at one of my future retreats, where you can relax in an inspiring environment, reimagine your future, and reconnect to the magic within you. It's time to take a step back from the grind and refill your well. You deserve to be happy, creatively expressed, and thriving. Something is calling you. Listen to it. Answer the call to what you will create next.

The future belongs to women who are committed to building in a new way. I'm on a mission to redefine the way we work, lead, and love. Collectively, we know that the hustle culture isn't working for us. We build differently; we Build with L.O.V.E.

For the Builders

This is for the builders
The bold ones who speak their dreams out loud
And continue to face failure
This is for the difference makers and the imperfect action
  takers

This is for the visionary rule breakers
The wild ones who dream a better world
And believe in something greater
This is for the movement starters and the trail blazers

This is for the daring creators
The resilient ones who pave their own path
And trust life's flow
This is for the answer seekers and truth speakers

This is for the courageous leaders
The brave ones who won't give up
And surrender when it's time to let go
This is for the movers and the shakers

This is for the freedom chasers
The unapologetic ones who are unshakeable
And have nothing to prove because they are enough
This is for the builders who build with love

ACKNOWLEDGMENTS

It takes a beautiful tapestry of humans to build something meaningful. I am deeply thankful for the many hands and hearts that supported me on this journey.

George Brian, thank you for continuing to be a solid rock of support and a safe place for me to be messy and imperfect. You give me the space to grow, evolve, and creatively express myself. You are the joy maker in my day. I love the life we have cocreated together. Seventeen years of marriage and counting! #chooselove

Zoe, I'm the luckiest mama to raise someone as creative, kind, and brave as you. It's a gift to watch you grow. I love our hot tub and "milk and bookie" dates. I can't wait to see what you build next.

To my mom and bonus dad, "Popo" and "Big Mike" (Joy and Michael Jonah)—thank you for always supporting my big ideas and dreams—including Little Sprouts Playhouse when it was just a seed of an idea. To my in-laws, "Lolo" and "Lola" (George and Beckie Sellner)—thank you for opening your home to us, so we could rebuild our lives. To my father, Darrell Whigham, for planting the belief that I can do what I love. To my siblings, Jamila, Isaiah, Trinity, and Max.

To my chosen family and Support Squad: I feel like the wealthiest woman in the world to have amazing support and friendships. Thank you . . . Nikki Elledge Brown for being my Polly Pocket, cheerleader, co-coach, and coworking buddy (Voxer holds all of our deepest wishes, secrets, and #authorpants pep talks); Michelle Long for hiring me as your front desk receptionist in 2012 while I built my next venture and becoming one of my best friends; Jen Kem for unlocking so many doors inside my heart and in the world—your generosity, gems, and genius inspire me; Rebecca McLoughlin for emotionally and spiritually stewarding this book by my side; Voge Smith for helping me heal and release trauma, so I could fully step into my power. And to my soul sisters who mastermind with me about business and hold me up in life: Amy Ahlers, Amy Groome, Briana Borten, Julie Santiago, Kate Northrup, Kavita Patel, Nicole Walters, Nisha Moodley, Sarah Jenks, Tara Mohr, and so many more brilliant women.

To my Dream Team. Thank you . . . Michele Morales for being my amazing right hand for more than seven years—you are the biggest advocate for my ideas and your dedication to making them happen with such ease and grace inspires me to create and serve even more; Rachel Pesso for integrating my visual brand into the book and sprinkling your creative solutions and designs throughout the pages; Heidi and Tara at In Her Image Photography for capturing my essence and reimagining the next level of my brand.

To my magical book team who brought *She Builds* to life. Thank you . . . David Fugate for being my literary agent and believing in this book in 2014 at World Domination Summit before I saw it myself—I am beyond thankful for your patience and chill California vibes; Azul Terronez for helping me mind map the stories brewing in my heart as my book coach in the early stages; Jennifer Lauck and Blackbird Studio for creating the space for me to write my personal stories; Elaine Pofeldt for your edits that saved me from drowning in Google Doc quicksand; AJ Harper and her editorial retreat to make sure I put the reader first; Jessica Sindler, "the magical word wizard unicorn," for swooping in and pulling all the pieces together; the HarperBusiness team: Rebecca Raskin and Hollis Heimbouch for believing in the message that love and business can coexist; Wendy Wong for being committed to the vision with your developmental and line edits (thank you for your grace and extended timelines to honor the anti-hustle way); Sydney Lewis and Hannah Gómez's support in guiding me to make this book more inclusive;

Kirby Sandmeyer and the production team for taking this book to the finish line.

To my clients and community who inspire and sustain me. Thank you for not only trusting me to support you in your business and life as a mentor and coach but also for being brave enough to share your story to show others what's possible. To Jen Hansard for being an essential part of my entrepreneurial journey (from The Valley Moms Social Club Meetup group to becoming published authors). I also appreciate the early readers who took the time to read and give generous feedback (Addie Spahr Kim, Adela Hussain, Alionka Polanco, Andrea Empey, Aysegul Sanford, Carol Gavhane, Cathy Axibal-Cordero, Chelle Lynn Temple, Dahye Lee, Jayme Johnson, Julia Foerster, Kim Hanlon, Michelle Courtney Berry, Rochelle Cooper, Susan Kerstan-DeVito, and Tomesha Campbell).

Christina Rasmussen, thank you for the divine download over a meal at True Food Kitchen to buy the domain "She Builds." I had no idea what I'd use it for, but I trusted the wink from the universe. I am also grateful to my loved ones who crossed over to the other side of the rainbow. I felt each of you, Max, Big Daddy, and my father, cheering for me every step of the way through hummingbirds, dragonflies, and butterflies.

This book was written with care on Yokuts Land (Walnut Creek, California) and fueled by Java Shakes, MUD\WTR, green juices, green smoothies, and a whole lotta love.

Warm hugs,
Jadah

P.S. I created a list of people who have influenced and supported me on this book journey (including people I may have forgotten) here: jadahsellner.com/gratitude.

APPENDIX

She Builds Exercises

Here's a list to reference the exercises mentioned in the book quickly. You can also download and print out all of the interactive worksheets at shebuilds.com/resources.

REVENUE MAP

THIS YEAR'S REVENUE GOAL

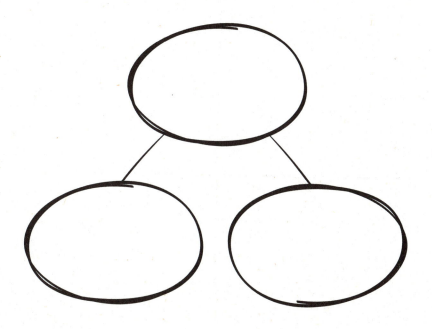

NEXT-LEVEL VISION

FEEL

ENJOY

LEARN

SERVE

WEEKLY TIME LOG

🕐	SUN	MON	TUE	WED	THU	FRI	SAT
6AM							
7AM							
8AM							
9AM							
10AM							
11AM							
12PM							
1PM							
2PM							
3PM							
4PM							
5PM							
6PM							
7PM							
8PM							
9PM							
10PM							

ENERGY AUDIT

Activities	Energizing, Draining, or Neutral	Notes

WEEKLY WORKFLOW PLAN

	Monday	Tuesday	Wednesday	Thursday	Friday	Saturday	Sunday
THEME							
ACTIVITIES							

PRODUCT SUITE

PRODUCT	PRICE	REVENUE	RESULT	EFFORT	CROSS-SELL

CORE CUSTOMER JOURNEY

1 Core Customer

_____

2 Core Dance Floor

_____

3 Core Love Magnet

_____

4 Core Offer

_____

QUARTERLY PLAN

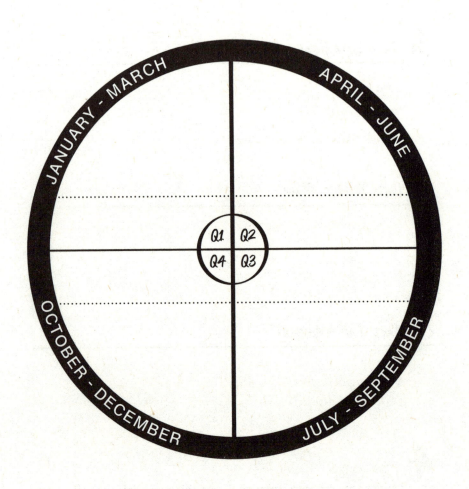

NOTES

INTRODUCTION: FROM F.E.A.R. TO L.O.V.E.

1. Juli Fraga, "Why the WHO's Decision to Redefine Burnout Is Important," Healthline, June 5, 2019, https://www.healthline.com/health/mental-health/burnout-definition-world-health-organization.

CHAPTER 1: DETOX FROM HUSTLE CULTURE

1. Dan Millman, *Way of the Peaceful Warrior: A Book That Changes Lives* (California: H J Kramer, Inc., Publishers Group West, 1984), 113.
2. Alyson Colón, "The Damaging Effect of Gendered Views of Work-Life Balance," Gender and the Economy, December 2017, https://www.gendereconomy.org/the-damaging-effect-of-gendered-views-of-work-life-balance.
3. Timothy Ferriss, *The 4-Hour Workweek: Escape 9–5, Live Anywhere, and Join the New Rich* (New York: Harmony, 2009).
4. Eva de Mol, Jeff Pollack, and Violet T. Ho, "What Makes Entrepreneurs Burn Out," *Harvard Business Review*, April 10, 2018, https://hbr.org/2018/04/what-makes-entrepreneurs-burn-out.
5. "Coping with High-Functioning Anxiety Disorders," Sprout Health Group, https://www.sprouthealthgroup.com/disorders/coping-with-high-functioning-anxiety.
6. Amy Ahlers, *Reform Your Inner Mean Girl: 7 Steps to Stop Bullying Yourself and Start Loving Yourself* (New York: Atria Books/Beyond Words, 2019).
7. Tosha Silver, *It's Not Your Money: How to Live Fully from Divine Abundance* (Carlsbad, NM: Hay House, 2020).

CHAPTER 2: SIMPLIFY YOUR LIFE

1. Paulo Coelho, "The Fisherman and the Businessman," Paulo Coelho Stories & Reflections, https://paulocoelhoblog.com/2015/09/04/the-fisherman-and-the-businessman.
2. "Chris Witherspoon's interview with Oprah Winfrey for 'The Butler' Part 1." Chris Witherspoon, November 12, 2015, https://www.youtube.com/watch?v=1maPYYEubkQ.

CHAPTER 3: ARCHITECT YOUR FUTURE VISION

1. A. J. Adams, "Seeing Is Believing: The Power of Visualization," *Psychology Today*, December 3, 2009, https://www.psychologytoday.com/us/blog/flourish/200912/seeing-is-believing-the-power-visualization.

2. Mark Murphy, "Neuroscience Explains Why You Need to Write Down Your Goals If You Actually Want to Achieve Them," *Forbes*, April 15, 2018, https://www.forbes.com/sites/markmurphy/2018/04/15/neuroscience-explains-why-you-need-to-write-down-your-goals-if-you-actually-want-to-achieve-them/?sh=a99e90a79059.

3. Anna Williams, "8 Successful People Who Use the Power of Visualization," mindbodygreen, July 8, 2015, https://www.mindbodygreen.com/0-20630/8-successful-people-who-use-the-power-of-visualization.html.

4. Anna Almendrala, "Lin-Manuel Miranda: It's 'No Accident' Hamilton Came to Me on Vacation," Huffpost, June 23, 2016, https://www.huffpost.com/entry/lin-manuel-miranda-says-its-no-accident-hamilton-inspiration-struck-on-vacation_n_576c136ee4b0b489b-b0ca7c2; Liz Steelman, "Here's Everything Lin-Manuel Miranda Read on Vacation," *Real Simple*, August 11, 2017, https://www.realsimple.com/work-life/entertainment/lin-manuel-miranda-vacation-reads.

5. Bill Frist, "The Science Behind How Nature Affects Your Health," *Forbes*, June 15, 2017, https://www.forbes.com/sites/billfrist/2017/06/15/the-science-behind-how-nature-affects-your-health/?sh=251aced15aeb.

CHAPTER 4: GATHER YOUR SUPPORT SQUAD

1. Minda Harts, *The Memo: What Women of Color Need to Know to Secure a Seat at the Table* (New York: Seal Press, 2019).

2. Napoleon Hill, *Think and Grow Rich* (Shippensburg, PA: Sound Wisdom, 1937), 251-252.

3. "Literary Britain: The 20th Century," The Great Courses Daily, October 18, 2018, https://www.thegreatcoursesdaily.com/literary-britain-the-20th-century.

4. "*Ted Lasso* - Keeley wants advice," Ted Lasso Clips, October 8, 2021, https://www.youtube.com/watch?v=pWNZvwV2RIA.

CHAPTER 5: RECLAIM YOUR TIME AND ENERGY

1. Cal Newport, *Deep Work: Rules for Focused Success in a Distracted World* (New York: Grand Central Publishing, 2016).

CHAPTER 7: STREAMLINE YOUR BUSINESS

1. "Consumer Trust in Online, Social and Mobile Advertising Grows," Nielsen, April 11, 2012, https://www.nielsen.com/us/en/insights /article/2012/consumer-trust-in-online-social-and-mobile-adver tising-grows.
2. Simon Sinek, "Lead a Crusade," Start with Why, April 2010, https:// blog.startwithwhy.com/refocus/2010/04/lead_a_crusade.html.

CHAPTER 8: BUILD YOUR QUARTERLY PLAN

1. John Ailanjian, "We Cannot Stop the Winter or the Summer from Coming...." Next Play Capital, accessed July 18, 2022; https://next playcapital.com/huddle/we-cannot-stop-the-winter-or-the-summer -from-coming..
2. "Why Writing Down Your Goals Is Essential to Achieving Them," SuccessGrid, October 11, 2020, https://successgrid.net/writing-down -your-goals-is-essential; Michael Hyatt, "5 Reasons Why You Should Commit Your Goals to Writing," Full Focus, July 22, 2019, https:// michaelhyatt.com/5-reasons-why-you-should-commit-your-goals-to -writing.
3. "B. J. Novak of *The Office* on Creative Process, Handling Rejection, and Good Comedy," *The Tim Ferriss Show*, November 25, 2015, https:// tim.blog/wp-content/uploads/2018/08/121-bj-novak.pdf.

CHAPTER 9: TAKE VISIONARY ACTION

1. Stephen Covey, *The 7 Habits of Highly Effective People: Powerful Lessons in Personal Change* (New York: Free Press, 2004).
2. Francesco Cirillo, *The Pomodoro Technique: The Acclaimed Time-Management System That Has Transformed How We Work* (New York: Currency, 2018).
3. "How Does Music Stimulate Left and Right Brain Function? Why Is This Important?," Fun Music Company, https://funmusicco.com /how-does-music-stimulate-left-and-right-brain-function-and-why-is -this-important-in-music-teaching/; "Can Music Help You Study and Focus?," Northcentral University, March 27, 2017, https://www.ncu .edu/blog/can-music-help-you-study-and-focus#gref; "Studying to Music Can Put Your Brain in the Right Frame of Mind," Vaughn College, September 17, 2018, https://www.vaughn.edu/blog/best-study -music-and-benefits.
4. Debbie Hampton, "How Watching Movies Can Help Your Mental Health," The Best Brain Possible, November 24, 2018, https://thebest brainpossible.com/movie-help-mental-health-therapy.

CHAPTER 10: REVIEW, REFLECT, AND REALIGN

1. "Heartbeat Retrospective," Agile Alliance, https://www.agilealliance .org/glossary/heartbeatretro.

CHAPTER 11: REFILL YOUR WELL

1. Michael A. Emmons and Michael E. McCullough, "Counting Bless- ings versus Burdens: An Experimental Investigation of Gratitude and Subjective Well-Being in Daily Life," *Journal of Personality and Social Psychology* 84, no. 2 (February 2003): 377–89, https://doi.org /10.1037/0022-3514.84.2.377

2. Camonghne Felix, "Simone Biles Chose Herself: 'I Should Have Quit Way Before Tokyo,'" The Cut, September 27, 2021, https://www.the cut.com/article/simone-biles-olympics-2021.html.

3. Quinci Legardye, "Simone Biles Learned 'How to Say No' at the Tokyo Olympics," *Harper's Bazaar,* September 27, 2021, https://www .harpersbazaar.com/celebrity/latest/a37755678/simone-biles-on -saying-no-at-tokyo-olympics.

4. Daniel Van Boom, "Simone Biles Wins Bronze in the Olympics Bal- ance Beam Final," CNET, August 3, 2021, https://www.cnet.com /news/simone-biles-wins-bronze-in-the-olympics-balance-beam-final.

5. James Clear, *Atomic Habits: An Easy & Proven Way to Build Good Habits & Break Bad Ones* (New York: Random House, 2018).

6. "The 'Loneliness Epidemic,'" Health Resources & Services Admin- istration, January 2019, https://www.hrsa.gov/enews/past-issues/2019 /january-17/loneliness-epidemic.

7. Debra Umberson and Jennifer Karas Montez, "Social Relation- ships and Health: A Flashpoint for Health Policy," *Journal of Health and Social Behavior* 51 (2010) (suppl.): S54–S66, https://doi .org/10.1177/0022146510383501.

8. Julia Cameron, *The Artist's Way: 25th Anniversary Edition* (New York: TarcherPerigee, 2016).

9. "Morning Pages," The Artist's Way, https://juliacameronlive.com /basic-tools/morning-pages.

10. "The Benefits of Play for Adults," The Beacon, https://living.aahs .org/behavioral-health/the-benefits-of-play-for-adults/; Michael For- man, "The Importance of Play in Adulthood," Wanderlust, https:// wanderlust.com/journal/the-importance-of-play-in-adulthood.

11. Jennifer Wallace, "Why It's Good for Grown-ups to Go Play," *Washington Post,* May 20, 2017, https://www.washingtonpost.com

/national/health-science/why-its-good-for-grown-ups-to-go
-play/2017/05/19/99810292-fd1f-11e6-8ebe-6e0dbe4f2bca_story.html.

12. Alison Escalante, "Men Are Just as Emotional as Women, Study Suggests," *Forbes*, November 12, 2021, https://www.forbes.com/sites
/alisonescalante/2021/11/12/men-are-just-as-emotional-as-women
-says-new-research/?sh=489beac72e96.

13. Joaquín Selva, "How to Set Healthy Boundaries: 10 Examples + PDF Worksheets," PositivePsychology.com, August 12, 2021, https://pos
itivepsychology.com/great-self-care-setting-healthy-boundaries.

14. Audre Lorde, *A Burst of Light and Other Essays* (New York: Ixia Press, 2017).

15. Michelle Obama, https://www.vogue.com/article/michelle-obama
-best-quotes-health-fitness.

CHAPTER 12: EMBRACE YOUR PACE

1. Steven Pressfield, *The War of Art: Break Through the Blocks and Win Your Inner Creative Battles* (New York: Black Irish Entertainment, 2012).

2. Mihaly Csikszentmihalyi, *Flow: The Psychology of Optimal Experience* (New York: HarperPerennial Modern Classics, 2008), 3.

3. Maharishi International University, "Jim Carrey at MIU: Commencement Address at the 2014 Graduation," May 30, 2014, https://
www.youtube.com/watch?v=V80-gPkpH6M.

CHAPTER 13: DEEPEN YOUR ROOTS

1. Derek Lidow, "Why Two-Thirds of the Fastest-Growing Companies Fail," *Fortune*, March 6, 2016, https://fortune.com/2016/03/07/fast
-growth-companies-fail.

2. Alex Konrad, "Canva Raises at $40 Billion Valuation—Its Founders Are Pledging Away Most of Their Wealth," *Forbes*, September 14, 2021, https://www.forbes.com/sites/alexkonrad/2021/09/14
/canva-raises-at-40-billion-valuation-and-founders-pledge-away-their
-wealth/?sh=6f8dd7d07ba9; Jemima Whyte, "Canva's Billion-Dollar Giveaway Will Be Nation's Most Generous," *Financial Review*, September 15, 2021, https://www.afr.com/wealth/people/canva-s-billion-dollar
-giveaway-will-be-nation-s-most-generous-20210915-p58rvj.

3. Melanie Perkins, "A Message for Those Who Feel They're on the Outside, from Canva Co-founder Melanie Perkins," SmartCompany, September 24, 2018, https://www.smartcompany.com.au/startupsmart
/advice/canva-co-founder-melanie-perkins-message/.

4. Karen Gilchrist, "How a 32-Year-Old Turned a High School Year-book Idea into a $3.2 Billion Business," CNBC, January 8, 2020, https://www.cnbc.com/2020/01/09/canva-how-melanie-perkins -built-a-3point2-billion-dollar-design-start-up.html.

5. Steven Johnson, "How an Australian Tech Start-up Launched from a Bedroom Is Now Bigger than Telstra after Being Valued at $54BILLION—as Glamorous Founders Reveal What They'll Do with Their Incredible Wealth," *Daily Mail*, September 15, 2021, https:// www.dailymail.co.uk/news/article-9991775/Canva-founder-Melanie -Perkins-wants-away-30-cent-wealth-firm-bigger-Telstra.html.

6. Konrad, "Canva Raises at $40 Billion Valuation."

INDEX

NOTE: Page numbers in *italics* indicate a chart or table.

JADAH SELLNER (rhymes with Prada) is a business coach, sought-after international speaker, TEDx presenter, poet, and host of the *Lead with Love* podcast. She is the bestselling author of *Simple Green Smoothies* and has been featured in *Forbes*; *O, The Oprah Magazine*; and the *Wall Street Journal*. As the founder of She Builds Collective, a leadership program for entrepreneurs, Jadah helps women to build their businesses and their lives in a way that works for them—with love. She lives in the San Francisco Bay Area with her husband, daughter, and dog, Beesly. Learn more at jadahsellner.com and stay connected on social media @jadahsellner.

Next steps

If you've made it all the way to the end, I'd love to hear from you!

1. Share the book online and use the #shebuilds hashtag.

2. Send my team and me a personal message saying, "I am ready to Build with L.O.V.E." at shebuilds.com/share. We'd love to celebrate with you. You can share a win or a personal story on how the book has impacted you.

3. Visit jadahsellner.com to hire me to speak at an event or attend one of my future retreats.